# BUDGET OF THE U.S. GOVERNMENT

## FISCAL YEAR 2023

### OFFICE OF MANAGEMENT AND BUDGET

## Bernan
Press

Lanham • Boulder • New York • London

Published by Bernan Press
An imprint of The Rowman & Littlefield Publishing Group, Inc.
4501 Forbes Boulevard, Suite 200, Lanham, Maryland 20706
www.rowman.com

86-90 Paul Street, London EC2A 4NE

ISBN 978-1-63671-094-5 (paperback)

∞™ The paper used in this publication meets the minimum requirements of American National Standard for Information Sciences—Permanence of Paper for Printed Library Materials, ANSI/NISO Z39.48-1992.

## THE BUDGET DOCUMENTS

***Budget of the United States Government***, Fiscal Year 2023, contains the Budget Message of the President, information on the President's priorities, and summary tables.

***Analytical Perspectives***, Budget of the United States Government, Fiscal Year 2023, contains analyses that are designed to highlight specified subject areas or provide other significant presentations of budget data that place the budget in perspective. This volume includes economic and accounting analyses, information on Federal receipts and collections, analyses of Federal spending, information on Federal borrowing and debt, baseline or current services estimates, and other technical presentations.

***Appendix, Budget of the United States Government***, Fiscal Year 2023, contains detailed information on the various appropriations and funds that constitute the budget and is designed primarily for the use of the Appropriations Committees. The Appendix contains more detailed financial information on individual programs and appropriation accounts than any of the other budget documents.

### GENERAL NOTES

1. All years referenced for budget data are fiscal years unless otherwise noted. All years referenced for economic data are calendar years unless otherwise noted.

2. At the time the Budget was prepared, none of the full-year appropriations bills for 2022 have been enacted, therefore, the programs and activities normally provided for in the full-year appropriations bills were operating under a continuing resolution (Public Law 117-43, division A, as amended by Public Law 117-70, division A; Public Law 117-86, division A; and Public Law 117-95).

3. The estimates in the 2023 Budget do not reflect the effects of the Ukraine Supplemental Appropriations Act, 2022 (included in Public Law 117-103) due to the late date of enactment.

4. Detail in this document may not add to the totals due to rounding.

# Table of Contents

# THE BUDGET MESSAGE OF THE PRESIDENT

To the Congress of the United States:

There is no greater testament to the grit and resilience of the American people than the extraordinary progress we have made together over the last year.

America entered 2021 in the midst of a devastating health crisis, on the heels of the worst economic crisis since the Great Depression. We ended 2021 having created over 6.5 million new jobs, the most our Nation has ever recorded in a single year. Our economy grew at a rate of 5.7 percent, the strongest growth in nearly 40 years. As of February, the unemployment rate has fallen from 6.4 percent when I took office to 3.8 percent—the fastest decline in recorded history. We are bringing everyone along, and leaving no one behind; child poverty is projected to reach the lowest level ever recorded, while long-term unemployment, youth unemployment, and Black and Hispanic unemployment have all dropped at record rates. Though family budgets are still tight, millions more Americans are earning paychecks today—and families have more money in their pockets than they did a year ago.

This progress was no accident. It was a direct result of the new economic vision for America I ran on—to build our economy from the bottom up and the middle out.

That vision was reflected in the American Rescue Plan Act of 2021, which lifted our Nation out of crisis; fueled our efforts to vaccinate America and combat the COVID-19 pandemic globally; enabled small businesses and State and local governments to hire, rehire, and retain workers; and delivered immediate economic relief to tens of millions of Americans—to put food on their tables, keep a roof over their heads, enable them to work by keeping schools and child care providers open, and maintain their dignity in the face of the pandemic.

That vision was also reflected in the Bipartisan Infrastructure Law—the most sweeping investment to rebuild America in history. After years of merely talking about fixing our infrastructure, we brought together Democrats and Republicans to finally get it done. Already, that law is paving the way for better jobs for millions of Americans—modernizing roads, bridges, ports, and airports; building a national network of charging stations, so America can own the electric car market; replacing lead pipes across the Nation, so every child can drink clean water at home and at school; providing affordable high-speed internet for every American; and strengthening our resilience to withstand both cyber and physical threats, including the devastating effects of the climate crisis.

There have been challenges as we have recovered from the COVID-19 pandemic. Due to the speed of our recovery, businesses have had a hard time hiring workers quickly enough to keep pace with resurgent demand. Disruptions to global supply chains have also contributed to higher prices. As a result, America was not immune to the worldwide inflation that has followed the pandemic—leaving too many families struggling to keep up with their bills. Since January, that pain has also been compounded by the anticipation and aftermath of Vladimir Putin's invasion of Ukraine—from the time he began amassing troops on Ukraine's borders, triggering a response in global oil markets, the price of a gallon of gas has risen by more than a dollar here at home as of mid-March.

Today, however, as a result of the new economic vision we are building our economy around, we are well-positioned to meet the challenges and seize the opportunities of this decisive decade. We are competing with China from a position of strength, while leading a global coalition united in condemnation of Russian aggression against Ukraine. We are tackling the climate crisis with urgency, strengthening the global health architecture to combat COVID-19 and future pandemics, and enhancing cybersecurity and addressing emerging cyber threats. We are joining with allies and partners to write the rules of 21st Century economics, trade, and technology.

My Budget details the next steps forward on our journey to execute a new economic vision, reduce costs for families, reduce the deficit, and build a better America. It is a Budget anchored in my bedrock belief that America is at its best when we invest in the backbone of our Nation: the hardworking people in every community who make our Nation run.

My Budget lays out detailed investments to build on a record-breaking year of broad-based, inclusive growth—and meet the challenges of the 21st Century. It is a call to reduce costs for families' biggest expenses; grow, educate, and invest in our workforce; bolster our public health infrastructure; save lives by investing in strategies such as community policing and community violence interventions, strategies proven to reduce gun crime; and advance equity, environmental justice, and opportunity for all Americans.

As I discussed in my 2022 State of the Union Address, my Budget also reflects a bipartisan unity agenda—areas where we can all come together to make progress. That includes investments to help beat the opioid epidemic; take on the invisible costs of the mental health crisis, especially among our children; support our veterans; and end cancer as we know it. My super-charged Cancer Moonshot plan has a goal of cutting cancer death rates by at least 50 percent over the next 25 years—while my vision for ARPA-H, the Advanced Research Projects Agency for Health, seeks breakthroughs in cancer, Alzheimer's, diabetes, and more.

Critically, my Budget would also keep our Nation on a sound fiscal course. It fights inflation and helps families deal with rising costs by growing our economy, making more goods in America, and lowering the costs families face. Its bold ideas are fully paid for, with tax reforms that more than offset the cost of new investments. It fulfills my ironclad promise that no one earning less than $400,000 per year would pay an additional penny in new taxes—while ensuring that the wealthiest Americans and the biggest corporations begin to pay their fair share. It keeps us on track to reduce the deficit this year to less than half of what it was before I took office.

After a year of historic progress, I am more optimistic about America today than I have ever been. We are on a path to win the competition for the 21st Century. We are prepared once again to turn a moment of crisis into a breathtaking opportunity. We are stronger today than we were a year ago—and we will be stronger a year from now than we are today.

All we have to do is keep coming together—to keep building, keep giving working families a fighting chance, and keep expanding the possibilities of our Nation. That is what my Budget is all about, and I look forward to working together to keep delivering for the American people.

JOSEPH R. BIDEN, JR.

THE WHITE HOUSE.

# CONFRONTING URGENT CRISES AND DELIVERING HISTORIC PROGRESS

When the President took office, the United States was confronting overlapping crises of unprecedented scope and scale: a once-in-a-century pandemic; a sharp economic downturn; an accelerating climate crisis; and a legacy of persistent inequity. On day one of his Administration, the President immediately got to work leveraging every tool at his disposal to tackle these crises head-on—mobilizing the Nation around an ambitious agenda to deliver results for working families. Under the President's leadership—and thanks to the grit and resilience of the American people in the face of significant challenges—America has made historic progress.

## POWERING A HISTORIC ECONOMIC RESURGENCE

When the President took office, he faced an economy that was struggling to recover from the most severe downturn since the Great Depression. The unemployment rate stood at 6.4 percent, with 10 million Americans unable to find a job. Factoring in workers who dropped out of the labor force or couldn't find full-time work, the unemployment rate was closer to 11 percent. Between February 2020 and January 2021, the labor force participation rate for women dropped by 3.7 percent overall, 6.4 percent for Black women, and 7.1 percent for Hispanic women, undoing more than 35 years of progress in labor force participation. More than 18 million Americans were receiving unemployment benefits, and more than half of the unemployed had been without a job for more than 15 weeks. Thousands of small businesses—the backbone of the American economy—were forced to close their doors, some permanently. Millions of Americans reported that they were struggling to pay their rent or mortgage, put food on the table, and cover basic expenses.

In the face of these challenges, the President took decisive action—not only to put a floor under the immediate economic fallout, but to begin rebuilding the economy from the bottom-up and the middle-out. The President's strategy helped rescue the economy, delivered urgently needed relief to families and small businesses, fueled record-breaking economic growth and job creation, and bolstered American competitiveness and manufacturing.

### Fueling Record-Breaking Economic Growth and Job Creation

Thanks to the American Rescue Plan Act of 2021 (American Rescue Plan) and the President's vaccination program, the American economy is recovering faster than other advanced economies around the world, with record-breaking economic growth and job creation. In 2021, the Administration achieved the best record of job creation in American history, with the single largest calendar year decrease in the unemployment rate on record. As of February 2022, the unemployment rate had fallen to 3.8 percent. Prior to passage of the American Rescue Plan, the Congressional Budget Office did not project the unemployment rate dropping to 3.8 percent at any point over this entire decade. Since the

President took office, the economy has created 7.4 million jobs. The number of long-term unemployed Americans decreased by two million during the President's first year in office—a record decline. More than 1.6 million women have reentered the workforce.

As more Americans have gotten back to work, the economy has come roaring back to life. In 2021, the American economy grew at 5.7 percent, the fastest rate in nearly four decades. For the first time in 20 years, the economy grew faster than China's. Applications for new small businesses increased 30 percent since before the pandemic. Retail sales rose by $90 billion. Between the American Rescue Plan's tax cuts for families that are raising children and rising wages for middle class families, the average American had more money in their pocket each month in 2021 than they did in 2020—after accounting for inflation.

### Strengthening Supply Chains, Promoting Competition, and Bolstering Manufacturing

To sustain and build on this economic momentum, the President has taken aggressive actions to address other global challenges triggered by the COVID-19 pandemic and expand the productive capacity of the economy—strengthening domestic supply chains, promoting competition and innovation to help lower prices, and bolstering American manufacturing.

In the face of global supply chain bottlenecks and global inflation, last year the President issued an Executive Order 14017, "America's Supply Chains," to strengthen the Nation's supply chains and launched the Supply Chain Disruptions Task Force to address disruptions linked to the COVID-19 pandemic. Thanks to those efforts, more cargo is moving through American ports than at any time in the Nation's history. The number of containers sitting on the docks at the Ports of Los Angeles and Long Beach—two of the largest ports in America—for more than eight days has been cut by more than 70 percent since the beginning of November 2021. Holiday

sales surged 14 percent last year—a new record. Despite dire predictions about delivery delays at the end of last year, holiday season delivery times dropped below their pre-pandemic levels, while retail inventories hit an all-time record. In addition, the Administration's Action Plan for America's Ports and Waterways and Trucking Action Plan to Strengthen America's Trucking Workforce continue to help American port operators move a record amount of goods from ships to shelves as quickly as possible and connect more Americans to good jobs in the trucking industry.

The President has also taken key steps to promote greater competition, protect consumers, and lower prices. In July 2021, the President signed a historic Executive Order 14036, "Promoting Competition in the American Economy," to encourage competition across industries, including travel, healthcare, food, internet service, and more. Executive Order 14036 includes 72 initiatives by more than a dozen Federal agencies to promptly tackle some of the most pressing competition problems across the economy. In the months since, the Administration has worked to lower prices for hearing aids and has taken on meat processors that are raking in record profits while raising prices for consumers at the grocery store. Also, enforcement agencies like the Federal Trade Commission and the Department of Justice (DOJ) have taken strong actions to protect consumers from anti-competitive mergers that could have raised prices for consumers and businesses.

The President has also relentlessly focused on implementing an industrial strategy to revitalize America's manufacturing base. During his first week in office, the President signed Executive Order 14005, "Ensuring the Future is Made in All of America by All of America's Workers," that created the first-ever Made in America Office within the Office of Management and Budget and launched a Government-wide initiative to leverage the Federal Government's procurement power to support American manufacturing and American workers. To help translate that commitment into action, the President announced the most robust changes to the Buy American Act of

1933 in more than 70 years—raising the domestic content threshold, strengthening domestic supply chains for critical goods, and increasing transparency and accountability. Since the President took office, the economy has added more than 423,000 new manufacturing jobs. Manufacturing as a share of Gross Domestic Product has returned to pre-pandemic levels. In recent months, major companies have announced significant investments in new manufacturing lines and factories that will create thousands of good-paying jobs in the United States.

## MOUNTING A FORCEFUL RESPONSE TO THE PANDEMIC

In January 2021, the United States lacked the tools to fully protect people against COVID-19. Less than one percent of Americans—some two million people—were fully vaccinated. Less than half of our Nation's schools were open for in-person instruction. Zero at-home tests were on the market. The Nation faced shortages of protective equipment for frontline workers and didn't have enough vaccines, vaccinators, or locations where people could get vaccinated. Meanwhile, the rapid spread of the virus had disrupted the education of millions of students, forced an estimated 1-in-4 child care providers to close their doors, taken a significant toll on Americans' mental health, produced a massive surge in domestic violence incidents and overdose deaths, worsened food and housing insecurity, and deepened long-standing health inequities in communities across the Nation.

From the day he took office, the President has been unrelenting in his focus on ensuring that the American people have the tools necessary to protect themselves against COVID-19: more vaccines, boosters, tests, masks, and treatments. Through the American Rescue Plan, the Administration secured $160 billion to support the President's vaccination program, therapeutics, testing and mitigation, personal protective equipment, and the broader COVID-19 response. These resources have played a key role in preventing hospitalizations and deaths from COVID-19 and combatting the Delta and Omicron variants.

As a result of these efforts, the United States is moving forward safely. As of March 2022, more than 216 million Americans—including more than 75 percent of adults—had been fully vaccinated. Vaccines are approved or authorized for all Americans five years of age and older. There are more than 90,000 vaccination locations in communities across the Nation, with 90 percent of Americans living within five miles of a site. The Administration is securing millions of doses of a highly effective pill to treat COVID-19. In addition, the President's focus on equity is delivering results: the latest CDC data show that gaps in vaccination rates among Latino, Black, and White adults have been effectively closed.

After a year of children falling behind on learning, the President took action to open schools and get kids and teachers back into their classrooms. The American Rescue Plan provided $130 billion to schools to allow for their safe operation and address the COVID-19 pandemic's impacts on learning, as well as an additional $10 billion to support COVID-19 testing. The Administration has also ensured schools have the flexibility and resources they need to ensure children are fed healthy meals. As a result, about 99 percent of schools are now open, full-time and in person—up from just 46 percent when the President took office. This progress has been crucial to ensuring that all students can safely be back where they belong—learning alongside their peers—and to helping them recover from any learning loss or mental health setbacks they experienced since the onset of the COVID-19 pandemic.

As the Administration combats the COVID-19 pandemic at home, the United States is also leading the international effort to respond to the Global COVID-19 pandemic and vaccinate the world. At the President's direction, the United States has committed to donating 1.2 billion vaccine doses for free with no strings attached—the largest commitment in the world—and has already shipped 500 million doses to 112 countries, four times more doses than any other country. The Administration is also working to expand access to tests, treatments, and personal protective equipment globally. These efforts are saving lives, improving our national and economic security, and helping prevent the emergence and spread of other dangerous variants and future biological catastrophes like pandemics.

### Delivering Urgent Relief

With the passage of the American Rescue Plan, the Administration quickly mobilized vital resources to help families and small businesses weather the worst of the pandemic and create a bridge to an economic recovery.

In 2021, the Administration delivered more than 175 million economic impact payments of $1,400 to the vast majority of Americans—totaling over $400 billion in relief. The American Rescue Plan expanded the Child Tax Credit for families of more than 61 million children, with up to $3,600 available for families with children under six, and $3,000 for families with children 6 to 17 years old. For the first time—and beginning just four months after the American Rescue Plan's passage—these payments were made on a monthly basis, providing a reliable boost to working families to help cover essential expenses. The American Rescue Plan also helped make quality health insurance coverage through the Affordable Care Act more affordable than ever—with

families saving an average of $2,400 on their annual premiums, and 4 out of 5 consumers finding quality coverage for under $10 a month.

At the same time, the American Rescue Plan provided funding to all 50 States and more than 34,000 cities, towns, and counties to help prevent layoffs and get workers back on the job. It provided $28 billion through the Restaurant Revitalization Fund (RRF) to help more than 100,000 restaurants and bars keep their doors open. The RRF was part of the more than $450 billion in emergency relief delivered to more than six million small businesses in 2021 through the Administration's implementation of the Paycheck Protection Program, COVID Economic Injury Disaster Loan (EIDL) program, the COVID EIDL Targeted and Supplemental Advance programs, and the Shuttered Venue Operators Grants program.

The Administration also implemented the Emergency Rental Assistance program, which delivered 3.8 million payments totaling over $33 billion to eligible households in 2021. Over 80 percent of the assistance was delivered to lowest-income households (those earning 50 percent of area median income and below). As a result of these efforts, the Administration has built a nationwide infrastructure for rental assistance and eviction prevention, helping keep eviction filings below 60 percent of historical levels and preventing households from experiencing further economic setbacks associated with housing insecurity.

## DELIVERING PROGRESS AT HOME

Under the President's leadership, our Nation has not only risen to meet urgent crises, but we have begun building a better and more resilient America. Since taking office, the President has advanced an agenda to bring more dignity, opportunity, security, and prosperity to working families across the Nation—from rebuilding America's infrastructure and laying a new foundation for growth, to taking historic action to combat the

climate crisis, to embedding equity as a priority across the Federal Government.

### Rebuilding America's Crumbling Infrastructure

After decades of talk in Washington about rebuilding our crumbling infrastructure, last year the President worked with members of both parties in the Congress to pass and sign into law the Infrastructure Investment and Jobs Act (Bipartisan Infrastructure Law)—a once-in-a-generation investment in our Nation's infrastructure and competitiveness that will help build a better America, create good-paying union jobs, ease inflationary pressures, and grow the economy sustainably and equitably so that everyone has the chance to get ahead for decades to come.

For the up to 10 million American households that lack safe drinking water, the Bipartisan Infrastructure Law invests $55 billion to deliver clean water to all American families and eliminate the Nation's lead service lines—including in tribal, rural, and disadvantaged communities. To ensure that every American has access to reliable, affordable, high-speed internet, it invests a historic $65 billion for broadband deployment to help lower the cost of internet service and to close the digital divide. To fix and rebuild our roads and bridges, it reauthorizes surface transportation programs for five years and makes the single largest investment in repairing and reconstructing our Nation's bridges since the construction of the interstate highway system.

The Bipartisan Infrastructure Law also: includes crucial resources to improve transportation options for millions of Americans and reduce greenhouse emissions through the largest investment in public transit in U.S. history; upgrades the Nation's airports and ports to strengthen domestic supply chains; makes the largest investment in passenger rail since the creation of Amtrak; builds a national network of electric vehicle chargers; makes our Nation's infrastructure resilient against the impacts of climate change, cyber-attacks, and extreme weather events; and includes more for our Nation.

In the months since the President signed the Bipartisan Infrastructure Law into law, the Administration has hit the ground running to deliver results. Already, the Administration has mobilized resources to: connect tribal Nations to reliable, affordable high-speed internet; replace, repair, and rehabilitate bridges across the Nation;

upgrade critical infrastructure at 3,075 airports; update America's aging water infrastructure, sewerage systems, pipes and service lines; and stop toxic waste from harming communities.

## Taking Aggressive Action to Tackle the Climate Crisis

When the President took office, he made tackling the climate crisis a central priority across the entire Federal Government. At his direction, the Administration has launched an unprecedented effort to reduce climate pollution while creating good-paying union jobs, advancing environmental justice, strengthening the Nation's resilience, and protecting public health.

On the first day of his Administration, the President rejoined the Paris Agreement. The President set an ambitious goal to reduce greenhouse gas pollution 50 to 52 percent from 2005 levels by 2030, while rallying countries around the world to make their own bold contributions. At the 2021 United Nations Climate Change Conference, the President launched the *U.S. Methane Emissions Reduction Action Plan* in support of the Global Methane Pledge of September 18, 2021 (Global Methane Pledge) to reduce the world's methane emissions 30 percent from 2020 levels by 2030. To advance the global phasedown of hydrofluorocarbons, the President secured domestic action to reduce emissions of these super pollutants by 85 percent within 15 years. Also, to reward clean manufacturing in the global marketplace, the President announced a groundbreaking commitment to negotiate the world's first carbon-based arrangement on steel and aluminum trade with the European Union.

The President also set a target to eliminate carbon pollution from the electricity sector by 2035 and is fast-tracking clean energy—including the launch of the American offshore wind industry, with the first approvals of large-scale projects on the path to 30 gigawatts by 2030. The President's support for innovation and deployment of wind, solar, storage, transmission, and more is creating good-paying union jobs and lowering energy bills for consumers. To jumpstart an electric transportation future that's Made in America, the President brought together automakers and autoworkers around a new ambitious goal for 50 percent electric vehicle sales share in 2030. The President also launched a Federal Sustainability Plan to lead by example through the Federal Government's vehicle fleet, buildings, and purchasing power. The President has pursued new climate-smart agriculture and forestry initiatives, protections for cherished monuments and habitats, and the America the Beautiful initiative to conserve 30 percent of U.S. lands and waters by 2030. Also, the President launched whole-of-Government efforts to build resilience to intensifying climate impacts, protect the economy and financial systems from climate-related financial risks, and secured emergency funding last year to help communities recover from disasters and related crop losses.

The President is also making good on his Justice40 commitment to deliver 40 percent of the benefits from Federal investments in climate and clean energy to disadvantaged communities to build their economies. To create good-paying union jobs in hard-hit energy communities, the President has driven Federal resources to coal, oil and gas, and power plant communities. The President made environmental justice and economic revitalization a centerpiece of the Bipartisan Infrastructure Law, which includes the largest investment in addressing legacy pollution in American history, including capping orphaned oil and gas wells that are major sources of methane emissions and local air pollution. The Environmental Protection Agency has committed to cleanup and clear the backlog of 49 previously unfunded Superfund sites and accelerate cleanup at dozens of other sites across the Nation.

Through the Bipartisan Infrastructure Law, the Administration also secured the largest investments ever in the Nation's water infrastructure, power grid, public transit, and resilience. The law will help replace lead service lines and reduce exposure to the dangerous per- and poly-fluoroalkyl chemical substances. It will make communities safer and our infrastructure more resilient to the impacts of climate change and cyber-attacks, with an investment of over $50 billion to protect against droughts, heat, floods, and wildfires, in addition to a major investment in weatherization. It invests more than $65 billion through the Department of Energy to upgrade our power infrastructure, facilitate the expansion of renewables and clean energy, and fund new programs to support the development, demonstration, and deployment of cutting-edge clean energy technologies to accelerate our transition to a zero-emission economy. Also, it will deliver thousands of electric school buses nationwide, including in rural communities, helping school districts across the Nation buy clean, American-made, zero-emission buses, and replace the yellow school bus fleet for America's children.

### Advancing Equity across the Economy and Nation

The promise of our Nation is that every American has an equal chance to live to their full potential. Yet persistent systemic inequities and barriers to opportunity have denied this promise for so many. That is why the President has taken historic steps to put equity at the center of his agenda—and why the President assembled the most diverse cabinet in American history to deliver on this Government-wide effort.

Beginning on his first day in office, the President took a series of landmark executive actions to advance equity. The President signed a day-one Executive Order 13985, "Advancing Racial Equity and Support for Underserved Communities Through the Federal Government," on advancing equity and racial justice across the Federal Government; a day-one Executive Order 13988, "Preventing and Combating Discrimination on the Basis of Gender Identity or Sexual Orientation," directing Federal agencies to extend protections against discrimination based on gender identity and sexual orientation, upon which agencies have already acted in the areas of housing, lending services, education, healthcare, and more; and Executive Order 14035, "Diversity, Equity, Inclusion, and Accessibility in the Federal Workforce," on advancing diversity, equity, inclusion, and accessibility (DEIA) across the Federal workforce. In the months since, Federal agencies have been hard at work implementing these orders—delivering more equitable external work, revised DEIA policies and trainings, and updated civil rights guidance and regulations.

The Administration set a Government-wide goal of increasing the share of Federal contracts to small disadvantaged businesses, including those owned by people of color, by 50 percent by 2025—which would translate to an increase of $100 billion to these firms over five years. The Bipartisan Infrastructure Law made permanent the Minority Business Development Agency, the only Federal entity focused exclusively on promoting growth and competitiveness of minority-owned businesses, and elevated the head of the Agency to the Under Secretary level. The Administration provided $32 billion specifically for tribal communities and Native Americans as part of the American Rescue Plan, as well as $13 billion in direct investments in tribal communities through the Bipartisan Infrastructure Law. Also, the American Rescue Plan's $122 billion Elementary and Secondary School Emergency Relief Fund, in addition to providing critically needed funds to safely reopen and operate schools and support students, included landmark maintenance of equity requirements that protected high-poverty districts and schools from disproportionate funding reductions and the highest poverty districts from any reductions.

On International Women's Day in March 2021, the President signed Executive Order 14020, "Establishment of the White House Gender Policy Council," establishing the first White House Gender Policy Council within the Executive Office of the President and charged the office with leading a Government-wide effort to advance gender equity and equality. To guide that work, last year the Administration issued the first ever *National Strategy on Gender Equity and Equality* in the United Sates to advance equal opportunity for people of all genders—now, agencies are developing action plans to achieve their top priorities for advancing gender equity and equality. The Administration has also: taken critical steps to eliminate racial disparities in maternal health; advanced historic military justice reform; deployed resources from the American Rescue Plan for domestic violence and sexual assault prevention and services; and announced bold commitments to advance women's economic security, gender-based violence prevention and response, and sexual and reproductive health and rights both at home and around the world.

The President has also moved decisively to condemn racism, xenophobia, and intolerance against Asian Americans (AA) and Native Hawaiian and Other Pacific Islanders (NHOPI). In his first week in office, the President signed a Presidential Memorandum establishing an official policy to ensure the Federal Government stands up against racism, xenophobia, nativism, and bias. The memorandum directed all Federal agencies to take steps to ensure their actions mitigate anti-Asian bias and xenophobia, especially in the response to the COVID-19 pandemic, and charged DOJ to partner with AA and NHOPI communities to respond to and prevent hate crimes and violence. In May 2021, the President signed into law the COVID-19 Hate Crimes Act, bipartisan legislation that makes significant improvements to the Nation's response to hate crimes.

The Administration is also creating opportunity and building wealth in rural communities. For example, the American Rescue Plan's Coronavirus State and Local Fiscal Recovery Fund has enabled States to invest in critical rural broadband and water infrastructure. In addition, the Administration's efforts to strengthen the food system through American Rescue Plan funding are opening up new markets for farmers and ranchers in rural America and supporting a fairer, more competitive, and more resilient meat and poultry supply chain. The Administration is also working to keep rural hospitals open, supporting rural providers, expanding rural healthcare coverage, and making it more affordable than ever, with nearly 700,000 rural Americans gaining coverage through the Patient Protection and Affordable Care Act in 2021 alone and families saving an average of $2,400 per year due to the American Rescue Plan.

## RESTORING AMERICAN LEADERSHIP ON THE WORLD STAGE

As the President has restored the Nation's strength at home, he has revitalized our alliances and partnerships around the world, brought American leadership to bear on the defining issues of our time, and invested in our military advantage. The President has prioritized strategic competition with China and worked with allies and partners to resist coercion and deter aggression from Beijing and Moscow, and ended America's 20-year war in Afghanistan while removing all U.S. troops. The President has led a global response to the COVID-19 pandemic and made historic investments to confront the climate crisis. As the United States enters what will be a decisive decade, the President is positioning America to win the competition for the 21st Century.

The President strengthened our foundational partnership with Europe on the full range of global challenges, including climate, health security, trade and technology, and our collective and decisive response to Russian aggression against Ukraine. In the Indo-Pacific, America is strengthening its role and expanding its cooperation with longtime allies and partners, including new diplomatic, defense and security, critical and emerging technology and supply chain, and climate and global health initiatives, while supporting stronger ties between our European and Indo-Pacific allies. Closer to home, the United States has invested in relationships in the Western Hemisphere, including by reviving the North American Leaders' Summit to consult with neighboring countries, committing to work together on major regional migration efforts, and collaborating on health security, democratic renewal, and shared economic growth. In the Middle East and North Africa, the United States is working to de-escalate tensions, curb Iran's destabilizing activities, and help regional partners lay the foundation for greater security, prosperity, and opportunity for their people. The United States is partnering with African nations and publics to solve problems of common interest—from health security to shared economic prosperity to countering terrorism—mindful of the continent's importance to critical global issues.

From his first days in office, the President has restored U.S. leadership to the most significant global challenges of our time. At the President's direction, the United States has served as the world's vaccine arsenal, pledging more than 1.2 billion COVID-19 vaccines to countries around the world, providing lifesaving supplies, and hosting a Global COVID-19 Summit to build better health security for the future. The President renewed U.S. leadership on climate, including by rejoining the Paris Agreement. Alongside the Group of Seven partners, the United States launched the Build Back Better World Initiative to meet the developing world's infrastructure needs transparently, sustainably, and with high standards. The President convened 110 governments in the first Summit for Democracy to catalyze action to strengthen democracy at home and abroad. The United States rejoined and reinforced international institutions such as the World Health Organization and the United Nations Human Rights Council. In addition, the Administration reprioritized cybersecurity by strengthening resilience at home and accelerating cooperation with allies and the private sector.

Under the President's leadership, the United States has resolved significant trade disputes, including on airplanes, steel, and aluminum, and protected American workers by centering them in our foreign policy. Last year, the United States rallied more than 100 countries to join the Global Methane Pledge to cut emissions by 30 percent by 2030. In addition to fueling the global economic recovery, America secured a historic win for workers and middle-class families through the agreement of 130 countries to support a global minimum tax for the world's largest corporations.

As America leads with diplomacy, we are also investing in our military—the strongest fighting force the world has ever known. We are investing in our warfighting advantages, understanding that a combat-credible military is the foundation of deterrence and America's ability to prevail in conflict. At the same time, the United States is making disciplined choices about the use of military force and focusing its attention on the military's primary responsibilities: to defend the homeland; deter conflict; and to fight and win the Nation's wars, while remaining committed to the wellbeing of its servicemembers and their families.

# BUILDING A BETTER AMERICA

Under the President's leadership, America is on the move again. Together, in the face of unprecedented crises and ongoing challenges, we have begun to change the trajectory of our economy to finally make it work for working people—with historic job creation, faster economic growth, and more money in workers' pockets. We are moving forward safely, continuing to combat the pandemic and building better preparedness for the next health emergency. We have mobilized the Federal Government to tackle the climate crisis with the urgency that the science demands. We have launched a Government-wide effort to advance equity and expand opportunity across our Nation and economy. We have revitalized our global alliances and our leadership on the world stage. While much work remains, we are poised to meet the challenges and opportunities ahead.

The President's Budget details his vision for how to carry this momentum forward and build a better America. It is a Budget anchored in the President's bedrock belief that the economy grows from the bottom up and the middle out, and that America is at its best when all Americans— not just the wealthiest few—can get ahead and pursue their promise and potential.

In last year's Budget, the President put forward a set of proposals designed to ensure America emerged from the pandemic even stronger than before. Just months later, the President's proposals to rebuild America's crumbling infrastructure, expand access to clean drinking water, and invest in communities too often left behind were enacted in the Infrastructure Investment and Jobs Act (Bipartisan Infrastructure Law). Earlier this month, the Congress reached a bipartisan agreement to fund the Government for 2022, ending a damaging series of short-term continuing resolutions and taking a first step to reinvest in research, education, public health, and other core functions of the Government.

In the State of the Union, the President reiterated his commitment to work with the Congress to pass legislation to lower costs for American families, reduce the deficit, and expand the productive capacity of the American economy. The President supports legislation that: cuts costs for prescription drugs, healthcare premiums, child care, long-term care, housing, and college, including tuition-free community college and expanded support for Historically Black Colleges and Universities (HBCUs), Tribally Controlled Colleges and Universities (TCCUs), and Minority-Serving Institutions (MSIs); reduces energy costs by combatting climate change and accelerating the transition to a clean energy economy while creating good-paying jobs for American workers; supports families with access to free, high-quality preschool and paid family and medical leave and by continuing the enhanced Child Tax Credit and Earned Income Tax Credit; and provides health coverage to millions of uninsured Americans. The President believes these proposals must be paired with reforms that ensure corporations and the wealthiest Americans pay their fair share, including by paying the taxes they already owe and closing loopholes that they exploit.

Because discussions with the Congress continue, the President's Budget includes a deficit neutral reserve fund to account for future legislation, preserving the revenue from proposed tax and prescription drug reforms for the investments needed to bring down costs for American families and expand our productive capacity. This approach reflects the President's continued commitments to: advancing the policies that strengthen our economy and reduce costs for American families; working collaboratively with the Congress to shape this legislation; and fully paying for the long-term costs of all new investments and reducing the deficit. As the President said in the State of the Union, he is committed to working with the Congress on legislation that both cuts costs for families and reduces the Federal deficit. To be conservative, however, the Budget reflects this reserve fund as deficit neutral.

In addition, the President's 2023 Budget proposes other targeted investments that would: help expand the productive capacity of our economy to create jobs, bring down prices, and continue our historic recovery; improve our public health infrastructure and spur transformational medical research; combat and prevent gun violence and other violent crime; drive action to lead the world in combating the climate crisis; and make higher education more affordable and accessible while advancing equity, opportunity, and security for all Americans. (Due to the timing of enactment, the 2023 Budget does not reflect the details of the 2022 appropriations bill, and investment levels in the Budget are compared to 2021 funding.)

The Budget also provides the resources necessary to deliver on our commitments to the American people's security and prosperity by revitalizing American leadership on the world stage. We are at the beginning of a decisive decade that will determine the future of strategic competition with China, the trajectory of the climate crisis, and whether the rules governing technology, trade, and international economics enshrine or violate our democratic values. The Budget enables us to meet these challenges by investing both in our domestic and international sources of strength—from our dynamic and diverse workforce, to our industrial and innovation base, to our military and development enterprise, to our unparalleled network of allies and partners. In doing so, the Budget enables us to marshal global coalitions to act from a position of strength, whether in the face of Russian aggression or transnational threats.

The Budget also delivers on the President's commitment to fiscal responsibility. The deficit is on track to drop by more than $1 trillion this year, the largest-ever one-year decline. Under the Budget policies, annual deficits would fall to less than half of last year's levels as a share of the economy, while the economic burden of debt would remain low. The Budget's investments are more than paid for through additional tax reforms that ensure corporations and the wealthiest Americans pay their fair share, allowing us to cut costs for American families, strengthen our economy, and cut deficits and debt by more than $1 trillion over the coming decade.

## PROMOTING JOB CREATION, REDUCING COST PRESSURES, AND BOOSTING THE PRODUCTIVE CAPACITY OF THE ECONOMY

In 2021, America saw the strongest monthly job growth ever recorded, the largest decline in unemployment ever recorded, and the strongest economic growth in nearly four decades. Importantly, the benefits from this growth were broadly shared, and not only concentrated among those at the very top. At the same time, the United States—like virtually all advanced economies

around the world—is facing pandemic-driven price increases that strain family budgets. That is why the President is laser focused on building a more productive economy that can deliver more goods and services to the American people while bringing down costs and driving growth and job creation. The Budget builds on the progress the Administration has already made—as well as additional steps the President is pursuing—through a package of investments that would bolster the supply-side of the economy, create jobs and address cost pressures, and expand the economy's capacity over the medium- and long-term.

### Strengthening Supply Chains, Bolstering Manufacturing, and Improving Infrastructure

**Strengthens the Nation's Supply Chains through Domestic Manufacturing.** To help ignite a resurgence of American manufacturing and strengthen domestic supply chains, the Budget provides $372 million, an increase of $206 million over the 2021 enacted level, for the National Institutes of Standards and Technology's manufacturing programs to launch two additional manufacturing innovation institutes in 2023 and continue support for the two institutes funded in 2022. The Budget includes a $125 million increase for the Manufacturing Extension Partnership to make America's small and medium manufacturers more competitive, as well as $200 million for a new Solar Manufacturing Accelerator at the Department of Energy (DOE) to build domestic capacity in solar energy supply chains while moving away from imported products manufactured using unacceptable labor practices. The Budget provides $30 million to support programs that help ensure entrepreneurs have the tools and networks they need to bring cutting-edge innovation to the market.

**Accelerates Efforts to Move More Goods Faster through American Ports and Waterways.** The Budget continues support for the historic levels of Federal investment to modernize America's port and waterway infrastructure provided under the Bipartisan Infrastructure Law. The Budget includes $230 million for the Port Infrastructure Development Program to strengthen maritime freight capacity. In addition to keeping the Nation's supply chain moving by improving efficiency, the Department of Transportation will prioritize projects that also lower emissions—reducing environmental impact in and around America's ports. The Budget also includes $1.7 billion for the Harbor Maintenance Trust Fund to facilitate safe, reliable, and environmentally sustainable navigation at the Nation's coastal ports.

**Reduces Bottlenecks and Commute Times through Investments in Competitive Programs.** The Budget provides robust support for transportation projects that reduce commute times, improve safety, reduce freight bottlenecks, better connect communities, and reduce transportation-related greenhouse gas emissions. For example, investments include $4 billion for the new Bipartisan Infrastructure Law-authorized National Infrastructure Investments grant programs to support transportation projects with significant benefits across multiple modes.

**Modernizes and Upgrades Roads and Bridges.** To modernize, repair, and improve the safety and efficiency of the Nation's network of roads and bridges, the Budget provides $68.9 billion for the Federal-aid Highway program, including: $9.4 billion provided by the Bipartisan Infrastructure Law for 2023; $8 billion to rebuild the Nation's bridges; $1.4 billion to deploy a nationwide, publicly-accessible network of electric vehicle chargers and other alternative fueling infrastructure; $1.3 billion for a new carbon reduction grant program; and $1.7 billion for a new resiliency grant program to make surface transportation infrastructure more resilient to hazards such as climate change.

**Invests in Reliable Passenger and Freight Rail.** To ensure the safety and performance of the rail industry today and deliver the passenger rail network of the future, the Budget provides a historic $17.9 billion, a $15 billion increase over the 2021 enacted level. This includes $4.7 billion in additional funding on top of the $13.2 billion already provided by the Bipartisan Infrastructure Law for 2023. These resources would support $7.4 billion to significantly improve Amtrak's rolling stock and facilities, and $10.1 billion for existing and new competitive grant programs to support passenger rail modernization and expansion, address critical safety needs, and support the vitality of the freight rail network.

**Connects All Americans to High-Speed, Affordable, and Reliable Internet.** The President is committed to ensuring that every American has access to broadband, which would not only strengthen rural economies, but also create high-paying union jobs installing broadband. Building on key investments in the Bipartisan Infrastructure Law, the Budget provides $600 million for the ReConnect program, which provides grants and loans to deploy broadband to unserved areas—especially tribal areas—and $25 million to help rural telecommunications cooperatives refinance their Rural Utilities Service debt and upgrade their broadband facilities.

### Addressing Cost Pressures and Expanding Economic Capacity

**Increases Affordable Housing Supply.** To address the critical shortage of affordable housing in communities throughout the Nation, the Budget proposes $50 billion in mandatory funding and additional Low-Income Housing Tax Credits (LIHTC) to address market gaps, increase housing supply, and help to stabilize housing prices over the long-term. Specifically, the Budget provides $35 billion in mandatory funding at the Department of Housing and Urban Development (HUD) for State and local housing finance agencies and their partners to provide grants, revolving loan funds and other streamlined financing tools, as well as grants to advance State and local jurisdictions' efforts to remove barriers to affordable housing development. In addition, the Budget proposes $5 billion in mandatory funding for the Department of the Treasury's Community Development Financial Institutions Fund to support financing of new construction and substantial rehabilitation that creates net new units of affordable rental and for sale housing. The Budget also proposes modifying LIHTC to better incentivize new unit production, with a 10-year cost of nearly $10 billion. The Budget also provides more than $1.9 billion in discretionary funding for the HOME Investment Partnerships Program to construct and rehabilitate affordable rental housing and provide homeownership opportunities—the highest funding level for HOME in nearly 15 years.

**Fosters Competitive and Productive Markets and Targets Corporate Concentration.** The Budget reflects the Administration's commitment to vigorous marketplace competition through robust enforcement of antitrust law by including historic increases of $88 million for the Antitrust Division of the Department of Justice (DOJ) and $139 million for the Federal Trade Commission. The President also supports legislation that would align executives' interests with the long-term interests of shareholders, workers, and the economy by requiring executives to hold on to company shares that they receive for several years after receiving them, and prohibiting them from selling shares in the years after a stock buyback. This would discourage corporations from using profits to repurchase stock and enrich executives, rather than investing in long-term growth and innovation.

**Builds a Competitive and Resilient Food Supply Chain.** The Budget strengthens market oversight through investments in the Agricultural Marketing Service and the Animal and Plant Health Inspection Service, resulting in competitive meat and poultry product prices for American families and increased protection against invasive pests and zoonotic diseases. These programs build on the pandemic and supply chain assistance funding in the American Rescue Plan Act of 2021 (American Rescue Plan) to address pandemic-related vulnerabilities in the food system and create new market opportunities and good-paying jobs.

**Promotes Innovation and Science in Underrepresented Communities.** The Budget supports programs, including community-led capacity building and training, that expand equitable inclusion in Federal science and technology programs and the use of scientific and technological innovation to advance equitable outcomes. The Budget provides $393 million for the National Science Foundation (NSF), an increase of $172 million or 78 percent above the 2021 enacted level, for programs dedicated to increasing the participation of historically underrepresented communities in science and engineering fields. The Budget also provides $260 million for DOE initiatives to build science and technology capacity in underserved institutions, including HBCUs, Hispanic Serving Institutions (HSIs), and TCCUs. In addition, the Budget provides $315 million through the U.S. Department of Agriculture (USDA) in agriculture research, education, and extension grants to build capacity in underserved institutions, including HBCUs, HSIs, and TCCUs.

## Expanding Opportunities for Workers and Small Businesses

**Expands Access to Capital for Small Businesses.** The Budget addresses the need for greater access to affordable capital, particularly in underserved communities. The Budget increases the authorized lending levels in key Small Business Administration (SBA) programs by a total of $9.5 billion to significantly expand the availability of working capital, fixed capital, and venture capital funding for small businesses. The Administration looks forward to working with the Congress to ensure small manufacturers have sufficient working capital to help them meet human resource needs and purchase raw materials/inventory, while incentivizing them to finance renewable energy equipment projects.

**Supports Minority-Owned Businesses to Narrow Racial Wealth Gaps.** The Budget elevates the stature and increases the capacity of the Minority Business Development Agency by providing the full $110 million authorized in the Bipartisan Infrastructure Law. This funding would bolster services provided to minority-owned enterprises by expanding the Business Center program, funding Rural Business Centers, opening new regional offices, and supporting innovative initiatives to foster economic resiliency.

**Creates New Global Markets for American Goods.** The Budget provides an additional $26 million over 2021 enacted levels to bolster commercial diplomacy and enhance export promotion through a targeted expansion of the Foreign Commercial Service at the International Trade Administration, which would help American businesses seeking to increase exports abroad, navigate new foreign markets, or find market opportunities.

**Equips Workers with Skills They Need to Obtain High-Quality Jobs.** The Budget invests $100 million to help community colleges work with the public workforce development system and employers to design and deliver high-quality workforce programs. The Budget also provides $100 million for a new Sectoral Employment through Career Training for Occupational Readiness program, which would support training programs focused on growing industries, enabling disadvantaged workers to enter on-ramps to middle class jobs, and creating the skilled workforce the economy needs to thrive.

**Expands Access to Registered Apprenticeships (RA).** RA is a proven earn-and-learn model that raises participants' wages and puts them on a reliable path to the middle class. The Budget invests $303 million, a $118 million increase above the 2021 enacted level, to expand RA opportunities in high growth fields, such as information technology, advanced manufacturing, healthcare, and transportation, while increasing access for historically underrepresented groups, including people of color and women. To improve access to RA for women, the Budget doubles the Department of Labor's (DOL) investment in its Women in Apprenticeship and Nontraditional Occupations grants, which provide pre-apprenticeship opportunities to boost women's participation in RA.

**Provides Youth Training and Employment Pathways.** The Budget invests in programs that provide young people with equitable access to high-quality training and career opportunities, including $75 million for a new National Youth Employment Program to create high-quality summer and year-round job opportunities for underserved youth. The Budget also provides $145 million for YouthBuild, $48 million above the 2021 enacted level, to enable more at-risk youth to gain the education and occupational skills they need to obtain good jobs. To further advance equity and inclusion, the Budget also provides $15 million to test new ways to enable low-income youth with disabilities—including youth who are in foster care, involved in the justice system, or are experiencing homelessness—to successfully transition to employment.

# RESTORING AMERICAN LEADERSHIP AND CONFRONTING GLOBAL THREATS

To ensure and strengthen American security, prosperity, and democracy, we must both deliver at home and lead on the world stage. The Budget invests in the key pillars of our international strength in order to position us to contend with determined competitors, address transnational threats, and manage crises as they arise. The Budget invests in deepening and modernizing our alliances and partnerships, as we are stronger in managing challenges—whether in the form of China's trade abuses, Russian aggression, or the worsening climate crisis—when we work in concert with those who share our values or interests. The Budget bolsters our cybersecurity and strengthens our military by ensuring we have the resources necessary to sustain deterrence and backstop our diplomacy, as well as fight and win the Nation's wars if necessary. Also, the Budget renews our commitment to sustainable and inclusive development, including through the President's Build Back Better World initiative, which supports building stronger infrastructure to confront the climate crisis, strengthening global health security, working toward gender equality, and shaping the rules of the road for digital connectivity. In addition, the Budget makes critical investments in addressing the root causes of migration while strengthening our immigration system, and in meeting the sacred commitments we have made to our Nation's veterans.

## Confronting 21ˢᵗ Century Threats

**Supports United States' European Allies and Partners.** The Budget supports Ukraine, the United States' strong partnerships with North Atlantic Treaty Organization (NATO) allies, and other European partner states by bolstering funding to enhance the capabilities and readiness of U.S. forces, NATO allies, and regional partners in the face of Russian aggression.

**Promotes Integrated Deterrence in the Indo-Pacific and Globally.** The Budget proposes $773 billion for the Department of Defense (DOD). To sustain and strengthen deterrence, the Budget prioritizes China as the Department's pacing challenge. The 2023 Pacific Deterrence Initiative highlights some of the key investments that DOD is making that are focused on strengthening deterrence in the Indo-Pacific region. Also, DOD is building the concepts, capabilities, and posture necessary to meet these challenges, working in concert with the interagency and America's allies and partners to ensure that deterrence is integrated across domains, theaters, and the spectrum of conflict.

**Defends Freedom Globally.** To support American leadership in defending democracy, freedom, and security worldwide, the Budget includes nearly $1.8 billion to support a free and open, connected, secure, and resilient Indo-Pacific Region and the Indo-Pacific Strategy, and $400 million for the Countering the People's Republic of China Malign Influence Fund. In addition, the Budget provides $682 million for Ukraine, an increase of $219 million above the 2021 enacted level, to counter Russian malign influence and to meet emerging needs related to security, energy, cybersecurity issues, disinformation, macroeconomic stabilization, and civil society resilience.

**Supports Democracy Globally.** In response to political fragility and increasing authoritarianism around the world, the Budget provides more than $3.2 billion to support global democracy, human rights, anti-corruption, and governance programming, consistent with the commitments made during the President's Summit for Democracy. The Budget advances the Presidential Memorandum on Advancing the Human Rights of Lesbian, Gay, Bisexual, Transgender, Queer, and Intersex Persons around the World, the U.S. Strategy on Countering Corruption, and the Presidential Initiative on Democratic Renewal.

**Counters Persistent Threats.** While focused on maintaining robust deterrence against China and Russia, the Budget would also enable DOD to counter other persistent threats including those posed by North Korea, Iran, and violent extremist organizations.

**Advances U.S. Cybersecurity.** The Budget invests in cybersecurity programs to protect the Nation from malicious cyber actors and cyber campaigns. Last year, the President signed Executive Order 14028, "Improving the Nation's Cybersecurity," charting a new course to improve the Nation's cybersecurity. Executive Order 14028 prioritizes protecting and modernizing Federal Government systems and data, improving information-sharing between the U.S. Government and the private sector, enhancing standards for secure software development, improving detection of cyber threats and vulnerabilities on Federal systems, and strengthening the United States' ability to respond to incidents when they occur.

**Modernizes the Nuclear Deterrent.** The Budget maintains a strong, credible nuclear deterrent, as a foundational aspect of integrated deterrence, for the security of the Nation and U.S. allies. The Budget supports the U.S. nuclear triad and the necessary ongoing nuclear modernization programs, to include the nuclear command, control, and communication networks.

## Marshalling American Leadership to Tackle Global Challenges

**Renews America's Leadership in International Institutions.** The Budget continues the Administration's efforts to lead through international organizations by meeting the Nation's commitments to fully fund U.S. contributions and to pay United Nations peacekeeping dues on time and in full. The Budget also provides $1.4 billion for the World Bank's International Development Association (IDA). This investment restores the United States' historical role as the largest World Bank donor to support the development of low- and middle-income countries, which benefits the American people by increasing global stability, mitigating climate and health risks, and developing new markets for U.S exports. The U.S. contribution would also support the United States' $3.5 billion pledge to the next IDA replenishment, a critical component of the global response to the devastating impacts of the COVID-19 pandemic on developing countries.

**Advances American Leadership in Global Health, Including Global Health Security and Pandemic Preparedness.** The Budget includes $10.6 billion to bolster U.S. leadership in addressing global health and health security challenges, a $1.4 billion increase above the 2021 enacted level. Within this total, the Budget demonstrates U.S. leadership by supporting a $2 billion contribution to the Global Fund's seventh replenishment, for an intended pledge of $6 billion over three years, to save lives and continue the fight against HIV/AIDS, tuberculosis, and malaria, and to support the Global Fund's expanding response to the COVID-19 pandemic and global health strengthening. This total also includes $1 billion to prevent, prepare for, and respond to future infectious disease outbreaks, including the continued expansion of Global Health Security Agenda capacity-building programs and a multilateral financial intermediary fund for health security and pandemic preparedness. The Budget also invests in the global health workforce and systems to enhance countries' abilities to provide core health services, improve health systems resiliency, and respond to crises while mitigating the impacts of crises on routine health services. In addition, the Budget includes $6.5 billion in mandatory funding for the Department of State and the U.S. Agency for International Development over five years to make transformative investments in pandemic and other biological threat preparedness globally in support of U.S. biodefense and pandemic preparedness strategies and plans. This pandemic preparedness funding would strengthen the global health workforce, support pandemic preparedness research and development (R&D), advance global R&D capacity, and support health security capacity and financing to prevent, detect, and respond to future COVID-19 variants and other infectious disease outbreaks.

**Advances Equity and Equality Globally.** The Budget provides $2.6 billion to advance gender equity and equality across a broad range of sectors. This includes $200 million for the Gender Equity and Equality Action Fund to advance the economic security of women and girls. This total also includes funding to strengthen the participation of women in conflict prevention, resolution, and recovery through the implementation of the Women, Peace, and Security Act of 2017.

**Continues Collaborative U.S. Leadership in Central America and Haiti.** As part of a comprehensive strategy to drive systemic reform while addressing the root causes of irregular migration from Central America to the United States, the Budget invests $987 million in the region to continue meeting the President's four-year commitment of $4 billion. Further, in response to deteriorating conditions and widespread violence in Haiti, the Budget invests $275 million to strengthen Haiti's recovery from political and economic shocks, such as strengthening the capacity of the Haitian National Police, combating corruption, strengthening the capacity of civil society, and support services for marginalized populations. These investments would ensure that the United States is able to revitalize partnerships that build economic resilience, democratic stability, and citizen security in the region.

**Strengthens U.S. Leadership on Refugee and Humanitarian Issues.** The Budget provides more than $10 billion to respond to the unprecedented need arising from conflict and natural disasters around the world to serve over 70 countries and approximately 240 million people. The Budget continues rebuilding the Nation's refugee admissions program and supports up to 125,000 admissions in 2023.

### Strengthening America's Immigration System

**Ensures a Fair and Efficient Immigration System.** The Administration is committed to ensuring that United States Citizenship and Immigration Services (USCIS) meets its mission of administering the Nation's lawful immigration system and safeguarding its integrity and promise by efficiently and fairly adjudicating requests for immigration benefits. The Budget provides $765 million for USCIS to efficiently process increasing asylum caseloads, address the immigration application backlog, and improve refugee processing.

**Supports America's Promise to Refugees.** The Budget provides $6.3 billion to the Office of Refugee Resettlement (ORR) to help rebuild the Nation's refugee resettlement infrastructure and support the resettling of up to 125,000 refugees in 2023. The Budget would also help ensure that unaccompanied immigrant children are unified with relatives and sponsors as safely and quickly as possible and receive appropriate care and services while in ORR custody.

**Improves Border Processing and Management.** The Budget provides $15.3 billion for the U.S. Customs and Border Protection and $8.1 billion for the U.S. Immigration and Customs Enforcement to enforce the immigration laws, further secure the border, and effectively manage irregular migration along the Southwest border, including $309 million for border security technology and $494 million for noncitizen processing and care costs.

**Improves Immigration Courts.** The Budget invests $1.4 billion, an increase of $621 million above the 2021 enacted level, in the Executive Office for Immigration Review (EOIR) to continue addressing the backlog of over 1.5 million cases that are currently pending in the immigration courts. This funding supports 100 new immigration judges, including the support personnel required to create maximum efficiencies in the court systems, as well as an expansion of EOIR's virtual court initiative. The Budget would also invest new resources in legal access programming, including $150 million in discretionary resources to provide access to representation for adults and families in immigration proceedings. Complementing this new program is a proposal for $4.5 billion in mandatory resources to expand these efforts over a 10-year period. Providing resources to support legal representation in the immigration court system creates greater efficiencies in processing cases while making the system fairer and more equitable.

### Delivering on Our Commitments to Veterans

**Prioritizes Veteran Medical Care.** The Budget provides $119 billion—a historic 32-percent increase above the 2021 enacted level for the Department of Veterans Affairs (VA). In addition to fully funding inpatient, outpatient, mental health, and long-term care services, the Budget supports programs that improve VA healthcare quality and delivery, including investments in training programs for clinicians, health professionals, and medical students. With more women choosing VA for their healthcare than ever before, the Budget also invests $9.8 billion for all of women veterans' healthcare, including $767 million toward women's gender specific care. The Budget also further supports VA's preparedness for regional and national public health emergencies.

**Prioritizes Veteran Suicide Prevention.** The Budget provides $497 million to support the Administration's veteran suicide prevention initiatives, including: implementation of the Veterans Crisis Line's 988 expansion initiative;

the suicide prevention 2.0 program to grow public health efforts in communities; a lethal means safety campaign in partnership with other agencies; and the Staff Sergeant Parker Gordon Fox Suicide Prevention Grant Program to enhance community-based clinical strategies.

**Bolsters Efforts to End Veteran Homelessness.** The Budget increases resources for veterans' homelessness programs to $2.7 billion, with the goal of ensuring every veteran has permanent, sustainable housing with access to healthcare and other supportive services to prevent and end veteran homelessness.

**Invests in Caregivers Support Program.** The Budget recognizes the important role of family caregivers in supporting the health and wellness of veterans. The Budget provides funding for the Program of General Caregivers Support Services. The Budget also provides $1.8 billion for the Program of Comprehensive Assistance for Family Caregivers, which includes stipend payments and support services to help empower family caregivers of eligible veterans.

**Supports Research Critical to Veterans' Health Needs.** Extensive research at VA medical centers, outpatient clinics, and nursing homes each year has significantly contributed to advancements in healthcare for veterans and all Americans. The Budget provides $916 million to continue the development of VA's research enterprise, including research in support of the *American Pandemic Preparedness: Transforming Our Capabilities* plan's goals. The Budget also invests $81 million within VA research programs for precision oncology to provide access to the best possible cancer care for veterans.

**Continues and Enhances Efficient Delivery of Veterans Benefits.** The Budget would ensure that veterans receive the benefits they have earned and deserve, such as disability compensation, education and employment training, and home loan guarantees. The Budget invests $120 million for VA to support automating the disability compensation claims process from submission to authorization which would increase VA's ability to deliver faster and more accurate claim decisions for veterans.

**Addresses Environmental Exposures.** The Budget increases resources for new presumptive disability compensation claims related to environmental exposures from military service. The Budget also invests $51 million within VA research programs and $63 million within the VA medical care program for Health Outcomes Military Exposures to increase scientific understanding of and clinical support for veterans and healthcare providers regarding the potential adverse impacts from environmental exposures during military service.

**Honors the Memory of All Veterans.** The Budget includes $430 million to ensure veterans and their families have access to exceptional memorial benefits, including two new and replacement national cemeteries. These funds maintain national shrine standards at the 158 VA managed cemeteries and provide the initial operational investment required to open new cemeteries.

# STRENGTHENING AMERICA'S PUBLIC HEALTH INFRASTRUCTURE

From the President's first days in office, the Administration has mounted a forceful response to the COVID-19 pandemic and taken action to advance the health and well-being of the American people. Through the American Rescue Plan, the Administration secured critical resources to support the President's historic vaccination program, testing and mitigation, therapeutics, and personal protective equipment—and to help make quality health insurance available through the Patient Protection and Affordable Care Act more affordable. To build on this progress and bolster America's public health infrastructure, the Budget includes key investments to ensure the United States is prepared to confront future pandemics and other biological threats domestically and globally, expand access to critical health services, address other diseases and epidemics, and advance and accelerate transformative medical research.

## *Ensuring World-Class Public Health Infrastructure*

**Prepares for Future Pandemics and Other Biological Threats.** While combatting the ongoing COVID-19 pandemic, the United States must catalyze advances in science, technology, and core capabilities to prepare the Nation for the next biological threat and strengthen U.S. and global health security. The Budget makes transformative investments in pandemic preparedness across the Department of Health and Human Services (HHS) public health agencies—$81.7 billion available over five years—to enable an agile, coordinated, and comprehensive public health response to protect American lives, families, and the economy and to prevent, detect, and respond to emerging biological catastrophes. The Budget builds toward a goal of making effective vaccines and therapeutics available within 100 days of identifying a new pathogen by investing in basic and advanced R&D of medical countermeasures for high priority viral families and biological threats, including expansion and modernization of clinical trial infrastructure and regulatory capacity necessary to inform evaluation and subsequent authorizations or approvals, as well as expansion of domestic manufacturing capacity to ensure sufficient supply is available. The Budget also enhances public health infrastructure by making significant investments in public health laboratory capacity, domestic and global threat surveillance, and public health workforce development that would enable States, localities, tribal nations, and Territories to mount a rapid and robust response to future threats. Further, the Budget encourages development of innovative antimicrobial drugs through advance market commitments for critical-need antimicrobial drugs. The President also supports extending telehealth coverage under Medicare beyond the COVID-19 Public Health Emergency to study its impact on utilization of services and access to care. In addition, the Budget supports enhanced DOD and DOE investments in: medical counter-measures, including vaccines, diagnostics, and therapeutics research and manufacturing; disease detection and biosurveillance; advanced computing; lab biosafety and biosecurity; and threat reduction activities with America's global partners.

**Builds Advanced Public Health Systems and Capacity.** The Budget includes $9.9 billion in discretionary funding to build capacity at the Centers for Disease Control and Prevention (CDC) and at the State and local levels, an increase of $2.8 billion over the 2021 enacted level. These resources would improve the core immunization program, expand public health infrastructure in States and Territories, strengthen the public health workforce, support efforts to modernize public health data collection, increase capacity for forecasting and analyzing future outbreaks, including at Center for Forecasting and Outbreak Analytics, and conduct studies on long COVID conditions to inform diagnosis and treatment options. In addition, to advance health equity, the Budget invests in CDC programs related to viral hepatitis, youth mental health, and sickle cell disease. To address gun violence as a public health epidemic, the Budget invests in community violence intervention and firearm safety research.

**Expands Access to Vaccines.** The Budget establishes a new Vaccines for Adults (VFA) program, which would provide uninsured adults with access to all vaccines recommended by the Advisory Committee on Immunization Practices at no cost. As a complement to the successful Vaccines for Children (VFC) program, the VFA program would reduce disparities in vaccine coverage and promote infrastructure for broad, access to routine and outbreak vaccines. The Budget would also expand the VFC program to include all children under age 19 enrolled in the Children's Health Insurance Program and consolidate vaccine coverage under Medicare Part B, making more preventive vaccines available at no cost to Medicare beneficiaries.

**Guarantees Adequate and Stable Funding for the Indian Health Service (IHS).** The Budget significantly increases IHS's funding over time, and shifts it from discretionary to mandatory funding. For the first year of the proposal, the Budget includes $9.1 billion in mandatory funding, an increase of $2.9 billion above 2021. After that, IHS funding would automatically grow to keep pace with healthcare costs and population growth and gradually close longstanding service and facility shortfalls. Providing IHS stable and predictable funding would improve access to high quality healthcare, rectify historical underfunding of the Indian Health system, eliminate existing facilities backlogs, address health inequities, and modernize IHS' electronic health record system. This proposal has been informed by consultations with tribal nations on the issue of IHS funding and will be refined based on ongoing consultation.

**Advances Maternal Health and Health Equity.** The United States has the highest maternal mortality rate among developed nations, with an unacceptably high mortality rate for Black and American Indian and Alaska Native women. The Budget includes $470 million to: reduce maternal mortality and morbidity rates; expand maternal health initiatives in rural communities; implement implicit bias training for healthcare providers; create pregnancy medical home demonstration projects; and address the highest rates of perinatal health disparities, including by supporting the perinatal health workforce. The Budget also extends and increases funding for the Maternal, Infant, and Early Childhood Home Visiting Program, which serves approximately 71,000 families at risk for poor maternal and child health outcomes each year, and is proven to reduce disparities in infant mortality. To address the lack of data on health disparities and further improve access to care, the Budget strengthens collection and evaluation of health equity data. Recognizing that maternal mental health conditions are the most common complications of pregnancy and childbirth, the Budget continues to support the maternal mental health hotline and the screening and treatment for maternal depression and related behavioral health disorders. The Administration also looks forward to working with the Congress to advance the President's goal of doubling the Federal investment in community health centers, which would help reduce health disparities by expanding access to care.

**Supports Survivors of Domestic Violence and Other Forms of Gender Based-Violence.** The Budget proposes significant increases to support and protect survivors of gender-based violence, including $519 million for the Family Violence Prevention and Services (FVPSA) program to support domestic violence survivors—more than double the 2021 enacted level. This amount continues funding availability for FVPSA-funded resource centers, including those that support the Lesbian, Gay, Bisexual, Transgender, Queer, and Intersex community. The Budget would provide additional funding for domestic violence hotlines and cash assistance for survivors of domestic violence, as well as funding to support a demonstration project evaluating services for survivors at the intersection of housing instability, substance use coercion, and child welfare. In addition, the Budget would provide over $66 million for victims of human trafficking and survivors of torture, an increase of nearly $21 million over the 2021 enacted level. The Budget also proposes a historic investment of $1 billion to support Violence Against Women Act of 1994 (VAWA) programs, a $487 million or 95-percent increase over the 2021 enacted level. The Budget supports substantial increases for longstanding VAWA programs, including in legal assistance for victims, transitional housing, and sexual assault services. The Budget also provides resources for new programs to support transgender survivors, build community-based organizational capacity, combat online harassment and abuse, and address emerging issues in gender-based violence.

**Expands Access to Healthcare Services for Low-Income Women.** The Budget provides $400 million, an increase of nearly 40 percent over the 2021 enacted level, to the Title X Family Planning program, which provides family planning and other healthcare to low-income individuals. This increase in Title X funding would improve overall access to vital reproductive and preventive health services and advance gender and health equity.

### Addressing Other Diseases and Epidemics

**Transforms Mental Healthcare.** Mental health is essential to overall health, and the United States faces a mental health crisis that has been exacerbated by the COVID-19 pandemic. To address this crisis, the Budget proposes reforms to health coverage and major investments in the mental health workforce. For people with private health insurance, the Budget requires all health plans to cover mental health and substance use disorder benefits and ensures that plans have an adequate network of behavioral health providers. For Medicare, TRICARE, the VA healthcare system, health insurance issuers, group health plans, and the Federal Employees Health Benefit Program, the Budget lowers costs for mental health services for patients. The Budget also requires parity in coverage between mental health and substance use disorder—or behavioral health—and other medical benefits, and expands the types of providers covered under Medicare to treat these conditions. The Budget invests in increasing the number of mental health providers serving Medicaid beneficiaries, as well as in behavioral health workforce development and service expansion, including in primary care clinics and at non-traditional sites. The Budget also provides sustained and increased funding for community-based centers and clinics, including a State option to receive enhanced Medicaid reimbursement on a permanent basis. In addition, the Budget makes historic investments in youth mental health and suicide prevention programs and in training, educational loan repayment, and scholarships that help address the shortage of behavioral health providers, especially in underserved communities. The Budget also strengthens access to crisis services by building out the National Suicide Prevention Lifeline, which will transition from a 10-digit number to 988 in July 2022.

**Accelerates Innovation through the Advanced Research Projects Agency for Health (ARPA-H).** The Budget proposes a major investment of $5 billion for ARPA-H, significantly increasing direct Federal R&D spending in health to improve the health of all Americans. With an initial focus on cancer and other diseases such as diabetes and dementia, this major investment would drive transformational innovation in health technologies and speed the application and implementation of health breakthroughs. Funding for ARPA-H, along with additional funding for the National Institutes of Health, total a $49 billion request to continue to support research that enhances health, lengthens life, reduces illness and disability, and spurs new biotechnology productions and innovation.

**Advances the Cancer Moonshot Initiative.** The Budget proposes investments in ARPA-H, the National Cancer Institute, CDC, and the Food and Drug Administration to accelerate the rate of progress against cancer by working toward reducing the cancer death rate by at least 50 percent over the next 25 years and improving the experience of people who are living with or who have survived cancer.

**Commits to Ending the HIV/AIDS Epidemic.** The *National HIV/AIDS Strategy for the United States 2022–2025* commits to a 75-percent reduction in HIV infection by 2025.

To meet this ambitious target and ultimately end the HIV/AIDS epidemic in the United States, the Budget includes $850 million across HHS to aggressively reduce new HIV cases by increasing access to HIV prevention and care programs and ensuring equitable access to support services. This includes increasing access to pre-exposure prophylaxis (also known as PrEP) among Medicaid beneficiaries, which is expected to improve health and lower Medicaid costs for HIV treatment. The Budget also proposes a new mandatory program to guarantee PrEP at no cost for all uninsured and underinsured individuals, provide essential wrap-around services through States and localities, and establish a network of community providers to reach underserved areas and populations.

**Addresses the Opioid and Drug Overdose Epidemic.** The drug overdose epidemic claimed an estimated 104,000 lives in the 12-month period ending in September, 2021. To end this epidemic, a full range of service and supports are needed for individuals who use or are at risk of using substances that cause overdose, and their families. The Budget invests in services that prevent substance use disorder, expand quality evidence-based treatment, and help individuals sustain recovery. The Budget also includes $663 million specific to VA's Opioid Prevention and Treatment programs, including programs in support of the Jason Simcakoski Memorial and Promise Act.

## TAKING HISTORIC STEPS TO COMBAT THE CLIMATE CRISIS AND ADVANCE ENVIRONMENTAL JUSTICE

The President has not only taken bold action to confront the climate crisis, but he has turned it into an opportunity to create good-paying union jobs, advance environmental justice, and position America to lead the industries of the future. At his direction, the Administration has moved swiftly and decisively to restore America's global climate leadership, accelerate clean energy to lower costs and create jobs, jumpstart an electric future that is Made in America, advance environmental justice in line with Justice40 and economic

revitalization, and bolster our Nation's resilience in the face of accelerating extreme weather and natural disasters. To build on this progress, the President's Budget invests a total of $44.9 billion to tackle the climate crisis, a $16.7 billion increase over 2021 enacted. The Budget also makes historic investments in environmental justice, coal and powerplant communities facing energy transition, and innovation. These investments would enhance U.S. competitiveness and put America on a path to reduce greenhouse gas emissions 50 to 52 percent by 2030—all while supporting communities that have been left behind and ensuring that 40 percent of the benefits from tackling the climate crisis are targeted toward addressing the disproportionately high cumulative impacts on disadvantaged communities.

### *Advancing Clean Energy, Climate Data, and Resilience*

**Invests in Clean Energy Infrastructure and Innovation.** The Budget invests $3 billion to support clean energy projects that would create good-paying jobs and drive progress toward the Administration's climate goals. Investments include $502 million to weatherize and retrofit low-income homes, including $100 million for a new Low Income Home Energy Assistance Program (LIHEAP) Advantage pilot to electrify and decarbonize low-income homes. In addition, the Budget funds $150 million to electrify tribal homes and transition tribal colleges and universities to renewable energy, and $90 million for a new Grid Deployment Office to build the grid of the future. In addition, the Budget provides $150 million in credit subsidy for the DOE Title XVII Innovative Technology Loan Guarantee Program to support up to $5 billion in loans to eligible projects that avoid, reduce, or sequester greenhouse gas emissions. DOE would also launch a new Net-Zero Laboratory Initiative with a $58 million competition to reduce emissions across the national laboratory complex.

**Strengthens Domestic Clean Energy Manufacturing.** Meeting the challenge of climate change will require a dramatic scale-up in domestic manufacturing of key climate and clean energy equipment, providing opportunities for U.S. workers. The Budget includes $200 million to launch a new Solar Manufacturing Accelerator that would help create a robust domestic manufacturing sector capable of meeting the Administration's solar deployment goals without relying on imported goods manufactured using unacceptable labor practices. At the same time, it is imperative that the United States partners with its allies to create resilient clean energy supply chains. In addition, the Budget proposes a new $1 billion mandatory investment to launch a Global Clean Energy Manufacturing effort that would build resilient supply chains for climate and clean energy equipment through engagement with allies, enabling an effective global response to the climate crisis while creating economic opportunities for the United States to increase its share of the global clean technology market.

**Increases Demand for American Made, Zero-Emission Vehicles through Federal Procurement.** The Budget invests $757 million for zero-emission fleet vehicles and supporting charging or fueling infrastructure in the individual budgets of 19 Federal agencies to provide an immediate, clear, and stable source of demand to help accelerate American industrial capacity to produce clean vehicles and components. This includes $300 million for dedicated funds at the General Services Administration for other agencies and for charging infrastructure at the United States Postal Service (USPS).

**Provides Resources, Tools, and Coordination to Reduce Greenhouse Gas Emissions.** To help reduce greenhouse gas emissions and make the Nation's infrastructure more resilient, the Budget invests $100 million in grants to States and Tribes that would support the implementation of on-the-ground efforts to reduce and prevent greenhouse gas emissions in communities across the Nation, such as ensuring safe and effective oil and gas well pollution management and prevention, and supporting State and local government development of zero emissions vehicle charging infrastructure. The Budget also provides an additional $35 million over the 2021 enacted level to continue phasing out potent greenhouse gases known as hydrofluorocarbons, as well as resources to spur the development of a Federal climate data portal with support from the Department of the Interior (DOI) that would provide the public with accessible information on historical and projected climate impacts. The Budget also supports multi-agency efforts to integrate science-based tools into conservation planning in order to measure, monitor, report, and verify carbon sequestration, greenhouse gas reduction, wildlife stewardship, and other environmental services at the farm level and on Federal lands. In addition, the Budget supports enhancement of greenhouse monitoring and measurement capabilities, as well as efforts to make greenhouse gas data more accessible to a broad range of users.

**Strengthens Climate Resilience.** The Budget provides more than $18 billion for climate resilience and adaptation programs across the Federal Government, including $3.5 billion for the Department of Homeland Security, $5.9 billion at DOI, $1 billion for HUD, and $376 million for the National Oceanic and Atmospheric Administration (NOAA). These critical investments would reduce the risk of damages from floods and storms, restore the Nation's aquatic ecosystems, and make HUD-assisted multifamily homes more energy and water efficient and climate resilient. Resources include $507 million, $93 million above the 2021 enacted level, for the Federal Emergency Management Agency's (FEMA) flood hazard mapping program to incorporate climate science and future risks and robust investments in FEMA programs that help disadvantaged communities build resilience against natural disasters. The Budget also sustains funding for key conservation and ecosystem management initiatives, including the Civilian Climate Corps, alongside a historic $1.4 billion investment in the Bipartisan Infrastructure Law for ecosystem restoration across America.

**Invests in Conservation and Carbon Sequestration.** The Budget invests in the Administration's America the Beautiful Initiative, a multi-agency, multi-jurisdictional ecosystem management effort that would strengthen conservation partnerships between communities and Federal partners such as DOI, USDA, and NOAA. The President's historic goal of conserving and restoring 30 percent of America's lands and waters by 2030 incentivizes America's farmers, ranchers, and forest landowners to sequester carbon in soils and vegetation, and support the efforts and visions of States and tribal nations.

**Bolsters the Nation's Frontline Defenses against Catastrophic Wildfires.** Protecting communities, ecosystems, and infrastructure from wildfire requires a resilient and reliable Federal workforce. The Budget provides nearly $3.9 billion for Forest Service Wildland Fire Management, an increase of $778 million, plus an additional $2.6 billion authorized in the suppression cap adjustment. The Budget upholds the President's commitment that no Federal firefighter will make less than $15 an hour, and increases the size of the Federal firefighting workforce by providing $1.8 billion for personnel and preparedness. Consistent with the President's commitment to use the latest technologies in the fight against wildfires, the Budget also permanently sustains a pilot program that leverages sensitive satellite imagery to rapidly detect wildfires. The Budget also invests $646 million in Hazardous Fuels Management and Burned Area Rehabilitation programs to help reduce the risk and severity of wildfires and restore lands that were devastated by catastrophic fire over the last several years. This funding complements the $2.5 billion for hazardous fuels management and $650 million for burned area rehabilitation projects provided through the Bipartisan Infrastructure Law.

## Securing Environmental Justice and Delivering for Communities Left Behind

**Advances Equity and Environmental Justice.** The Budget provides historic support for underserved communities, and advances the President's Justice40 commitment to ensure 40 percent of the benefits of Federal investments in climate and clean energy reach disadvantaged communities. The Budget includes more than $12 million to coordinate implementation of the Justice40 initiative at impacted agencies. The Budget bolsters the Environmental Protection Agency's (EPA) environment justice efforts by investing over $1.5 billion across numerous programs that would help create good-paying jobs, clean up pollution, implement Justice40, advance racial equity, and secure environmental justice for communities that too often have been left behind, including rural and tribal communities. To better align with this vision, EPA's Budget structure includes the new Environmental Justice National Program Manager to help administer this work. The Budget also provides over $670 million for EPA's enforcement and compliance assurance efforts, including funding to implement an enforcement plan for climate and environmental justice inspections and community outreach. The Budget invests over $3 billion in DOI programs covered under the Justice40 initiative, such as tribal housing improvements, wildlife conservation grants, and energy infrastructure development in insular communities. In addition, the Budget provides DOE with $47 million to strengthen the Agency's environmental justice mission, $100 million to launch a new LIHEAP Advantage pilot to retrofit low-income homes with efficient electric appliances and systems, and $31 million for a new Equitable Clean Energy Transition initiative to help energy and environmental justice communities navigate and benefit from the transition to a clean energy economy. The Budget also provides $1.4 million for DOJ to establish an Office for Environmental Justice to further this important work.

**Supports the Clean Energy Transition in Rural America.** The Budget provides $300 million in new funding for grants, loans, and debt forgiveness for rural electric providers as they transition to clean energy, as well as $6.5 billion in loan authority for rural electric loans, an increase of $1 billion over the 2021 enacted level. The Budget also provides $20 million to support the new Rural Clean Energy Initiative, to provide technical assistance and promote coordination between USDA, DOE, and DOI that is necessary to achieve the President's de-carbonization goals and ensure clean energy funding is implemented effectively in rural areas. The Budget also supports multi-agency efforts to integrate science-based tools into conservation planning in order to measure, monitor, report, and verify carbon sequestration, greenhouse gas reduction, wildlife stewardship, and other environmental services at the farm level and on Federal lands.

**Supports Legacy Energy Communities.** The Budget includes over $9 billion in discretionary funding for priority programs and initiatives across the Federal Government that support economic revitalization and job creation in hard-hit coal, oil and gas, and power plant communities. This includes $100 million to support DOL's role in the multi-agency POWER+ Initiative, which aims to assist displaced workers and transform local economies and communities transitioning away from fossil fuel production to new, sustainable industries. The Budget also includes $35 million, administered by DOL in partnership with the Appalachian Regional Commission and the Delta Regional Authority, to help Appalachian and Delta communities develop local and regional workforce development strategies that promote long-term economic stability and opportunities for workers, especially those connected to the energy industry.

**Upgrades Drinking Water and Wastewater Infrastructure Nationwide.** The Budget provides roughly $4 billion for EPA water infrastructure programs, an increase of $1 billion over the 2021 enacted level. This includes full funding of grant programs authorized by the Drinking Water and Wastewater Infrastructure Act of 2021, an increase of $160 million over 2021 enacted for EPA's Reducing Lead in Drinking Water grant program. Outside of EPA, the Budget also includes $717 million in direct appropriation and $1.5 billion in loan level for USDA's Water and Wastewater Grant and Loan Program. These resources would help upgrade drinking water and wastewater infrastructure nationwide, with a focus on underserved communities that have historically been overlooked.

**Protects Communities from Hazardous Waste and Environmental Damage.** Preventing and cleaning up environmental damage that harms communities and poses a risk to public health and safety is a top Administration priority. The Budget includes $7.6 billion for DOE's Environmental Management program to support the cleanup of community sites used during the Manhattan Project and Cold War for nuclear weapons production, including $40 million for a new initiative to support historically under-served communities. The Budget also provides $1.2 billion for the Superfund program for EPA to continue cleaning up some of the Nation's most contaminated land, respond to environmental emergencies and natural disasters, and begin to adjust for revenue from the Superfund Tax. The Budget also provides $215 million for EPA's Brownfields program to enable EPA to provide technical assistance and grants to communities, including disadvantaged communities, so they can safely clean up and reuse contaminated properties. These funds complement Brownfields funding provided in the Bipartisan Infrastructure Law. These programs also support presidential priorities such as the Cancer Moonshot Initiative, by addressing contaminants that lead to greater cancer risk.

**Tackles Per- and Polyfluoroalkyl Substances (PFAS) Pollution.** PFAS are a set of man-made chemicals that threaten the health and safety of communities across the Nation, disproportionately impacting historically disadvantaged communities. As part of the President's commitment to tackling PFAS pollution, the Budget provides approximately $126 million, $57 million over the 2021 enacted level, for EPA to: increase the understanding of PFAS impacts to human health, as well as its ecological effects; restrict use to prevent PFAS from entering the air, land, and water; and remediate PFAS that have been released into the environment.

## Investing in Innovation and Climate Science

**Improves Climate Data and Forecasting.** The Budget significantly improves the Nation's ability to predict extreme weather and climate events so that American businesses and communities can have accurate and accessible information to allow them to better prepare for such events. This includes a bold investment of $2.3 billion for the next generation of weather satellites at NOAA which would help support the development of next generation technologies, and $2.4 billion for the Earth Science program at the

National Aeronautics and Space Administration, including more than $200 million to develop an Earth System Observatory that would provide a three-dimensional, holistic view of Earth to better understand natural hazards and climate change. The Budget also provides an additional $13 million over 2021 enacted levels to bolster EPA's abilities to forecast where smoke from wildfires could harm people and communicate where smoke events are occurring.

**Makes Historic Investments in Innovation and Climate Research.** To support the Administration's whole-of-Government approach to tackle the climate crisis, the Budget provides a historic investment of $17 billion for climate science and innovation, including more than $9 billion to DOE for clean energy research, development and demonstration, an increase of more than 33 percent over the 2021 enacted level. Within this total, the Budget provides $700 million for the Advanced Research and Projects Agency – Energy (ARPA-E) and proposes expanded authority for ARPA-E to more fully address innovation gaps around adaptation, mitigation, and resilience to the impacts of climate change. The Budget provides $913 million at NSF for research to better understand climate change and its adverse impacts and $500 million for R&D in clean energy and emission mitigation technologies. The Budget invests $6 million in USDA's climate hubs, a multi-agency undertaking to leverage climate science and increase landowner awareness of—and engagement in—efforts to combat climate change. In addition, the overall budget for DOE's Office of Science would grow 11 percent over 2021 enacted levels.

## Restoring America's Global Climate Leadership

**Advances the President's Historic Climate Pledge.** The Budget request includes over $11 billion in international climate finance, meeting the President's pledge to quadruple international climate finance a year early. U.S. international climate assistance and financing would: accelerate the global energy transition to net-zero emissions by 2050; help developing countries build resilience to the growing impacts of climate change, including through the *President's Emergency Plan for Adaptation and Resilience (PREPARE)* and other programs; and support the implementation of the President's *Plan to Conserve Global Forests: Critical Carbon Sinks*. Among these critical investments are $1.6 billion for the Green Climate Fund, a critical multilateral tool for financing climate adaptation and mitigation projects in developing countries and support for a $3.2 billion loan to the Clean Technology Fund to finance clean energy projects in developing countries.

## EXPANDING ECONOMIC OPPORTUNITY, ADVANCING EQUITY, AND STRENGTHENING AMERICAN DEMOCRACY

From his first days in office, the President has pursued an agenda to ensure all Americans can lead lives of dignity and extend the reach of America's promise. To further that agenda, the Budget includes a range of crucial investments to help ensure that all Americans can pursue their potential and fully participate in our economy and our democracy—improving education and supporting students; advancing equity, dignity, and security across our Nation and economy; expanding housing opportunities; and ensuring safety and justice and reinvigorating American democracy.

### *Improving Education*

**Makes Historic Investments in High-Poverty Schools.** To advance the goal of providing a high-quality education to every student, the Budget provides $36.5 billion for Title I, more than doubling the program's funding compared to the 2021 enacted level, through a combination of discretionary and mandatory funding. Title I helps schools provide students in low-income communities the learning opportunities and supports they need to succeed. This substantial new support for the program, which serves 25 million students in nearly 90 percent of school districts across the Nation, would be a major step toward fulfilling the President's commitment to addressing long-standing funding disparities between under-resourced schools—which disproportionately serve students of color—and their wealthier counterparts.

**Makes Historic Investments in College Affordability and Completion.** To help low- and middle-income students overcome financial barriers to postsecondary education, the Budget proposes to double the maximum Pell Grant by 2029. This begins with a historic $2,175 increase for the 2023-2024 school year, compared to the 2021-2022 school year, thereby expanding access and reaching nearly 6.7 million students. The Budget would also support strategies to improve the retention, transfer, and completion of students by investing the Federal TRIO Programs, Gaining Early Awareness and Readiness for Undergraduate Programs, and new retention and completion grants. The Budget also invests in institutional capacity at HBCUs, TCCUs, MSIs, and low-resourced institutions such as community colleges, by providing an increase of $752 million over the 2021 enacted level. This funding includes $450 million in four-year HBCUs, TCCUs, and MSIs to expand research and development infrastructure at these institutions. The Administration also looks forward to working with the Congress on changes to the Higher Education Act that ease the burden of student debt, including through improvements to the Income Driven Repayment and Public Service Loan Forgiveness programs.

**Expands Access to Affordable, High-Quality Early Child Care and Learning.** The Budget provides $20.2 billion for HHS's early care and education programs, an increase of $3.3 billion over the 2021 enacted level. This includes $7.6 billion for the Child Care and Development

Block Grant, an increase of $1.7 billion over the 2021 enacted level, to expand access to quality, affordable child care for families. In addition, the Budget helps young children enter kindergarten ready to learn by providing $12.2 billion for Head Start, an increase of $1.5 billion over the 2021 enacted level. The Budget also helps States identify and fill gaps in early education programs by funding the Preschool Development Grants program at $450 million, an increase of $175 million over the 2021 enacted level.

**Prioritizes the Health and Well-Being of Students.** Disruptions caused by the COVID-19 pandemic continue to take a toll on the physical and mental health of students, teachers, and school staff. Recognizing the profound effect of physical and mental health on academic achievement, the Budget includes a $1 billion investment to increase the number of school counselors, psychologists, social workers, nurses, and other health professionals in schools.

**Increases Support for Children with Disabilities.** The President is committed to ensuring that children with disabilities receive the services and support they need to thrive in school and graduate ready for college or a career. The Budget provides an additional $3.3 billion over 2021 enacted levels—the largest two-year increase ever—for Individuals with Disabilities Education Act (IDEA) Grants to States, with a total of $16.3 billion to support special education and related services for students in grades Pre-K through 12. The Budget also doubles funding to $932 million for IDEA Part C grants, which support early intervention services for infants and families with disabilities that have a proven record of improving academic and developmental outcomes.

## *Advancing Equity, Dignity, and Security*

**Expands Opportunities for Minority- and Women-Owned Businesses.** The Budget provides a $31 million increase over the 2021 enacted level to support women, people of color, veterans, and other underserved entrepreneurs through SBA's Entrepreneurial Development programs. This bold commitment ensures entrepreneurs have access to counseling, training, and mentoring services. The Budget also provides $331 million for the Department of the Treasury's Community Development Financial Institutions (CDFI) Fund, an increase of $61 million, or 23 percent, above the 2021 enacted level. CDFIs provide historically underserved and often low-income communities access to credit, capital, and financial support to grow businesses, increase affordable housing, and reinforce healthy neighborhood development.

**Supports Economic Development and Invests in Underserved Communities.** The Budget provides $3.8 billion for the Community Development Block Grant program to help communities modernize infrastructure, invest in economic development, create parks and other public amenities, and provide social services. The Budget includes a targeted increase of $195 million to spur equitable development and the removal of barriers to revitalization in 100 of the most underserved neighborhoods in the United States.

**Empowers and Protects Workers.** To ensure workers are treated with dignity and respect in the workplace, the Budget invests $2.2 billion, an increase of $397 million above the 2021 enacted level, in DOL's worker protection agencies. Between 2016 and 2020, these agencies lost approximately 14 percent of their staff, limiting their ability to perform inspections and conduct investigations. The Budget would enable DOL to conduct the enforcement and regulatory work needed to ensure workers' wages and benefits are protected, address the misclassification of workers as independent contractors, and improve workplace health and safety. The Budget also ensures fair treatment for millions of workers by restoring resources to oversee and enforce the equal employment obligations of Federal contractors, including protections against discrimination based on race, gender, disability, gender identity, and sexual orientation.

**Reduces Lead and Other Home Health Hazards for Vulnerable Families.** The Budget provides $400 million, an increase of $40 million above the 2021 enacted level, for States, local governments, and nonprofits to reduce lead-based paint and other health hazards in the homes of low-income families with young children. The Budget also includes $25 million to address lead-based paint and $60 million to prevent and mitigate other housing-related hazards, such as fire safety and mold, in Public Housing.

**Provides Robust Support for Tribal Communities.** The Budget requests $4.5 billion for DOI tribal programs, more than $1 billion above the 2021 enacted level. These investments would support public safety and justice, social services, climate resilience, and educational needs to uphold Federal trust responsibilities and promote equity for historically underserved communities. This includes a $156 million increase to support reconstruction work at seven Bureau of Indian Education schools. This funding complements Bipartisan Infrastructure Law investments to address climate resilience needs in tribal communities. The Budget proposes to reclassify Contract Support Costs and Indian Self-Determination and Education Assistance Act of 1975 Section 105(l) leases as mandatory spending, providing certainty in meeting these ongoing needs through dedicated funding sources. The Budget further proposes to provide mandatory funding to the Bureau of Reclamation for operation and maintenance of previously enacted Indian Water Rights Settlements, and the Administration is interested in working with the Congress on an approach to provide a mandatory funding source for future settlements. The Budget also complements Bipartisan Infrastructure Law investments to address climate resilience needs in tribal communities with $673 million in tribal climate funding at DOI.

**Advances Child and Family Well-Being in the Child Welfare System.** The Budget proposes to expand and incentivize the use of evidence-based foster care prevention services to keep families safely together and to reduce the number of children entering foster care. For children who do

need to be placed into foster care, the Budget provides States with support and incentives to place more children with relatives or other adults who have an existing emotional bond with the child and fewer children in group homes and institutions, while also providing additional funding to support youth who age out of care without a permanent caregiver. The Budget proposes to nearly double flexible funding for States through the Promoting Safe and Stable Families program and proposes new provisions to expand access to legal representation for children and families in the child welfare system. The Budget also provides $100 million in competitive grants for States and localities to advance reforms that would reduce the overrepresentation of children and families of color in the child welfare system, address the disparate experiences and outcomes of these families, and provide more families with the support they need to remain safely together. In addition, the Budget provides $215 million for States and community-based organizations to respond to and prevent child abuse.

**Supports Health and Economic Security of America's Seniors and People with Disabilities.** The Budget provides $14.8 billion, an increase of $1.8 billion above the 2021 enacted level, to improve services at the Social Security Administration's field offices, State disability determination services, and teleservice centers for retirees, people with disabilities, and their families. At HUD, the Budget supports 2,000 units of new permanently affordable housing specifically for seniors and people with disabilities, supporting the Administration's priority to maximize independent living for people with disabilities. The Budget also includes nearly $500 million to Centers for Medicare and Medicaid Services Survey and Certification, a 24-percent increase, to support health and safety inspections at nursing homes and enhances Medicare for seniors by expanding behavioral health benefits, eliminating cost sharing for vaccines, and adding coverage of services from community health workers. The President also looks forward to working with the Congress on other policies to improve economic security and access to healthcare for seniors and people with disabilities.

**Strengthens the Unemployment Insurance (UI) Program and Combats Fraud.** The UI program has helped millions of Americans through periods of unemployment during the COVID-19 pandemic. The Budget invests $3.4 billion, an increase of $769 million above the 2021 enacted level, to modernize, protect, and strengthen this critical program. This includes several investments aimed at tackling fraud in the UI program, including funding to support more robust identity verification for UI applicants, help States develop and test fraud-prevention tools and strategies, and allow the Office of Inspector General to increase its investigations into fraud rings targeting the UI program.

**Improves Healthcare, Nutrition Assistance, and Economic Support for Americans in Puerto Rico and Other Territories.** The President supports: eliminating Medicaid funding caps for Puerto Rico and other Territories while aligning their matching rate with States; granting U.S. Territories the option to transition from current block grants to the Supplemental Nutrition Assistance Program; and providing parity to U.S. Territories in the Supplemental Security Income Program. The Administration will continue to work with the Congress to advance these policies.

## *Expanding Housing Opportunity*

**Expands the Housing Choice Voucher Program and Enhances Household Mobility.** The Housing Choice Voucher program currently provides 2.3 million low-income families with rental assistance to obtain housing in the private market. The Budget provides $32.1 billion, an increase of $6.4 billion—including emergency funding—over the 2021 enacted level, to maintain services for all currently assisted families and to expand assistance to an additional 200,000 households compared to the 2021 level, particularly those who are experiencing homelessness or fleeing, or attempting to flee, domestic violence or other forms of gender-based violence. The Budget also funds mobility-related supportive services to provide low-income families with greater options to move to higher-opportunity neighborhoods.

**Advances Efforts to End Homelessness.** To prevent and reduce homelessness, the Budget provides $3.6 billion, an increase of $580 million over the 2021 enacted level, for Homeless Assistance Grants to meet renewal needs and expand assistance to nearly 25,000 additional households, including survivors of domestic violence and homeless youth.

**Prevents and Redresses Housing Discrimination and Supports Access to Homeownership for First-Generation Homebuyers.** The Budget provides $86 million in grants to support State and local fair housing enforcement organizations and bolster education, outreach, and training on rights and responsibilities under Federal fair housing laws. The Budget supports access to homeownership for underserved borrowers, including many first-time and minority homebuyers, through Federal Housing Administration and Ginnie Mae credit guarantees. The Budget also provides $115 million for complementary loan and down payment assistance pilot proposals to expand homeownership opportunities for first-generation and/or low-wealth first-time homebuyers.

**Invests in Affordable Housing in Tribal Communities.** Native Americans are seven times more likely to live in overcrowded conditions and five times more likely to have inadequate plumbing, kitchen, or heating systems than all U.S. households. The Budget helps address poor housing conditions in tribal areas by providing $1 billion to fund tribal efforts to expand affordable housing, improve housing conditions and infrastructure, and increase economic opportunities for low-income families.

**Addresses Housing Needs in Rural America.** The Budget includes $1.9 billion for USDA's rural housing loan and grant programs, including increases for the rural multifamily housing programs which would help address housing insecurity, rent burdens, and the impacts of climate change in rural America, including through a new policy requiring construction practices to improve energy or water efficiency, implement green features, or strengthen climate resilience. The multifamily housing programs would fund the preservation or development of 224 affordable multifamily housing properties, totaling 11,100 units and provide rental assistance to 270,000 units. USDA's single-family housing loans would provide new homeownership opportunities to 171,000 rural borrowers. The Budget also provides $39 million to continue the Rural Partners Network initiative from 2022, which connects America's rural communities to a broad range of programs and resources throughout the Federal Government.

### Addressing Violent Crime, Ensuring Justice, and Strengthening American Democracy

**Invests in Federal Law Enforcement to Combat Gun Crime and Other Violent Crime.** The Budget once again makes robust investments to bolster Federal law enforcement capacity. The Budget includes $17.4 billion, an increase of $1.7 billion above the 2021 enacted level, for DOJ law enforcement, including a total of $1.7 billion for the Bureau of Alcohol, Tobacco, Firearms, and Explosives (ATF) to expand multijurisdictional gun trafficking strike forces with additional personnel, increase regulation of the firearms industry, enhance ATF's National Integrated Ballistic Information Network, and modernize the National Tracing Center. The Budget includes $1.8 billion for the U.S. Marshals Service to support personnel dedicated to fighting violent crime, including through fugitive apprehension and enforcement operations. The Budget also provides the Federal Bureau of Investigation with an additional $69 million to address violent crime, including violent crimes against children and crime in Indian Country. In addition, the U.S. Attorneys are provided with $72.1 million to prosecute violent crimes.

**Supports State and Local Law Enforcement and Community Violence Prevention and Intervention Programs to Make Our Neighborhoods Safer.** The Budget provides $3.2 billion in discretionary resources for State and local grants and $30 billion in mandatory resources to support law enforcement, crime prevention, and community violence intervention.

**Reinvigorates Federal Civil Rights Enforcement.** In order to address longstanding inequities and strengthen civil rights protections, the Budget invests $367 million, an increase of $101 million over the 2021 enacted level, in civil rights protection across DOJ. These resources support police reform, the prosecution of hate crimes, enforcement of voting rights, and efforts to provide equitable access to justice. Investments also provide mediation and conciliation services through the Community Relations Service.

**Reforms the Federal Criminal Justice System.** The Budget leverages the capacity of the Federal justice system to advance innovative criminal justice reform initiatives and serve as a model for reform that is not only comprehensive in scope, but evidence-informed and high-impact. The Budget supports key investments in First Step Act implementation, including $100 million for a historic collaboration with the Bureau of Prisons (BOP), DOJ, and DOL for a national initiative to provide comprehensive workforce development services to people in the Federal prison system, both during their time in the BOP facilities and after they are transferred to community placement. In support of Federal law enforcement reform and oversight, the Budget also proposes $106 million to support the deployment of body-worn cameras (BWC) to DOJ's law enforcement officers, as well as an impact evaluation to assess the role of BWC in advancing criminal justice reform.

**Protects U.S. Elections and the Right to Vote.** As America's democracy faces threats across the Nation, the State, county, and municipal governments that run Federal elections have struggled to obtain resources commensurate with the improved access and security that voters expect and deserve. Federal funding for the equipment, systems, and personnel that comprise the Nation's critical election infrastructure has been episodic or crisis-driven. To provide State and local election officials with a predictable funding stream for critical capital investments and increased staffing and services, the Budget proposes $10 billion in new elections assistance funding to be allocated over 10 years. The Budget also proposes to fund an expansion of USPS delivery capacity in underserved areas and support for vote-by-mail, including making ballots postage-free and reducing the cost of other election-related mail for jurisdictions and voters.

# PUTTING THE NATION ON A SOUND FISCAL AND ECONOMIC COURSE

When the President took office, the COVID-19 pandemic and resulting economic crisis had driven deficits to high levels: $3.1 trillion, or 14.9 percent, of Gross Domestic Product (GDP) in 2020. Thanks in part to the success of the American Rescue Plan and the President's economic strategy, strong economic growth has driven deficits down dramatically. The Budget projects a deficit of $1.4 trillion, or 5.8 percent, of GDP for 2022—less than half the deficit the President inherited and more than $1 trillion less than the deficit for 2021.

The Budget builds on this progress by proposing smart, targeted, and fully-offset investments designed to expand economic capacity, spur durable economic growth, create jobs, reduce cost pressures, and foster shared prosperity. The Budget reflects the President's belief that growing the economy from the bottom up and the middle out creates more growth, higher wages, more jobs, lower prices, less poverty, and makes it easier to achieve fiscal sustainability.

The Budget also reflects the President's commitment to put the Nation on a sound fiscal course by more than fully offsetting the cost of its new investments. Overall, the Budget's policies would reduce deficits by more than $1 trillion over 10 years through additional tax reforms that ensure corporations and the wealthiest Americans pay their fair share. Under the Budget policies, annual deficits would fall further as a share of the economy, while the economic burden of debt would stay low.

## Paying for Investments through a Fairer Tax System

The Budget's investments are more than paid for through reforms that would create a fairer tax system.

**Proposes a New Minimum Tax on Billionaires.** The tax code currently offers special treatment for the types of income that wealthy people enjoy. This special treatment, combined with sophisticated tax planning and giant loopholes, allows many of the very wealthiest people in the world to end up paying a lower tax rate on their full income than many middle-class households. To finally address this glaring problem, the Budget includes a 20 percent minimum tax on multi-millionaires and billionaires who so often pay indefensibly low tax rates. This minimum tax would apply only to the wealthiest 0.01 percent of households—those with more than $100 million—and over half the revenue would come from billionaires alone.

**Ensures Corporations Pay Their Fair Share.** The Budget also includes an increase to the rate that corporations pay in taxes on their profits. Corporations received an enormous tax break in 2017. While their profits have soared, their investment in the economy did not. Those tax breaks did not trickle down to workers or consumers. Instead of allowing some of the most profitable corporations in the world to avoid paying their fair share, the Budget would raise the corporate tax rate to 28 percent, still well below the 35 percent rate that prevailed for most of the last several decades. This increase is complemented by other changes to the corporate tax code that would incentivize job creation and investment in the United States and ensure that large corporations pay their fair share.

**Prevents Multinational Corporations from Using Tax Havens to Game the System.** For decades, American workers and taxpayers have paid the price for a tax system that has rewarded multinational corporations for shipping jobs and profits overseas. Last year, the Administration rallied more than 130 countries to agree to a global minimum tax that will ensure that profitable corporations pay their fair share and incentivizes U.S. multinationals to create jobs and invest in the United States. The Budget contains additional measures to ensure that multinationals operating in the United States cannot use tax havens to undercut the global minimum.

### Improving the Nation's Fiscal Outlook

The Budget's investments boost economic growth, reduce cost pressures, and promote shared prosperity in a way that improves the fiscal outlook of the United States and reduces fiscal risks over the long term.

The Administration is on track to becoming the first in history to reduce the deficit by more than $1 trillion in a single year. Under the Budget's policies, deficits would continue to decline from recent levels. Deficits would fall from 14.9 percent of GDP in 2020 to 5.8 percent of GDP this year and then decline further and remain below 5 percent of GDP through the 10-year window.

Moreover, under the Budget's policies, the medium-term economic burden of Federal debt would remain low. Real interest—the Federal Government's annual interest payments after adjusting for inflation—directly measures the cost of servicing the debt: the real resources that are going toward paying off old debt, instead of investing in the future.

The widespread, persistent, and global phenomenon of interest rates falling even as debt has risen has meant that the burden associated with debt over the near and medium term has decreased. Even as the economy has recovered and growth has come roaring back, interest rates remain well below historical averages.

Real interest has averaged about one percent of the economy since 1980 and was about two percent in the 1990s. Since then, the effective real interest rate on Federal debt has fallen ten-fold, from over 4 percent to 0.4 percent in the 2010s. As a result, real interest has fallen—and real interest costs are expected to remain negative in 2022. The Budget's economic assumptions anticipate that real interest rates would rise over the coming decade, using projections in line with private forecasters. Nevertheless, under these assumptions, the President's policies would keep real interest at or below the historical average over the coming decade. This means that we have the capacity to make fully-offset, critical investments that expand the productive capacity of the economy while also keeping real interest cost burdens low by historical standards.

At the same time, the United States does face fiscal challenges over the long term—driven largely by demographic pressures on health and retirement programs, an inequitable tax system, and rising healthcare costs. There is also uncertainty about the interest rate outlook. The Budget's proposals prudently address these future challenges by reforming the tax system and more than paying for all new policies, reducing deficits over the long run. In total, the Budget policies reduce deficits by more than $1 trillion over the next 10 years

Overall, the Budget details an economically and fiscally responsible path forward—addressing the long-term fiscal challenges facing the Nation while making investments that produce stronger economic growth and broadly shared prosperity well into the future.

# ENSURING AN EQUITABLE, EFFECTIVE, AND ACCOUNTABLE GOVERNMENT THAT DELIVERS RESULTS FOR ALL

Under the President's leadership, the Nation is rising to meet the full range of challenges and opportunities before us. As set forth in the President's Management Agenda (PMA), making the most of this historic moment and delivering on the President's agenda also requires strengthening the Government's capacity to meet the needs of all Americans—toward a Government that works for people by meeting them where they are. To help deliver that future, the President's Budget advances the goals of the PMA across three key priority areas: strengthening and empowering the Federal workforce; delivering excellent, equitable, and secure Federal services and customer experience; and managing the business of Government to build a better America. This work—including the investments the Budget puts forward in support of the PMA—is critical for bolstering the Federal Government's capacity and capabilities to deliver for the American people today and for years to come.

## *Values in Action*

The Administration's work to further develop and implement the PMA, including through the Budget, is guided by values: equity, dignity, accountability, and results. These values guide the Administration's work to deliver results for the public and strengthen the capacity of Federal agencies. For example, the Budget advances these values by:

**Advancing Equity as a Core Part of Government Management and Decision-Making Processes.** To support the Administration's whole-of-Government approach to advancing equity, the Budget provides resources to hire Federal agency talent and expertise needed to help embed equity in agency decision-making and policy-making, such as civil rights legal expertise, human-centered design, public engagement and participatory design, evaluation and evidence design, planning and analysis, and data science. For example, the Budget includes resources to: expand the Department of Labor's Civil Rights Center in order to begin establishing regional offices across the Nation that can be more responsive to regional equity challenges; promote greater equity in service delivery at the Veterans Benefits Administration by placing evaluation analysts to assess potential disparities among veterans who have historically been disadvantaged based on their race, ethnicity, sex, sexual orientation, or gender identity; and help to bolster the Federal Emergency Management Agency's capacity to identify inequities and barriers to access in the application process for disaster assistance.

**Treating Every Person with Dignity and Meeting the American People Where They Are.** The Administration values and respects the inherent dignity of all people. The Government of the United States is working to recommit to being "of the people, by the people, [and] for the people" in order to solve the complex challenges the Nation faces. Through the PMA and the President's Executive Order 14058, "Transforming Federal Customer Experience and Service Delivery to Rebuild Trust in Government," the Administration has developed an accountability framework for designing and delivering services with a focus on the actual experience of the people whom Federal agencies are meant to serve. The Budget supports agencies conducting activities in support of this framework, including building increased mechanisms for providing feedback and input from the public into the work of the Government, hiring for the skills and expertise required to conduct human centered design, and forming interagency teams to tackle pain points from the lens of how *people* experience the Government's role in important events in their lives.

**Managing Federal Funding with Accountability and Integrity.** The Administration is committed to improving program integrity and ensuring effective stewardship of taxpayer dollars, including through implementation of the American Rescue Plan Act of 2021 (American Rescue Plan) and the Infrastructure Investment and Jobs Act (Bipartisan Infrastructure Law). To deliver on those commitments, the Administration has provided comprehensive guidance to Federal agencies to ensure coordinated and consistent approaches to fostering program integrity and delivering on the intended outcomes for financial assistance programs. In addition, as the President has made clear, results and accountability go hand-in-hand. To that end, the Administration is committed to collaborating with the Congress and the oversight community, including Offices of Inspectors General and the U.S. Government Accountability Office, as appropriate, and across various sectors and levels of the Government. Also, the Administration will apply its commitment to accountability and transparency to implementation of the resources provided by the President's Budget as well, through sound financial management and a focus on delivering effective and equitable funding.

**Managing the Government to Deliver Results that Improve Lives.** As part of the Administration's commitment to deliver results for all, Federal agencies have worked with external stakeholders and their own workforces to create four-year strategic plans that define mission success, as well as two-year Agency Priority Goals (APGs), reflecting each agency's top implementation priorities. Concurrent with the President's

Budget, Federal agencies have identified strategic goals, strategic objectives, and APGs that reflect the bottom line of the Government advancing outcomes across key Administration priorities, including improving customer experience, advancing equity, combatting climate change, improving the Nation's infrastructure, and meeting the health, welfare, and economic challenges of the COVID-19 pandemic. In addition, the Office of Management and Budget (OMB) has deployed Cross-Agency Priority (CAP) Goals to establish cross-cutting targets that cover a limited number of mission and management areas where Government-wide direction will be helpful to drive collective action on these cross-cutting issues. The public will be able to follow progress toward PMA priorities, agency strategic plans, and APGs, on *https://Performance.gov*, which will be updated quarterly.

## *Strengthening and Empowering the Federal Workforce*

The strength of any organization rests on its people. As the Nation's largest employer, more than four million Americans work for the Federal Government, both at home in the United States and overseas. Those serving in Government today are dedicated and talented professional public servants. That is why the President has taken significant steps to protect, empower, and rebuild the career Federal workforce, and why the President charged the White House Task Force on Worker Organizing and Empowerment with developing steps to augment the voice of frontline Federal workers. The Budget makes further investments in the Federal workforce by providing agencies with new tools to help win the competition for highly-skilled talent. The Budget builds on this work and advances the first PMA priority—strengthening and empowering the Federal workforce—by:

**Making Every Federal Job a Good Job, Where All Employees are Engaged, Supported, Heard, and Empowered.** Federal agencies must cultivate the passion of their employees and empower them to advance agency missions—and the Federal Government must be a model employer with respect to worker organizing, collective bargaining, and labor-management partnership. The voices of Federal employees are critical to agency management, which is why the Administration is strengthening the annual Federal Employee Viewpoint Survey and piloting a Government-wide pulse survey of Federal employees. These efforts will help agencies retain qualified employees, empower workers to make their agencies better, create a pipeline of qualified leaders, and provide better services to the public. The Budget supports these objectives by ensuring that all those in Federal jobs earn at least $15 per hour and providing a pay increase of 4.6 percent for civilian and military personnel. The Budget also supports the Office of Personnel Management (OPM) and agencies' ability to answer the President's call for agencies to lead by example in supporting worker organizing and collective bargaining.

**Helping Agencies Attract and Hire Talent that Reflect America's Diversity across the Federal Government.** Federal agencies are focused on attracting more people to Federal service over the long term, while also addressing immediate agency hiring needs to rebuild capacity. The Federal Government is continuing to implement practices to hire based on skills rather than educational qualifications alone. Certain agency hiring practices are changing, including applicant assessment methods, to ensure that those most capable of performing the role do not get needlessly overlooked because they do not have a college degree. Agencies are also aligning with the *Government-wide Strategic Plan to Advance Diversity, Equity, Inclusion, and Accessibility in the Federal Workforce*, including through efforts to develop cultures within agencies that can foster a more diverse, equitable, inclusive, and accessible environment. To support hiring surges necessary to deliver on the Bipartisan Infrastructure Law and streamline hiring practices across the Federal Government, the Budget includes resources to help Federal agencies increase capacity for recruiting and talent management. This includes continued support for agency "talent teams" in each of the 24 Chief Financial Officers Act agencies. Given that internships can introduce students and those in the early stages of their careers to public service, the Budget prioritizes internships and equitable access to internships. Developing pipelines for internships would also be prioritized around the Nation through a reinvigorated vision and funding model for Federal Executive Boards, to ensure a pulse on the Federal impact in communities and support Federal employees and agencies across the Nation. The Budget also provides resources to support new requirements for personnel vetting and the Trusted Workforce 2.0 Initiative, which is designed to ensure all Americans can trust the Federal workforce to protect people, property, information, and mission.

**Reimagining and Building a Roadmap to the Future of Federal Work.** The Federal Government has an opportunity to reimagine the way Federal employees work. By utilizing expanded flexibilities in work arrangements such as: expanded telework and alternative work schedules; increased adoption of technology, such as cloud computing collaboration tools; and automation supported by information technology investments in the Budget the Government can enhance its ability to recruit and retain top talent, staying competitive with broader trends in how Americans work. A changing world has proven that innovation is possible in the way Federal employees work and operate, including changing needs and uses for Federal workplaces, which agencies will continue to evaluate and assess.

**Building the Personnel System and Support Required to Sustain the Federal Government as a Model Employer.** As the Government faces increasingly complex challenges, the need for Federal leaders, managers, and front-line staff with the right skills in the right jobs has never been greater. To meet this need, the Budget supports OPM in enhancing its ability to lead Federal human capital management, and serve as a central, strategic leader in Federal human resources, in alignment with OPM's Strategic Plan. In support of this work, the Budget requests $418 million, a $88 million increase over the 2021 enacted level, for OPM's Salaries and Expenses account, its primary discretionary appropriation. This funding would support staffing to enhance customer service provided by OPM to Federal agencies, allowing further collaboration in support of the Federal Government's strategic workforce planning and talent acquisition functions.

### Delivering Excellent, Equitable, and Secure Federal Services and Customer Experience

Every interaction between the Government and the public is an opportunity to deliver the value and competence Americans expect and deserve. The American people rely on Federal services to support them through disasters, advance their businesses, provide opportunities for their families, safeguard their rights, and help rebuild their communities. That is why the President signed Executive Order 14058 that will help agencies center services around those who use them—toward delivering simple, secure, effective, equitable, and responsive solutions. The Budget advances these efforts and the second PMA priority—delivering excellent, equitable, and secure Federal services and customer experience—by:

**Improving the Service Design, Digital Products, and Customer-Experience Management of Federal High-Impact Service Providers.** The Budget supports Federal High Impact Service Providers—those services that serve the largest percentage of people, conduct the greatest volume of transactions annually, and have an outsized impact on the lives of the individuals they serve. Focusing on these high-impact services would yield capabilities, tools, and practices that cascade to other Federal programs and services Government-wide. For example, the Budget includes an additional $2 million to build the Office of Customer Experience at the U.S. Department of Agriculture, which would improve delivery of critical programs for farmers, producers, and ranchers, as well as support for the nutrition of more than six million participants in the Women, Infants, and Children program. The Budget supports the Small Business Administration's efforts to establish baseline customer experience measures for application processes across the Agency's loan, grant, and

contracting programs, as well as streamlining the online disaster assistance application experience. The Budget also includes resources to advance customer experience efforts at the Department of Housing and Urban Development, to help deliver on the President's housing priorities, including eliminating barriers that restrict housing and neighborhood choice, furthering fair housing, and providing redress to those who have experienced housing discrimination. In addition, the Budget's investments in digital modernization would allow the U.S. Fish and Wildlife Service to enable Americans to access more permits online, and the Budget would help the Transportation Security Administration expand the use of innovative technologies to reduce passenger wait times at airport security checkpoints. The Budget also invests in the Social Security Administration's efforts to make it easier for individuals to file for Social Security retirement benefits, apply for replacement Social Security cards, and apply for need-based Supplemental Security Income disability payments. In addition, the Budget would also provide $2.7 billion to the Department of Education's Office of Federal Student Aid to provide better support to student loan borrowers by implementing customer experience improvements and ensuring the successful transition from the current short-term loan servicing contracts into a more stable long-term contract and servicing environment.

**Designing, Building, and Managing Government Service Delivery for Key Life Experiences that Reach across Federal Agencies.** When a person experiences a disaster, loses a job, or faces another key moment in their lives, Federal Government services should meet them where they are instead of forcing them to navigate Government siloes. By better coordinating service delivery based on the life experience of the customer, instead of around existing funding streams or organizational structures, Government can better serve the public. The Budget advances these efforts by providing funding for interagency teams to simplify the process of accessing Government services, such as, services for those surviving a natural disaster, approaching retirement, having a child, and navigating supports after a financial shock.

**Enabling Simple, Seamless, and Secure Customer Experiences across High Impact Service Providers.** The Budget supports efforts to develop shared products, services, and standards while designing safe and secure products that better meet customer needs. For example, these resources would support efforts at the Departments of Veterans Affairs and Defense to provide streamlined login credentials for servicemembers to access the benefits they have earned through their service as they transition to veterans status, as well as a $61 million increase over the 2021 enacted level for the Federal Citizen Services Fund at the General Services Administration (GSA) to power shared products and platforms that enable simple, seamless, and secure services across the Federal Government. As part of this request, GSA is investing an additional $35 million in the Public Experience Portfolio to continue to evolve *USA.gov* to deliver a seamless public experience when transacting with the Government and provide the public an optimal experience when seeking voting resources on *https://Vote.gov*.

## *Managing the Business of Government*

The Federal Government influences and re-shapes markets, supports key supply chains, drives technological advances, and supports domestic manufacturing. This scale creates an opportunity to leverage Federal systems for managing the business of Government—the goods and services the Government buys and the financial assistance and resources it provides and oversees—to create and sustain good quality union jobs, address persistent wealth and wage gaps, and tackle other challenges. The Administration has taken bold action to leverage Federal acquisition, financial assistance, and financial management systems to take on some of the Nation's most pressing challenges. That is why the Budget supports improvements that would make continued progress and improvements in these systems. The Budget supports this work and advances the

third PMA priority—managing the business of Government—by:

**Ensuring the Future is Made in America by America's Workers.** The Administration is working to ensure that Federal resources and programs advance domestic jobs and industries. Two recent examples of that work include the creation of a new review process to ensure Made in America waivers are transparent and consistently applied and a change in the Buy American Act rule for procurement to increase domestic content. The Made in America Office within OMB will continue its work with Federal agencies to maximize the use of Federal procurement and assistance on domestic goods and services that provide good value while strengthening the U.S. industrial base in critical sectors and creating good-paying jobs and economic opportunities in communities across the Nation.

**Leveraging Federal Contracting as a Catalyst to Drive Clean Energy Solutions, Support American Jobs, and Advance Equity.** Federal agencies spent over $619 billion in 2021 through millions of contracts for goods and services, providing an opportunity to transform the marketplace in ways that mitigate the effects of climate change, bolster American manufacturing, and increase opportunities for small disadvantaged businesses (SDBs) and other small businesses in underserved communities. The Administration is leveraging Federal procurement power to move toward a clean energy future, including 100 percent carbon pollution-free Federal electricity on a net annual basis by 2030, 100 percent zero-emission vehicle acquisitions by 2035, and a net-zero emissions in the Federal building portfolio by 2045. The Administration is also using the Federal acquisition system to increase the procurement of Made in America products to support domestic manufacturing, including through greater transparency in agency acquisition plans so domestic providers can help meet agency requirements, and a new Government-wide acquisition regulation that establishes an aggressive schedule to raise domestic content to 75 percent by 2029. In addition, the Administration is taking steps through Federal acquisitions to better disclose and mitigate the risks that climate change poses in Federal contracting. Agencies are taking aggressive actions to increase contract awards to SDBs and other underserved entrepreneurs to advance the President's commitment to break down barriers and build generational wealth for underserved communities through procurement and contracting. This includes increasing contract awards for SDBs from just over 10 percent to 15 percent of total Federal contract spend by 2025. Agencies will continue to apply category management principles for common goods and services to ensure strong stewardship of taxpayer dollars, supported by increased use of business intelligence and data analytics. The President has directed the Administration to explore additional actions that strengthen the United States as a buyer, improving the efficiency and effectiveness of the Federal procurement system, including, for example, by utilizing approaches such as skills-based hiring, Registered Apprenticeship, and work-based learning.

### Supporting Ongoing Improvements to Federal Government Capabilities and Systems in Support of the PMA

The Budget also supports ongoing improvements to Federal Government capabilities that support an equitable, effective, and accountable Government by:

**Modernizing Federal Information Technology (IT) Systems and Strengthening Federal Data Capabilities.** The Administration continues to prioritize the modernization of Federal IT systems to better deliver agency mission and services to the American public in an effective, efficient, and secure manner. This includes continued efforts by Federal agencies to leverage, utilize, and implement data as a resource and strategic asset, with focus on opening data, advancing equity through data collection, use, and management, and data sharing, accountability, and transparency in support of Administration priorities. The Budget supports the interagency driving data sharing practices project that promotes data sharing activities in support of the Administration's priorities on racial equity and climate. To support IT modernization efforts, the Budget also includes an additional $300 million for the Technology Modernization Fund (TMF). In the first tranche of TMF awards funded by the American Rescue Plan, the TMF Board invested $187 million in *Login.gov*, a secure sign-on service used by over 30 million citizens and businesses that: supports easy access to over 200 Government services spanning 27 agencies; reduces Government costs; prevents fraud; and protects individual privacy. This first tranche of TMF investments also is contributing to protecting the data and privacy of 100 million students and borrowers, two million civilian Federal employees, and millions of users of Government-wide shared services, as well as the security of hundreds of Federal facilities.

**Bolstering Federal Cybersecurity.** The Budget funds a strategic shift in the defense of Federal infrastructure and service delivery, better positioning agencies to guard against sophisticated adversaries. The Budget provides for investments across Federal agencies that align them to foundational cybersecurity practices and priorities as outlined in Executive Order 14028, "Improving the Nation's Cybersecurity." This includes funding to facilitate the ongoing transition to a "zero trust" approach, which would enable agencies to more rapidly detect, isolate, and respond to cyber threats. To support these efforts, the Budget provides $2.5 billion to the Cybersecurity and Infrastructure Security Agency, a $486 million increase above 2021 enacted, to: maintain critical cybersecurity capabilities implemented in the American Rescue Plan; expand network protection throughout the Federal Executive Branch; and bolster support capabilities, such as cloud business applications, enhanced analytics, and stakeholder engagement. The Budget also supports the Office of the National Cyber Director, which would improve national coordination in the face of escalating cyber attacks on Government and critical infrastructure.

**Promoting Evidence-Based Policymaking and Decision Making in Federal Agencies.**

The President has made clear that the Administration will make decisions guided by the best available science and data, which requires the Federal Government to foster and strengthen a culture of evidence where generation and use is routine and integrated across all agency functions. The Budget's investments have been informed by existing evidence of effectiveness. The Budget also includes investments to build evidence in critical areas where it is lacking and invests in agency capacity to execute priority studies, including those identified in publicly posted Learning Agendas and Annual Evaluation Plans required by the Foundations for Evidence-Based Policymaking Act of 2018. The Budget's investments in statistical infrastructure recognize the importance of Federal statistics in strengthening the evidence base. New investments also support cross-agency evaluation efforts aligned with Administration priorities, where policy and programmatic solutions span agencies and functions.

# DEPARTMENT OF AGRICULTURE

The U.S. Department of Agriculture (USDA) is responsible for providing nutrition assistance to low-income Americans and income support for the farm sector, and for conserving and preserving the Nation's forests and private agricultural lands. The President's 2023 Budget for USDA: invests in tackling the climate crisis while mitigating its ongoing impacts on communities; strengthens the food supply chain and nutrition safety net; advances environmental justice; creates new jobs and opportunities in rural communities; supports underserved farmers and producers; and restores America's advantage in agriculture.

The Budget requests $28.5 billion in discretionary funding for USDA, a $4.2 billion or 17.1-percent increase from the 2021 enacted level, excluding Food for Peace Title II Grants, which is included in the State and International Programs total. Resources provided through the 2023 Budget complement investments in conservation, forest management, and broadband deployment provided in the Infrastructure Investment and Jobs Act (Bipartisan Infrastructure Law).

**The President's 2023 Budget:**

- **Bolsters the Nation's Frontline Defenses against Catastrophic Wildfires.** Protecting communities, ecosystems, and infrastructure from wildfire requires a resilient and reliable Federal workforce. The Budget provides nearly $4.9 billion for Forest Service Wildland Fire Management, including $2.2 billion for the Wildfire Suppression Operations Reserve Fund. The Budget also upholds the President's commitment that no Federal firefighter would make less than $15 an hour, increases the size of the Federal firefighting workforce, and provides critical technological support for wildfire detection and response, including FireGuard satellite imagery. The Budget also complements investments provided in the Bipartisan Infrastructure Law to reduce the risk and severity of wildfires through smart investments in Forest Service hazardous fuels management and ecosystem restoration.

- **Builds a Fair and Resilient Food Supply Chain.** The Budget strengthens market oversight through investments in the Agricultural Marketing Service and the Animal and Plant Health Inspection Service, resulting in competitive meat and poultry product prices for American families and increased protection against invasive pests and zoonotic diseases. These programs build on the pandemic and supply chain assistance funding in the American Rescue Plan Act of 2021 to address pandemic-related vulnerabilities in the food system and create new market opportunities and good-paying jobs.

- **Spurs Climate Research.** To support the Administration's whole-of-Government approach to tackle the climate crisis, the Budget invests $24 million in USDA's climate hubs, a multi-agency undertaking to leverage climate science and increase landowner awareness of—and engagement in—efforts to combat climate change. The Budget also supports multi-agency efforts to integrate science-based tools into conservation planning in order to measure, monitor, report, and verify carbon sequestration, greenhouse gas reduction, wildlife stewardship, and other environmental services at the farm level and on Federal lands. In addition, the Budget increases funding for priority climate research and for innovative mechanisms to incentivize the adoption of innovative agricultural practices and open new markets for climate-smart commodities at scale, while complementing actions being undertaken by stakeholders and the private sector.

- **Advances Equity and Environmental Justice.** The Budget supports the Administration's ongoing work to advance racial justice and provide more equitable program delivery. Certain USDA programs and initiatives, such as High Cost Energy grants, Rural Energy for America grants and loan guarantees, Private Lands Conservation Operations, Urban Agriculture, and Water and Wastewater direct loans, would support the President's Justice40 Initiative, which directs that at least 40 percent of the overall benefits from climate and clean energy investments be directed to historically disadvantaged communities. In addition, the Budget includes $39 million for the Rural Partners Network, which would connect America's rural communities to a broad range of programs and resources throughout the Federal Government. The Budget also provides $31 million for USDA's Office of Civil Rights, an increase of $9 million over the 2021 enacted level.

- **Addresses Climate Change and Housing Insecurity in Rural Communities.** The Budget provides $1.8 billion for USDA multifamily housing programs, an increase of $259 million from the 2021 enacted level, including over twice the loan level as in 2021. This significant investment would help address housing insecurity, rent burdens, and the impacts of climate change in rural America, including through a new policy requiring construction practices to improve energy or water efficiency, implement green features, or facilitate climate resilience.

- **Helps Rural Communities Transition to Clean Energy.** Rural communities are critical to achieving the goal of transitioning to 100 percent zero carbon electricity by 2035. The Budget provides $300 million in new funding for grants, loans, and debt forgiveness for rural electric providers as they transition to clean energy. The Budget also provides $6.5 billion in loan authority for rural electric loans, an increase of $1 billion over the 2021 enacted level, to support additional clean energy, energy storage, and transmission projects that would create good-paying jobs and meet the ambitious climate progress that science demands. In addition, the Budget includes $15 million in new funding to support the creation of the Rural Clean Energy Initiative to help achieve the President's decarbonation goals and ensure clean energy funding is implemented effectively in rural areas.

- **Restores America's Advantage in Agriculture.** American farmers must be able to leverage new technologies to compete in world markets. The Budget provides $4 billion, $644 million above the 2021 enacted level, for USDA's research, education, and outreach programs, including $315 million targeted to under-served populations.

- **Connects All Americans to High-Speed, Affordable, and Reliable Internet.** The President is committed to ensuring that every American has access to broadband. High-speed internet strengthens rural economies, and the work of installing broadband creates high-paying union jobs. Building on the $2 billion for USDA broadband programs provided in the Bipartisan Infrastructure Law, the Budget provides $600 million for the ReConnect program, which provides grants and loans to deploy broadband to unserved areas, especially tribal areas. The Budget also provides $25 million to help rural telecommunications cooperatives refinance their Rural Utilities Service debt and upgrade their broadband facilities.

- **Protects America's Food Supply.** The Budget provides $1.2 billion for the Food Safety and Inspection Service (FSIS), an increase of $134 million from the 2021 enacted level. This funding would enable the hiring of more inspectors and Public Health Veterinarians, which would increase the strength and flexibility of FSIS to provide inspection services so that meat and poultry producers would be better able to respond to market demands and provide safe and healthy food products. The Budget is providing targeted funds to support smaller producers so that they may increase their production capacity, which in turn would create a more diverse food supply chain.

- **Invests in Tribal Communities.** The Budget invests $62 million for agriculture research, education, and extension grants to tribal institutions; $7 million to assist Native Americans with home ownership through the Single-Family Housing Native American Community Development Financial Institutions Re-lending Program, and $7 million to support Native American farmers and ranchers through the Intertribal Assistance Network. In addition, through the Tribal Forest Protection Act of 2004 and other authorities, the Forest Service would make initial investments of at least $11 million in 2023 to increase equity and expand tribal self-governance, allowing Tribes to participate in restoration activities under agreements and contracts.

- **Supports a Strong Nutrition Safety Net.** The Budget provides $6.8 billion for critical nutrition programs, including $6 billion for the Special Supplemental Nutrition Program for Women, Infants, and Children, to help vulnerable families put healthy food on the table and address racial disparities in maternal and child health outcomes.

- **Supports Economically Distressed Farmers.** USDA is committed to examining barriers faced by all underserved borrowers, especially those in economic distress, beginning farmers, and veterans. The Administration is interested in working with the Congress on legislative changes that would ease the debt burden for economically distressed farm loan borrowers to achieve a robust and competitive agriculture sector.

- **The 2023 Farm Bill.** The Administration looks forward to working this year with the Congress, partners, stakeholders, and the public to identify shared priorities for the 2023 Farm Bill that position USDA to live up to its moniker as "the People's Department" and deliver on its mission to serve all Americans by providing effective, innovative, science-based public policy leadership in agriculture, food and nutrition, natural resource protection and management, and rural development. The Administration also looks forward to working with the Congress to address climate change through climate-smart agriculture and forestry and investments in renewable energy that open new market opportunities and provide a competitive advantage for American producers of climate-smart commodities, including small and historically underserved producers and early adopters, and through voluntary incentives to reduce climate risk. The 2023 Farm Bill is also a critical opportunity to ensure that the wealth created in rural America stays there and to empower rural communities with the tools necessary to advance their locally-led vision. In addition, USDA's nutrition programs are among the most far-reaching tools available to improve health and well-being and to ensure that all Americans have access to healthy, affordable food. This is an important moment to reconsider barriers to food assistance for vulnerable groups that are likely undermining their chances of success, including low-income college students, individuals reentering society and seeking a second chance, youth who have aged out of foster care, kinship families, and low-income individuals in the U.S. Territories.

# DEPARTMENT OF COMMERCE

The Department of Commerce (Commerce) is responsible for: promoting job creation; supporting and overseeing international trade; and providing economic, environmental, and scientific information needed by businesses, citizens, and governments. The President's 2023 Budget for Commerce makes historic investments to strengthen domestic supply chains, help American entrepreneurs bring their products to the market, support minority business development, tackle the climate crisis, and promote opportunity and safety in space.

The Budget requests $11.7 billion in discretionary funding for Commerce, a $2.8 billion or 31.2-percent increase from the 2021 enacted level. Resources provided through the 2023 Budget complement major investments in broadband Internet access and climate resilience through the Infrastructure Investment and Jobs Act (Bipartisan Infrastructure Law).

**The President's 2023 Budget:**

- **Strengthens the Nation's Supply Chains through Domestic Manufacturing.** To help ignite a resurgence of American manufacturing, the Budget provides $372 million, an increase of $206 million from the 2021 enacted level, for the National Institutes of Standards and Technology's (NIST) manufacturing programs. These resources would help launch two additional Manufacturing Innovation Institutes in 2023 and continue support for two institutes funded in 2022 as part of the Administration's growing Manufacturing USA network, which brings together industry, academia, and Government to accelerate manufacturing innovation and commercialization. The Budget also expands the Manufacturing Extension Partnership, providing an increase of $125 million to make America's small and medium manufacturers more competitive and to ensure that the future is made in all of America by all of America's workers. The Budget also provides $11 million to the International Trade Administration (ITA) to build analytical capacity in meeting new requirements on supply chain resilience across the manufacturing and services industries, as well as $5 million for the Bureau of Economic Analysis (BEA) to develop new data tools to measure American competitiveness in global supply chains.

- **Revitalizes Coal Communities and Other Economically Distressed Communities.** To foster investment and economic revitalization in communities impacted by the transition from fossil fuel to a clean energy economy, the Budget provides more than $70 million in new funding to the Economic Development Administration (EDA) to create jobs and drive growth in economically distressed communities. This funding would allow EDA to more than double its Assistance to Coal Communities initiative. The Budget also provides $50 million for an EDA pilot program to address structural prime-age employment gaps and boost competitiveness in persistently distressed communities through innovative, flexible, and locally-led grants.

- **Supports Minority-Owned Business to Narrow Racial Wealth Gaps.** The Budget elevates the stature and increases the capacity of the Minority Business Development Agency by providing the full $110 million authorized in the Bipartisan Infrastructure Law. This funding would bolster services provided to minority-owned enterprises by expanding the Business Center program, funding Rural Business Centers, opening new regional offices, and supporting innovative initiatives to foster economic resiliency.

- **Creates New Markets for American Goods by Expanding Economic Engagement Abroad.** The Budget provides an additional $26 million from the 2021 enacted level to bolster commercial diplomacy and enhance export promotion through a targeted expansion of the Foreign Commercial Service at the ITA. With this funding, Commerce would augment staff to assist American businesses seeking to increase exports abroad, navigate new foreign markets, or find market opportunities. These activities would focus on areas of high economic and geostrategic value, including the Indo-Pacific.

- **Responds to the Impacts of Climate Change and Extreme Weather.** The Budget invests $6.9 billion in the National Oceanic and Atmospheric Administration (NOAA), an increase of $1.4 billion from the 2021 enacted level, supporting programs that would catalyze wind energy, restore habitats, protect the oceans and coasts, and improve NOAA's ability to predict extreme weather associated with climate change. This includes $45 million to support NOAA's role in deploying 30 gigawatts of offshore wind energy by 2030, and a $30 million increase in funding for marine sanctuaries and other marine protected areas to assess and address climate change impacts. The Budget also supports the Administration's America the Beautiful initiative, and $92 million for expanded climate competitive research grants. Through a bold investment of $2.3 billion in the next generation of weather satellites, the Budget also provides a robust and predictable long-term funding strategy to develop new weather detection capabilities to help plan for extreme weather events.

- **Safeguards America's Burgeoning Space Industry.** The Budget expands opportunities for civil space situational awareness and supports the long-term sustainability of the space environment by committing $88 million, a $78 million increase from the 2021 enacted level, for the Office of Space Commerce in order to improve real-time tracking and reporting of space objects and debris, helping the space industry safely navigate a congested space environment. The Budget also provides $2 million for BEA to develop new data tools to measure the space economy.

- **Advances Key Emerging Technologies and U.S. Leadership in International Standards Development.** The Budget supports U.S. industry competing in the global communications market by providing $13 million for cutting-edge advanced communications research and engineering at the National Telecommunications and Information Administration. The Budget also includes a $187 million increase for research initiatives at NIST that would focus on developing standards to accelerate adoption of critical and emerging technologies with a focus on artificial intelligence, quantum science, and advanced biotechnologies. As part of this investment, the Budget includes an $8 million increase to strengthen U.S. leadership in international standards development for critical and emerging technologies.

- **Secures the American Economy and American's Sensitive Data against Foreign Threats.** The Budget strengthens the Nation's national and economic security by protecting the information and communications technology (ICT) supply chain and improving the security of the commercial cyber ecosystem. This includes a $36 million increase to review ICT transactions that pose an undue risk to the United States, and an enforcement program to deter and mitigate foreign malicious cyber-enabled activities. The Budget also provides the Bureau of Industry and Security (BIS) with a $30 million increase to advance national security and secure trade by bolstering BIS's ability to implement and enforce export controls. In addition, BIS monitors industrial base and supply chain trends with regard to critical and emerging technologies, such as microelectronics.

- **Supports Evidence-Based Policymaking.** The Budget supports evidence-based policy making and strengthens the ability of the Census Bureau to deliver reliable, high-quality data and innovative statistical products that improve understanding of the Nation's people and economy. The Budget includes $408 million to finalize and evaluate the Decennial Census and lay the groundwork for a successful 2030 Census and $141 million for BEA to support the production of vital economic indicators such as Gross Domestic Product. In 2023, BEA will transition the prototype Annual National and Annual State Distribution of Personal Income measures into regular production, providing policymakers and the public with crucial new information about how families across the income distribution spectrum are faring.

# DEPARTMENT OF DEFENSE

The Department of Defense (DOD) is responsible for the military forces needed to safeguard U.S. vital national interests. The President's 2023 Budget for DOD provides the resources necessary to sustain and strengthen U.S. deterrence, advancing our vital national interests through integrated deterrence, campaigning, and investments that build enduring advantages. The Budget: supports America's servicemembers and their families; strengthens alliances and partnerships; preserves America's technological edge; bolsters economic competitiveness; and combats 21st Century security threats.

The Budget requests $773 billion in discretionary funding for DOD, a $69 billion or 9.8-percent increase from the 2021 enacted level. This two-year growth enables DOD to make the investments necessary to execute the Administration's *Interim National Security Strategic Guidance* and forthcoming National Security Strategy and National Defense Strategy.

## The President's 2023 Budget:

- **Supports United States' European Allies and Partners.** The Budget supports Ukraine, the United States' strong partnerships with North Atlantic Treaty Organization (NATO) allies, and other European partner states by bolstering funding to enhance the capabilities and readiness of U.S. forces, NATO allies, and regional partners in the face of Russian aggression.

- **Promotes Integrated Deterrence in the Indo-Pacific and Globally.** The Budget proposes $773 billion for DOD. To sustain and strengthen deterrence, the Budget prioritizes China as the Department's pacing challenge. DOD's 2023 Pacific Deterrence Initiative highlights some of the key investments the Department is making that are focused on strengthening deterrence in the Indo-Pacific region. DOD is building the concepts, capabilities, and posture necessary to meet these challenges, working in concert with the interagency and U.S. allies and partners to ensure U.S. deterrence is integrated across domains, theaters, and the spectrum of conflict.

- **Counters Persistent Threats.** While focused on maintaining robust deterrence against China and Russia, the Budget also enables DOD to counter other persistent threats including those posed by North Korea, Iran, and violent extremist organizations.

- **Modernizes the Nuclear Deterrent.** The Budget maintains a strong, credible nuclear deterrent, as a foundational aspect of integrated deterrence, for the security of the Nation and U.S. allies. The Budget supports the U.S. nuclear triad and the necessary ongoing nuclear modernization programs, to include the nuclear command, control, and communication networks.

- **Advances U.S. Cybersecurity.** The Budget invests in cybersecurity programs to protect the Nation from malicious cyber actors and cyber campaigns. These priorities include strengthening cyber protection standards for the defense industrial base and investing in the cybersecurity of DOD networks.

- **Takes Care of Servicemembers and the DOD Civilian Workforce.** The Budget invests in America's servicemembers and civilian workforce with robust 4.6 percent pay raises—the largest in a generation—and addresses economic insecurity by funding a newly authorized basic needs allowance. The Budget also continues to combat the COVID-19 pandemic.

- **Fulfills America's Commitment to Military Families.** Military families are key to the readiness and well-being of the All-Volunteer Force, and therefore are critical to national security. The Budget supports military families by prioritizing programs that directly support military spouses, children, caregivers, survivors, and other dependents.

- **Strengthens Programs to Prevent and Respond to Sexual Assault.** The Budget fully funds DOD's implementation of the recommendations of the Independent Review Commission on Sexual Assault in the Military to improve the Department's ongoing work to enhance accountability, prevention, climate and culture, and victim care and support. Examples of these efforts include the establishment of a violence prevention workforce and enabling servicemembers who experience sexual harassment to access services from a sexual assault victim advocate. The Budget also supports the establishment of an independent Office of Special Trial Counsel in each military department, as required under the National Defense Authorization Act for Fiscal Year 2022, to carry out changes to the military justice process for handling sexual assault, domestic violence, and other serious crimes.

- **Promotes Climate Resilience and Energy Efficiency to Support Warfighting Operations.** It is vital to examine the security implications of climate-induced extreme weather and to adapt DOD platforms and military installations to protect mission critical capabilities. The Budget supports efforts to plan for and mitigate the impacts of climate change and improve the resilience of DOD facilities and operations. The Budget invests in power and energy performance, which makes U.S. forces more agile, efficient, and survivable in this complex and changing environment.

- **Enhances Biodefense and Pandemic Preparedness.** The Budget provides robust funding for programs that support the Administration's biodefense and pandemic preparedness priorities as outlined in U.S. biodefense and pandemic preparedness strategies and plans, including the Office of the Assistant Secretary for Health Affairs, Chemical and Biological Defense Program, and Biological Threat Reduction Program. The Budget supports enhanced investments in medical countermeasures, including vaccines, diagnostics, and therapeutics research and manufacturing; clinical research and testing; early warning and real-time monitoring; biosafety and biosecurity; and threat reduction activities with global partners.

- **Builds the Air Forces Needed for the 21ˢᵗ Century.** The Budget procures a mix of highly capable aircraft while continuing to make investments in the fighter, bomber, and training aircraft of the future. Investing in this mix of aircraft provides an opportunity to reduce the future fleet's operational costs while increasing its resiliency and flexibility to meet future threats.

- **Optimizes U.S. Naval Shipbuilding.** Maintaining U.S. naval power is critical to reassuring allies and deterring potential adversaries. The Budget proposes executable and responsible investments in the U.S. Navy fleet. In addition, the Budget continues the recapitalization of the Nation's strategic ballistic missile submarine fleet while also investing in the submarine industrial base.

- **Supports a Ready and Modern Army.** The Budget maintains a ready Army capable of responding globally as part of the Joint Force through investments in Army modernization initiatives, force posture improvements, and deterrence capabilities.

- **Invests in Long-Range Fire Capabilities.** The safety and security of the Nation requires a strong, sustainable, and responsive mix of long-range strike capabilities. The Budget invests in the development and testing of hypersonic strike capabilities while enhancing existing long-range strike capabilities to bolster deterrence and improve survivability.

- **Increases Space Resilience.** Space is vital to U.S. national security and integral to modern warfare. The Budget maintains America's advantage by improving the resilience of U.S. space architectures to bolster deterrence and increase survivability during hostilities.

- **Ensures Readiness.** The Budget continues to ensure that U.S. Soldiers, Sailors, Airmen, Marines, and Guardians remain the best trained and equipped fighting force in the world. At the same time, the Budget strengthens and empowers DOD's civilian workforce as a critical contributor to the Nation's security.

- **Optimizes Force Structure.** In line with the forthcoming National Defense Strategy, the Budget optimizes force structure to build a Joint Force that is lethal, resilient, sustainable, survivable, agile, and responsive. The Budget supports DOD's plan to responsibly upgrade capabilities by redirecting resources to cutting edge technologies in high-priority platforms. Some force structure is too costly to maintain and operate, and no longer provides the capabilities needed to address the current and future national security challenges. The Budget enables DOD to reinvest savings associated with optimized force structure to higher priority investments.

- **Supports Defense Research and Development and the Defense Technology Industrial Base.** DOD plays a critical role in overall Federal research and development that spurs innovation, yields high-value technology, ensures American dominance over strategic competitors, and creates good-paying jobs. The Budget prioritizes defense research, development, test, and evaluation funding to invest in breakthrough technologies that drive innovation, support capacity in the defense technology industrial base, ensure American technological leadership, and underpin the development of next-generation defense capabilities.

- **Strengthens the U.S. Supply Chain and Industrial Base.** The Budget invests in key technologies and sectors of the U.S. industrial base such as microelectronics, casting and forging, and critical materials.

- **Empowers Small Disadvantaged Businesses and Underserved Communities.** The Budget advances equity and supports small disadvantaged businesses and underserved communities. DOD will continue to explore opportunities to serve the American people, with a focus on these communities, through supplier and contracting operations.

# DEPARTMENT OF EDUCATION

The Department of Education assists States, school districts, and institutions of higher education in providing a high-quality education to all students and addressing the inequitable barriers underserved students face in education. The President's 2023 Budget for the Department of Education makes historic investments in the Nation's future prosperity: increases aid for high-poverty schools; meets the needs of students with disabilities; and expands access to higher education.

The Budget requests $88.3 billion in discretionary funding for the Department of Education, a $15.3 billion or 20.9-percent increase from the 2021 enacted level.

**The President's 2023 Budget:**

## *K-12 Education*

- **Makes Historic Investments in High-Poverty Schools.** To advance the goal of providing a high-quality education to every student, the Budget provides $36.5 billion for Title I, including $20.5 billion in discretionary funding and $16 billion in mandatory funding, which more than doubles the program's funding compared to the 2021 enacted level. Title I helps schools provide students in low-income communities the learning opportunities and support they need to succeed. This substantial new support for the program, which serves 25 million students in nearly 90 percent of school districts across the Nation, would be a major step toward fulfilling the President's commitment to address long-standing funding disparities between under-resourced schools—which disproportionately serve students of color—and their wealthier counterparts.

- **Prioritizes the Health and Well-Being of Students.** Disruptions caused by the COVID-19 pandemic continue to take a toll on the physical and mental health of students, teachers, and school staff. Recognizing the profound effect of physical and mental health on academic achievement, the Budget includes a $1 billion investment to increase the number of counselors, nurses, school psychologists, social workers, and other health professionals in schools.

- **Increases Support for Children with Disabilities.** The President is committed to ensuring that children and youth with disabilities receive the services and support they need to thrive in school and graduate ready for college or a career. The Budget provides an additional $3.3 billion from the 2021 enacted level—the largest two-year increase ever—for Individuals with Disabilities Education Act (IDEA) grants to States, with a total of $16.3 billion to support special education and related services for students in grades Pre-K through 12. The

Budget also doubles funding to $932 million for IDEA Part C grants, which support early intervention services for infants and families with disabilities that have a proven record of improving academic and developmental outcomes. The increased funding would support States in implementing critical reforms to expand their enrollment of underserved children, including children of color, children from low-income families, and children living in rural areas. The increase also includes $200 million to expand and streamline enrollment of children at risk of developing disabilities, such as children born with very low-birth weight or who have been exposed to environmental toxins, which would help mitigate the need for more extensive services later in childhood and further expand access to the program for underserved children. The Budget also more than doubles funding to $250 million for IDEA Part D Personnel Preparation grants to support a pipeline of special educators at a time when the majority of States are experiencing a shortage of special educators.

- **Supports Full Service Community Schools.** Community schools play a critical role in providing comprehensive wrap-around services to students and their families, from afterschool to adult education opportunities, and health and nutrition services. The Budget includes $468 million for this program, an increase of $438 million from the 2021 enacted level. The increase would also help school districts implement integrated student supports to meet student and family mental health needs through partnerships with community-based organizations and other entities.

- **Invests in Education Recruitment and Retention.** While the education sector has faced shortages in critical staffing areas for decades, the COVID-19 pandemic and tight labor market has made shortages worse, which has negatively impacted students and fallen hardest on students in underserved communities. The Budget includes $514 million for the Education Innovation and Research program, $350 million of which the Department would target toward identifying and scaling models that improve recruitment and retention of staff in education. Such models include those that would improve support for educators and provide teacher access to leadership opportunities that improve teacher retention and maximize the impact of great teachers beyond their classrooms.

- **Supports Multi-Language Learners.** Students learning English as a second language were disproportionately impacted by the multiple transitions to and from remote learning during the COVID-19 pandemic. The Budget would provide $1.1 billion for the English Language Acquisition (ELA) program, an increase of $278 million, or 35 percent, from the 2021 enacted level, including additional funding to provide technical assistance and build local capacity to better support multilanguage learners and their teachers. The ELA program helps students learning English attain English proficiency and achieve academic success.

- **Fosters Diverse Schools.** The segregation of students by race and income undermines the promise that public schools provide an equal opportunity for all students to learn and succeed. The Budget includes $100 million for a grant program to help communities develop and implement strategies to promote racial and socioeconomic diversity in their schools.

## *Education Beyond High School*

- **Makes Historic Investments in College Affordability and Completion.** To help low- and middle-income students overcome financial barriers to postsecondary education, the Budget proposes to double the maximum Pell Grant by 2029. This begins with a historic $2,175 increase for the 2023-2024 school year compared to the 2021-2022 school year, thereby expanding access and reaching nearly 6.7 million students. The Budget would also support strategies to improve the retention, transfer, and completion rates of students by investing in the Federal TRIO Programs, Gaining Early Awareness and Readiness for Undergraduate Programs, and new retention and completion grants.

- **Increases Funding for Historically Black Colleges and Universities (HBCUs), Tribally Controlled Colleges and Universities (TCCUs), Minority-Serving Institutions (MSIs), and Community Colleges.** The Budget would increase institutional capacity at HBCUs, TCCUs, MSIs, and low-resourced institutions, including community colleges, by providing an increase of $752 million from the 2021 enacted level. This funding includes $450 million for four-year HBCUs, TCCUs, and MSIs to expand research and development infrastructure at these institutions.

- **Invests in Services for Student Borrowers.** The Budget provides $2.7 billion to the Department of Education's Office of Federal Student Aid (FSA), an $800 million, or 43-percent, increase compared to the 2021 enacted level. This additional funding is needed to provide better support to student loan borrowers. Specifically, the increase allows FSA to implement customer service improvements to student loan servicing and to ensure the successful transition from the current short-term loan servicing contracts into a more stable long-term contract and servicing environment.

## *Office for Civil Rights*

- **Strengthens Civil Rights Enforcement.** The Budget provides $161 million to the Department of Education's Office for Civil Rights, an 18-percent increase compared to the 2021 enacted level. This additional funding would ensure that the Department has the capacity to protect equal access to education through the enforcement of civil rights laws, such as Title IX of the Education Amendments of 1972.

# DEPARTMENT OF ENERGY

The Department of Energy (DOE) is responsible for supporting the Nation's prosperity by addressing its climate, energy, environmental, and nuclear security challenges through transformative science and technology solutions. The President's 2023 Budget for DOE: invests in domestic clean energy manufacturing; advances environmental justice; tackles the climate crisis; and modernizes and ensures the safety and security of the nuclear weapons stockpile.

The Budget requests $48.2 billion in discretionary funding for DOE, a $6.3 billion or 15.1-percent increase from the 2021 enacted level. Resources provided through the 2023 Budget complement major investments in clean energy demonstrations, advanced manufacturing, grid infrastructure, and low-income home weatherization funded in the Infrastructure Investment and Jobs Act (Bipartisan Infrastructure Law).

**The President's 2023 Budget:**

- **Enables Progress toward Climate Goals.** The Budget supports investments in research, development, demonstration, and deployment, which are central to enabling achievement of the Administration's climate goals of a 50- to 52-percent reduction from 2005 levels in economy-wide net greenhouse gas pollution in 2030 and zero emissions economy-wide by no later than 2050.

- **Creates Jobs through Support for Clean Energy Infrastructure.** The Budget invests $2.1 billion to support clean energy workforce and infrastructure projects across the Nation, including: $502 million to weatherize and retrofit low-income homes; $150 million to electrify tribal homes and transition tribal colleges and universities to renewable energy; and $90 million for a new Grid Deployment Office to build a grid that is more reliable and resilient and that integrates accelerating levels of renewable energy. In addition, the Budget includes $58 million to launch the Net-Zero Labs Initiative, competitively selecting clean energy deployment projects across the national laboratories. These investments would create good-paying jobs while driving progress toward the Administration's climate goals, including the President's goal of carbon pollution-free electricity by 2035.

- **Tackles the Climate Crisis through Clean Energy Innovation.** To support U.S. preeminence in developing innovative technologies that accelerate the transition to a clean energy economy, the Budget invests $9.2 billion in DOE clean energy research, development, and demonstration, an increase of more than 33 percent from the 2021 enacted level. These investments strengthen clean energy-enabling transmission and distribution systems, decarbonize transportation, advance carbon management technologies, improve energy efficiency in industry and buildings, and secure the availability of high-assay low-enriched uranium. Funding would also leverage the tremendous innovation capacity of the national laboratories, universities, and entrepreneurs to transform America's power, transportation, buildings, and industrial sectors to achieve a net-zero emissions economy by 2050.

- **Strengthens Domestic Clean Energy Manufacturing.** Meeting the challenge of climate change will require a dramatic scale-up in domestic manufacturing of key climate and clean energy equipment, providing opportunities for U.S. workers. Across the $11.3 billion in discretionary DOE clean energy investments described above, the Budget reflects the importance of strategically supporting the U.S. domestic manufacturing base through innovation, technical assistance, and training. Specifically, the Budget includes $200 million for a new Solar Manufacturing Accelerator that would help create a robust domestic manufacturing sector capable of meeting the Administration's solar deployment goals without relying on imported goods manufactured using unacceptable labor practices. The Budget also funds a new ManufacturingUSA institute and increases support for Industrial Assessment Centers, giving students valuable experience conducting energy audits for small and medium-sized manufacturers. In addition, the Budget also proposes a $1 billion mandatory investment to launch a Global Clean Energy Manufacturing effort that would build resilient supply chains for climate and clean energy equipment through engagement with allies, enabling an effective global response to the climate crisis while creating economic opportunities for the United States to increase its share of the global clean technology market.

- **Advances Environmental Justice and Equity.** The Budget provides historic support for underserved communities, including: $34 million for the Office of Economic Impact and Diversity to play a critical role in implementing the Department's Justice40 efforts and equity action plan; $40 million in new resources for capacity building assistance in areas of persistent poverty around the Department's cleanup sites; and $13 million for the Office of Legacy Management to strengthen its environmental justice mission. New programs, including Funding for Accelerated, Inclusive Research, would train and support a diverse and inclusive scientific workforce for the future. In addition, the newly established Office of State and Community Programs would launch Low Income Home Energy Assistance Program Advantage with a $100 million pilot to retrofit low-income homes with efficient electric appliances and systems; and the Office of Energy Efficiency and Renewable Energy would lead a $31 million Equitable Clean Energy Transition initiative to build capacity and provide technical assistance to help energy and environmental justice communities navigate and benefit from the transition to a clean energy economy. These investments would build healthy, culturally vibrant, sustainable, and resilient communities.

- **Supports Energy Communities.** The Budget provides $893 million for DOE's Office of Fossil Energy and Carbon Management to advance technologies that can provide economic revitalization opportunities in energy communities. This includes dedicated funding for the Interagency Working Group on Coal and Power Plant Communities and Economic Revitalization to coordinate interagency efforts and stakeholder engagement across at least 10 Federal agencies. This interagency effort would expand the delivery of Federal resources to those communities affected by the energy transition.

- **Advances Transformational Clean Energy and Climate Solutions.** The Budget provides $700 million for the Advanced Research and Projects Agency – Energy (ARPA-E). This investment in high-potential, high-impact research and development would help remove the technological barriers to advance energy and environmental missions. The Budget also proposes expanded authority for ARPA-E to more fully address innovation gaps around adaptation, mitigation, and resilience to the impacts of climate change.

- **Invests in Research and Innovation.** The Budget provides a historic investment of $7.8 billion for the Office of Science to support cutting-edge research at the national laboratories and universities to: advance the Nation's understanding of climate change; identify and accelerate novel technologies for clean energy solutions; provide new computing insight through quantum information science and artificial intelligence that would address scientific and environmental challenges; leverage data, analytics, and computational infrastructure to strengthen pandemic preparedness in support of U.S. biodefense and pandemic preparedness strategies and plans; and support the Nation's leading scientific user facilities. New programs would promote U.S. leadership in the industries of the future, including biotechnology and biomanufacturing, and support the Cancer Moonshot initiative.

- **Reduces Health and Environmental Hazards for At-Risk Communities.** The Budget includes $7.6 billion for the Environmental Management program to support the cleanup of communities used during the Manhattan Project and Cold War for nuclear weapons production. The Administration would ensure that investments in the remediation of legacy soil and groundwater contamination provide benefits to disadvantaged communities.

- **Strengthens the Nation's Nuclear Security, Biological Security, and Cybersecurity.** The Budget supports a safe, secure, and effective nuclear stockpile by robustly funding investments in the recapitalization of the National Nuclear Security Administration's physical infrastructure and essential facilities to modernize the U.S. nuclear deterrent. The Budget also increases funding for: key arms control and nuclear nonproliferation and counterterrorism programs; the Naval Nuclear Propulsion Program, which designs, builds, operates, maintains, and manages the reactor systems of the naval nuclear fleet; and biosecurity innovation, as well as highly-skilled staff capacity to carry out these missions. The Budget also invests in energy-sector cybersecurity through the Office of Cybersecurity, Energy Security, and Emergency Response.

# DEPARTMENT OF HEALTH AND HUMAN SERVICES

The Department of Health and Human Services (HHS) is responsible for protecting the health and well-being of Americans through its research, public health, and social services programs. The President's 2023 Budget for HHS invests in: mental healthcare and suicide prevention; healthcare access and outcomes for vulnerable populations; health research and innovation; public health systems and pandemic preparedness; ending the HIV/AIDS epidemic; social service equity; access to child care and early learning programs; and support services for survivors of domestic violence.

The Budget requests $127.3 billion in discretionary funding for HHS, a $26.9 billion or 26.8-percent increase from the 2021 enacted level, excluding amounts requested for the Indian Health Service (IHS), which the Budget proposes to shift from discretionary to mandatory funding. This request includes appropriations for 21st Century Cures Act and program integrity activities.

**The President's 2023 Budget:**

- **Accelerates Innovation through the Advanced Research Projects Agency for Health (ARPA-H).** The Budget proposes a major investment of $5 billion for ARPA-H, significantly increasing direct Federal research and development spending in health. With an initial focus on cancer and other diseases such as diabetes and dementia, this major investment would drive transformational innovation in health research and speed application and implementation of health breakthroughs. Funding for ARPA-H, along with additional funding for the National Institutes of Health, total a $49 billion request to continue to support research that enhances health, lengthens life, reduces illness and disability, and spurs new biotechnology productions and innovation.

- **Advances the Cancer Moonshot Initiative.** The Budget proposes investments in ARPA-H, the National Cancer Institute, the Centers for Disease Control and Prevention (CDC), and the Food and Drug Administration (FDA) to accelerate the rate of progress against cancer by working toward reducing the cancer death rate by at least 50 percent over the next 25 years and improving the experience of people who are living with or who have survived cancer.

- **Transforms Mental Healthcare.** Mental health is essential to overall health, and the United States faces a mental health crisis that has been exacerbated by the COVID-19 pandemic. To address this crisis, the Budget proposes reforms to health coverage and major investments in the mental health workforce. For people with private health insurance, the Budget requires all health plans to cover mental health benefits and ensures that plans have an adequate network of behavioral health providers. For Medicare, TRICARE, the

Department of Veterans Affairs healthcare system, health insurance issuers, group health plans, and the Federal Health Employee Benefit Program, the Budget lowers patients' costs for mental health services. The Budget also requires parity in coverage between behavioral health and medical benefits, and expands coverage for behavioral health providers under Medicare. The Budget invests in increasing the number of mental health providers serving Medicaid beneficiaries, as well as in mental health workforce development and service expansion, including at primary care clinics and non-traditional sites. The Budget also provides sustained and increased funding for community-based centers and clinics, including a State option to receive enhanced Medicaid reimbursement on a permanent basis. In addition, the Budget makes historic investments in youth mental health and suicide prevention programs and in training, educational loan repayment, and scholarships that help address the shortage of behavioral health providers, especially in underserved communities. The Budget also strengthens access to crisis services by building out the National Suicide Prevention Lifeline, which will transition from a ten-digit number to 988 in July 2022.

- **Commits to Ending the HIV/AIDS Epidemic.** The *National HIV/AIDS Strategy for the United States 2022–2025* commits to a 75-percent reduction in HIV infection by 2025. To meet this ambitious target and ultimately end the HIV/AIDS epidemic in the United States, the Budget includes $850 million across HHS to aggressively reduce new HIV cases, increase access to pre-exposure prophylaxis (also known as PrEP), and ensure equitable access to services and supports for those living with HIV. This includes increasing access to PrEP among Medicaid beneficiaries, which is expected to improve health and lower Medicaid costs for HIV treatment. The Budget also proposes a new mandatory program to guarantee PrEP at no cost for all uninsured and underinsured individuals, provide essential wrap-around services through States, IHS, tribal entities, and localities, and establish a network of community providers to reach underserved areas and populations.

- **Guarantees Adequate and Stable Funding for IHS.** As part of the Administration's commitment to honor the United States' trust responsibility to tribal nations and strengthen the Nation-to-Nation relationship, the Budget significantly increases IHS's funding over time, and shifts it from discretionary to mandatory funding. For the first year of the proposal, the Budget includes $9.1 billion in mandatory funding, an increase of $2.9 billion from the 2021 enacted level. After the first year, IHS funding would automatically grow to keep pace with healthcare costs and population growth and gradually close longstanding service and facility shortfalls. By providing IHS stable and predictable funding, the proposal would improve access to high-quality healthcare, rectify historical underfunding of the Indian health system, reduce existing facility backlogs such as the Healthcare Facilities Construction Priority List, address health inequities, and modernize IHS' electronic health record system. This proposal has been informed by consultations with tribal nations on the issue of mandatory funding and will be refined based on ongoing consultation.

- **Prepares for Future Pandemics and Advances Health Security for Other Biological Threats.** While combatting the ongoing COVID-19 pandemic, the United States must catalyze advances in science, technology, and core capabilities to prepare the Nation for the next biological threat and strengthen U.S. and global health security. The Budget makes transformative investments in pandemic preparedness and biodefense across HHS public health agencies—$81.7 billion available over five years—to enable an agile, coordinated, and comprehensive public health response to future threats, and to protect American lives, families and the economy. The Budget provides $40 billion to the Office of the Assistant Secretary for Preparedness and Response to invest in advanced development and manufacturing of vaccines, therapeutics, and diagnostics for high priority threats. The Budget provides $28 billion for CDC to enhance public health system infrastructure, domestic and global threat surveillance, public health workforce development, public health laboratory capacity, and global health security. The Budget provides $12.1 billion to NIH for: research and development of vaccines, diagnostics, and therapeutics against high priority biological threats; biosafety and biosecurity research and innovation to prevent biological incidents; and safe and secure laboratory capacity and clinical trial infrastructure. The Budget also includes $1.6 billion for FDA to expand and modernize regulatory capacity information technology and laboratory infrastructure to support the evaluation of medical countermeasures. Further, the Budget encourages the development of innovative antimicrobial drugs through advance market commitments for critical-need antimicrobial drugs.

- **Builds Advanced Public Health Systems and Capacity.** The Budget includes $9.9 billion in discretionary funding to build capacity at CDC and at the State and local levels, an increase of $2.8 billion over the 2021 enacted level. These resources would: improve the core immunization program; expand public health infrastructure in States and Territories and strengthen the public health workforce; support efforts to modernize public health data collection; including at the Center for Forecasting and Outbreak Analytics; and conduct studies on long COVID conditions to inform diagnosis and treatment options. In addition, to advance health equity, the Budget invests in CDC programs related to viral hepatitis, youth mental health, and sickle cell disease. To address gun violence as a public health epidemic, the Budget invests in community violence intervention and firearm safety research.

- **Expands Access to Vaccines.** The Budget establishes a new Vaccines for Adults (VFA) program, which would provide uninsured adults with access to all vaccines recommended by the Advisory Committee on Immunization Practices at no cost. As a complement to the successful Vaccines for Children (VFC) program, the VFA program would reduce disparities in vaccine coverage and promote infrastructure for broad access to routine and outbreak vaccines. The Budget would also expand the VFC program to include all children under age 19 enrolled in the Children's Health Insurance Program and consolidate vaccine coverage under Medicare Part B, making more preventive vaccines available at no cost to Medicare beneficiaries.

- **Advances Maternal Health and Health Equity.** The United States has the highest maternal mortality rate among developed nations, and rates are disproportionately high for Black and American Indian and Alaska Native women. The Budget includes $470 million to: reduce maternal mortality and morbidity rates; expand maternal health initiatives in rural communities; implement implicit bias training for healthcare providers; create pregnancy medical home demonstration projects; and address the highest rates of perinatal health disparities, including by supporting the perinatal health workforce. The Budget also extends and increases funding for the Maternal, Infant, and Early Childhood Home Visiting program, which serves approximately 71,000 families at risk for poor maternal and child health outcomes each year, and is proven to reduce disparities in infant mortality. To address the lack of data on health disparities and further improve access to care, the Budget strengthens collection and evaluation of health equity data. Recognizing that maternal mental health conditions are the most common complications of pregnancy and childbirth, the Budget continues to support the maternal mental health hotline and the screening and treatment for maternal mental depression and related behavioral disorders.

- **Expands Access to Healthcare Services for Low-Income Women.** The Budget provides $400 million, an increase of nearly 40 percent from the 2021 enacted level, to the Title X Family Planning program, which provides family planning and other healthcare to low-income communities. This increase in Title X funding would improve overall access to vital reproductive and preventive health services and advance gender and health equity.

- **Expands Access to Affordable, High-Quality Early Child Care and Learning.** The Budget provides $20.2 billion for HHS's early care and education programs, an increase of $3.3 billion, or 19 percent, from the 2021 enacted level. This includes $7.6 billion for the Child Care and Development Block Grant, an increase of $1.7 billion from the 2021 enacted level to expand access to quality, affordable child care for families across the Nation. In addition, the Budget helps young children enter kindergarten ready to learn by providing $12.2 billion for Head Start, an increase of $1.5 billion from the 2021 enacted level. The Budget also helps States identify and fill gaps in early education programs by funding the Preschool Development Grants program at $450 million, an increase of $175 million from the 2021 enacted level.

- **Advances Child and Family Well-Being in the Child Welfare System.** The Budget proposes to expand and incentivize the use of evidence-based foster care prevention services to keep families safely together and to reduce the number of children entering foster care. For children who do need to be placed into foster care, the Budget provides States with support and incentives to place more children with relatives or other adults who have an existing emotional bond with the children and fewer children in group homes and institutions, while also providing additional funding to support youth who age out of care without a permanent caregiver. The Budget proposes to nearly double flexible funding for States through the Promoting Safe and Stable Families program, and proposes new provisions to expand access to legal representation for children and families in the child welfare system. The Budget also provides $100 million in competitive grants for States and localities to advance reforms that would reduce the overrepresentation of children and families of color in the child welfare system, address the disparate experiences and outcomes of these families, and provide more families with the support they need to remain safely together. Further, the Budget provides $215 million for States and community-based organizations to respond to and prevent child abuse.

- **Supports Survivors of Domestic Violence and Other Forms of Gender Based-Violence.** The Budget proposes significant increases to support and protect survivors of gender-based violence, including $519 million for the Family Violence Prevention and Services (FVPSA) program to support domestic violence survivors—more than double the 2021 enacted level. This amount continues funding availability for FVPSA-funded resource centers, including those that support the Lesbian, Gay, Bisexual, Transgender, Queer, and Intersex community. The Budget would provide additional funding for domestic violence hotlines and cash assistance for survivors of domestic violence, as well as funding to support a demonstration project evaluating services for survivors at the intersection of housing instability, substance use coercion, and child welfare. In addition, the Budget would provide over $66 million for victims of human trafficking and survivors of torture, an increase of nearly $21 million from the 2021 enacted level.

- **Supports America's Promise to Refugees.** The Budget provides $6.3 billion to the Office of Refugee Resettlement (ORR). This funding would help rebuild the Nation's refugee resettlement infrastructure and support the resettling of up to 125,000 refugees in 2023. The Budget would also help ensure that unaccompanied immigrant children are unified with relatives and sponsors as safely and quickly as possible and receive appropriate care and services while they are in ORR's custody. The Budget makes additional investments in services, including expanded access to counsel to help children navigate complex immigration court proceedings, and enhanced case management and post-release services. The Budget also includes mandatory investments in the Unaccompanied Children (UC) program, including a multiyear contingency fund that would automatically provide additional resources when there are large increases in UC referrals, and a proposal to scale up to universal UC legal representation. The Budget redresses past wrongs by providing resources for critical reunification services—including trauma-related and mental health services—to children and families unduly separated from each other through policies of the previous administration.

- **Supports Families Struggling with Home Energy and Water Bills.** The Budget provides $4 billion, a $225 million increase from the 2021 enacted level, for the Low Income Home Energy Assistance Program (LIHEAP). LIHEAP helps families access home energy and weatherization assistance, vital tools for protecting vulnerable families' health in response to extreme weather and climate change. As part of the Justice40 pilot, HHS plans to increase efforts to prevent energy shutoffs and increase support for households with young children and older people, and high energy burdens. Since the Low Income Household Water Assistance Program (LIHWAP) expires at the end of 2023, the Budget proposes to expand LIHEAP to advance the goals of both LIHEAP and LIHWAP. Specifically, the Budget increases LIHEAP funding and gives States the option to use a portion of their LIHEAP funds to provide water bill assistance to low-income households.

# DEPARTMENT OF HOMELAND SECURITY

The Department of Homeland Security (DHS) is responsible for safeguarding the American people by: preventing terrorism and countering domestic violent extremism; securing and managing U.S. borders; administering and enforcing U.S. immigration laws; defending and securing Federal cyberspace and critical infrastructure; and ensuring disaster resilience, response, and recovery. The President's 2023 Budget for DHS advances key Administration priorities by: investing in climate resilience; research and development; Federal cybersecurity; maritime security; and secure and humane border management. The Budget also enhances DHS's capacity to prepare for and respond to pandemics and other biological threats.

The Budget requests $56.7 billion in discretionary funding for the Department of Homeland Security, a $2.9 billion or 5.4-percent increase from the 2021 enacted level. Resources provided through the 2023 Budget complement investments in cybersecurity, hazard mitigation, and others areas provided in the Infrastructure Investment and Jobs Act (Bipartisan Infrastructure Law).

## The President's 2023 Budget:

- **Bolsters Federal Cybersecurity and Critical Infrastructure Security.** The Budget provides $2.5 billion to the Cybersecurity and Infrastructure Security Agency (CISA), a $486 million increase from the 2021 enacted level, to maintain critical cybersecurity capabilities implemented in the American Rescue Plan Act of 2021, expand network protection throughout the Federal Executive Branch, and bolster support capabilities, such as cloud business applications, enhanced analytics, and stakeholder engagement. The Budget also provides significant enhancements across DHS to modernize protection of systems, networks, assets, and information, as required by Executive Order 14028, "Improving the Nation's Cybersecurity." In addition to bolstering Federal cybersecurity, the Budget includes funding to ensure safe and secure elections, build and maintain critical public-private partnerships, enhance critical infrastructure protection, and prioritize and reinforce CISA's role as the national risk manager.

- **Enhances Natural Disaster Resilience.** The Budget provides $3.5 billion for DHS's climate resilience programs. This includes $507 million, a $93 million increase from the 2021 enacted level, for the Federal Emergency Management Agency's (FEMA) flood hazard mapping program to incorporate climate science and future risks. The Budget also makes robust investments in FEMA's hazard mitigation grant programs, including the Building Resilient Infrastructure and Communities grant program, which helps communities build resilience against natural disasters, including disadvantaged communities who are disproportionately at risk from climate crises.

- **Expands U.S. Coast Guard (USCG) Capabilities.** The Budget provides $11.5 billion for the USCG, a $564 million increase from the 2021 enacted level, to address emerging national security concerns and goals. This includes expanding USCG cyber operations capacity to protect and respond to cyber threats in the maritime sector, as well as expanding its presence in the Pacific, the Atlantic, and the Arctic—including procuring a commercially available icebreaker. These efforts would expand the capabilities of partners and deepen U.S. ties in each of the above-mentioned regions in order to strengthen maritime security and governance, which would protect economic activity and counter transnational criminal organizations.

- **Upgrades Research Laboratory Infrastructure.** The Budget makes historic investments in research and development infrastructure, providing $89 million to improve and modernize laboratories in the DHS Science and Technology Directorate (S&T). This funding would allow S&T to replace and enhance mission-critical equipment, make necessary information technology improvements, and allow DHS to construct the Detection Sciences Testing and Applied Research Center, which would enable DHS to more efficiently and effectively test and evaluate threat screening devices and counter homemade explosives to further secure transportation systems and other public venues.

- **Modernizes Transportation Security Administration (TSA) Pay and Workforce Policies.** The Budget provides a total of $7.1 billion for TSA pay and benefits, an increase of $1.6 billion from the 2021 enacted level, to compensate TSA employees at rates comparable to their peers in the Federal workforce. By establishing salary parity with other Federal employees, the Budget addresses retention issues faced by the Transportation Security Officer workforce, improving service delivery. The Budget also supports expanding TSA workforce access to labor benefits such as collective bargaining and merit systems protection. These enhancements support the President's commitment to fostering diversity, equity, and inclusion in the Federal workforce.

- **Ensures a Safe, Humane, and Efficient Immigration System.** The Administration is committed to ensuring the U.S. Citizenship and Immigration Services (USCIS) meets its mission administering the Nation's lawful immigration system and safeguarding its integrity and promise by efficiently and fairly adjudicating requests for immigration benefits. The Budget provides $765 million in discretionary funding for USCIS to: efficiently process increasing asylum caseloads; address the backlog of applications for work authorization, naturalization, adjustment of status, and other immigration benefits; and improve refugee processing.

- **Improves Border Processing and Management.** The Budget provides $15.3 billion for the U.S. Customs and Border Protection and $8.1 billion for the U.S. Immigration and Customs Enforcement to enforce immigration law, further secure U.S. borders and ports of entry, and effectively manage irregular migration along the Southwest border, including through $309 million in modern border security technology and $494 million for noncitizen processing and care costs.

# DEPARTMENT OF HOUSING AND URBAN DEVELOPMENT

The Department of Housing and Urban Development (HUD) is responsible for creating healthy, safe, sustainable, inclusive communities and affordable homes for all. The President's 2023 Budget for HUD: significantly expands rental assistance to low-income households; advances efforts to end homelessness; increases affordable housing supply; expands homeownership opportunities for underserved borrowers; improves affordable housing by increasing climate resilience and energy efficiency; strengthens communities facing underinvestment; and prevents and redresses housing-related discrimination.

The Budget requests $71.9 billion in discretionary funding for HUD, a $12.3 billion or 21-percent increase from the 2021 enacted level.

## The President's 2023 Budget:

- **Expands the Housing Choice Voucher Program and Enhances Household Mobility.** The Housing Choice Voucher program currently provides 2.3 million low-income families with rental assistance to obtain housing in the private market. The Budget provides $32.1 billion, an increase of $6.4 billion (including emergency funding) over the 2021 enacted level, to maintain services for all currently assisted families and to expand assistance to an additional 200,000 households, particularly for those who are experiencing homelessness or fleeing, or attempting to flee, domestic violence or other forms of gender-based violence. The Budget also funds mobility-related supportive services to provide low-income families with greater options to move to higher-opportunity neighborhoods.

- **Increases Affordable Housing Supply.** To address the critical shortage of affordable housing in communities throughout the Nation, the Budget provides nearly $2 billion for the HOME Investment Partnerships Program (HOME), an increase of $600 million over the 2021 enacted level, to construct and rehabilitate affordable rental housing and provide homeownership opportunities. If enacted, this would be the highest funding level for HOME in nearly 15 years. In addition, the Budget provides $180 million to support 2,000 units of new permanently affordable housing specifically for the elderly and persons with disabilities, supporting the Administration's priority to maximize independent living for people with disabilities. To complement these investments, the Budget contains a total of $50 billion in mandatory funding and additional Low-Income Housing Tax Credits to increase affordable housing development. Specifically, the Budget provides $35 billion in HUD funding for State and local housing finance agencies and their partners to provide grants, revolving loan funds, and other streamlined financing tools that reduce transactional costs and increase housing supply, as well as grants to advance State and local jurisdictions' efforts to remove barriers to affordable housing development.

- **Advances Efforts to End Homelessness.** To prevent and reduce homelessness, the Budget provides $3.6 billion, an increase of $580 million over the 2021 enacted level, for Homeless Assistance Grants to meet renewal needs and expand assistance to nearly 25,000 additional households, including survivors of domestic violence and homeless youth.

- **Promotes Equity by Preventing and Redressing Housing Discrimination.** The Budget provides $86 million in grants to support State and local fair housing enforcement organizations and to further education, outreach, and training on rights and responsibilities under Federal fair housing laws. The Budget also invests in HUD staff and operations capacity to deliver on the President's housing priorities, including to lift barriers that restrict housing and neighborhood choice, affirmatively further fair housing, and provide redress to those who have experienced housing discrimination.

- **Supports Access to Homeownership.** The Budget supports access to homeownership for underserved borrowers, including many first-time and minority homebuyers, through Federal Housing Administration (FHA) and Ginnie Mae credit guarantees. The Budget, via FHA and HOME, also provides $115 million for complementary loan and down payment assistance pilot proposals to expand homeownership opportunities for first-generation and/or low-wealth first-time homebuyers.

- **Invests in Resilience and Energy Efficiency across HUD Multifamily Programs.** Multifamily properties with HUD rental assistance and Public Housing provide 2.3 million affordable homes to low-income families. The Budget not only fully funds operating costs across this portfolio and provides critical Public Housing capital investments, but also provides about $900 million in resources across HUD programs for modernization activities aimed at energy efficiency and resilience to climate change impacts. These investments would help improve the quality of public and HUD-assisted housing while creating good-paying jobs.

- **Reduces Lead and Other Home Health Hazards for Vulnerable Families.** The Budget provides $400 million, an increase of $40 million above the 2021 enacted level, for States, local governments, and nonprofits to reduce lead-based paint and other health hazards in the homes of low-income families with young children. The Budget also includes $25 million to address lead-based paint in Public Housing. The Centers for Disease Control and Prevention identifies the risk for lead exposure as greatest for children from racial and ethnic minority groups and children in families living below the poverty level, and the Lead Hazard and Healthy Homes grants complement additional Government-wide lead remediation investments included in the Infrastructure Investment and Jobs Act (Bipartisan Infrastructure Law), and target interventions to these most at-risk communities. In addition, the Budget targets $60 million specifically to prevent and mitigate housing-related health hazards, such as fire safety and mold, in HUD-assisted housing.

- **Supports Economic Development and Invests in Underserved Communities.** The Budget provides $3.8 billion for the Community Development Block Grant program to help communities modernize infrastructure, invest in economic development, create parks and other public amenities, and provide social services. The Budget includes a targeted increase of $195 million to spur equitable development and the removal of barriers to revitalization in 100 of the most underserved neighborhoods in the United States.

- **Invests in Affordable Housing in Tribal Communities.** Native Americans are seven times more likely to live in overcrowded conditions and five times more likely to have inadequate plumbing, kitchen, or heating systems than all U.S. households. The Budget helps address the poor housing conditions in tribal areas by providing $1 billion to fund tribal efforts to expand affordable housing, improve housing conditions and infrastructure, and increase economic opportunities for low-income families. Of this total, $150 million would prioritize activities that advance resilience and energy efficiency in housing-related projects.

# DEPARTMENT OF THE INTERIOR

The Department of the Interior (DOI) conserves and manages the Nation's natural resources and cultural heritage for the benefit and enjoyment of the American people. The President's 2023 Budget for DOI invests in climate change mitigation and adaptation, honors commitments to tribal nations, supports development in U.S. Territories and freely associated states, and funds reclamation and resilience work that ensures healthy lands and waters and creates good-paying jobs.

The Budget requests $17.5 billion in discretionary funding for DOI, a $2.8 billion or 19.3-percent increase from the 2021 enacted level, excluding amounts requested for Contract Support Costs and Indian Self-Determination and Education Assistance Act of 1975 Section 105(l) leases, which the Budget proposes to shift from discretionary to mandatory funding. Resources provided through the 2023 Budget complement major investments in wildfire management, tribal programs, methane emissions reduction, abandoned mine land reclamation, western water infrastructure, and ecosystem restoration through the Infrastructure Investment and Jobs Act (Bipartisan Infrastructure Law).

**The President's 2023 Budget:**

- **Strengthens Climate Resilience for Communities and Ecosystems.** As steward for 20 percent of the Nation's lands and waters and with a primary responsibility to uphold the Nation's commitments to American Indians and Alaska Natives, DOI plays an integral role in addressing the climate crisis through strengthened conservation partnerships, including the Administration's America the Beautiful Initiative, and science-based ecosystem management. The Budget invests $5 billion in climate adaptation and resilience, including for several priorities listed below, to mitigate the impacts of climate change—such as drought, wildfire and severe storms—on America's communities, lands, waters, and wildlife. The Budget also sustains funding for key conservation and ecosystem management initiatives, including the Civilian Climate Corps, alongside a historic $1.4 billion investment in the Bipartisan Infrastructure Law for ecosystem restoration across America.

- **Honors Trust and Treaty Responsibilities to Tribal Communities through Robust Program Funding.** The Budget makes the largest annual investment in tribal nations in history, reflecting input received from the first Government-wide tribal consultation on the development of the President's Budget. With $4.5 billion for DOI's tribal programs, more than $1 billion above the 2021 enacted level, investments would support public safety and justice, social services, climate resilience, and educational needs to uphold Federal trust responsibilities and advance equity for Native communities. This includes a $156 million increase to support construction work at seven Bureau of Indian Education schools, providing quality facilities for culturally-appropriate education with high academic standards, as well as $7 million for the Indian Boarding School Initiative, which takes preliminary steps to address the injustices of past Federal Indian boarding school policy. The Budget also includes $632 million in Tribal Public Safety and Justice funding at DOI, which collaborates closely with the Department of Justice, including on continued efforts to address the crisis of Missing and Murdered Indigenous Persons. The Budget also proposes to reclassify Contract Support Costs and Indian Self-Determination and Education Assistance Act of 1975 Section 105(l) leases as mandatory spending, providing certainty for tribal communities in meeting these ongoing needs through dedicated funding sources. The Budget further proposes to provide mandatory funding to the Bureau of Reclamation for operation and maintenance of previously enacted Indian Water Rights Settlements, and the Administration is interested in working with the Congress on an approach to provide a mandatory funding source for future settlements. The Budget also complements Bipartisan Infrastructure Law investments to address climate resilience needs in tribal communities.

- **Advances Climate Science.** The Budget invests $375 million at DOI to advance understanding of the impacts of climate change, unlock new opportunities to reduce climate risk through innovative mitigation and adaptation research, measure and monitor greenhouse gas emissions and sinks on Federal lands, and ensure that coastal, fire-prone, and other particularly vulnerable communities have accurate and accessible information to allow them to better respond to the climate crisis. The Budget also supports the development of a Federal climate data portal that would provide the public with accessible information on historical and projected climate impacts, inform decision-making, and strengthen community climate resilience.

- **Mitigates the Risk of Catastrophic Wildfires.** The Budget invests $325 million in Hazardous Fuels Management and Burned Area Rehabilitation programs to help reduce the risk and severity of wildfires, and restore lands that were devastated by catastrophic fire over the last several years. This funding complements the $878 million for hazardous fuels management and $325 million for burned area rehabilitation projects provided through the Bipartisan Infrastructure Law.

- **Invests in the Wildland Firefighting Workforce.** Protecting communities, ecosystems, and infrastructure from wildfire requires a resilient and reliable Federal workforce. The Budget includes $477 million, an increase of $130 million over the 2021 enacted level, to ensure that no Federal firefighter will make less than $15 an hour, to increase the Federal firefighting workforce, and to support these men and women with competitive compensation. This funding is further supported by $120 million made available in the Bipartisan Infrastructure Law to address firefighting workforce needs.

- **Increases Drought Resilience.** The Budget helps to ensure that all communities across the Nation have access to a resilient and reliable water supply by investing in water conservation, development of desalination technologies, and water recycling and reuse projects. In addition, nearly $1.7 billion provided through the Bipartisan Infrastructure Law for 2023, the Budget invests over $675 million in Western water resource infrastructure and to provide potable water to rural areas, serving both tribal and non-tribal communities. The Budget also provides funding to address the ongoing drought in the western United States, including funding to implement the Drought Contingency Plans to conserve water in the Colorado River System, which is at historically low levels.

- **Promotes Racial Justice and Equity.** The Budget supports DOI's ongoing work to advance racial justice and more equitably deliver services to all Americans with discrete investments in each bureau. The Budget provides over $3 billion to programs covered under the Justice40 initiative, such as tribal housing improvements, wildlife conservation grants, and energy infrastructure development in insular communities, which ensures that at least 40 percent of the overall benefits from certain Federal investments are delivered to disadvantaged communities. Moreover, the Budget includes a $48 million initiative to build a more equitable National Park System (NPS). Through this initiative, DOI would expand operations at parks that preserve and tell the story of historically underrepresented and marginalized groups, further integrate tribal viewpoints into park management, address transportation barriers to parks from underserved communities, and improve park accessibility for visitors and employees with disabilities.

- **Accelerates Renewable Energy Development on Public Lands.** The Budget includes $254 million, an increase of $151 million from the 2021 enacted level, to accelerate and expand activities that support economic development and the creation of thousands of good-paying jobs through clean energy deployment on public lands and offshore waters. Funding would support the leasing, planning, and permitting of solar, wind and geothermal energy projects, and associated transmission infrastructure that would help mitigate climate change impacts and meet the Administration's goal of deploying 30 gigawatts of offshore wind capacity by 2030.

- **Creates Jobs Remediating and Reclaiming Abandoned Wells and Mines.** The Budget provides over $321 million to remediate orphaned oil and gas wells and reclaim abandoned mine lands on Federal and non-Federal lands. The funding complements the $16 billion provided in the Bipartisan Infrastructure Law for orphaned well remediation and abandoned mine reclamation, and would help create good union jobs, mitigate climate change by reducing greenhouse gas emissions, and ultimately allow for more productive land uses.

- **Rebuilds Critical Capacity.** The Budget rebuilds core functions and capabilities across DOI, including science capacity at the U.S. Geological Survey, and land management operations of the NPS, Fish and Wildlife Service, and Bureau of Land Management.

# DEPARTMENT OF JUSTICE

The Department of Justice (DOJ) is responsible for defending the interests of the United States and protecting all Americans as the chief enforcer of Federal laws. The President's 2023 Budget for DOJ invests in: combating gun crime and other violent crime, terrorism, violence against women, and cyber threats; protecting civil rights; implementing Federal, State, and local criminal justice reforms; improving the immigration court system; bolstering antitrust enforcement; and advancing environmental justice.

The Budget requests $37.7 billion in discretionary funding for DOJ, a $4.2 billion or nearly 13-percent increase from the 2021 enacted level.

## The President's 2023 Budget:

- **Invests in Federal Law Enforcement to Combat Gun Crime and Other Violent Crime.** The Budget makes robust investments to bolster Federal law enforcement capacity. The Budget includes $17.4 billion, an increase of $1.7 billion above the 2021 enacted level, for DOJ law enforcement including a total of $1.7 billion for the Bureau of Alcohol, Tobacco, Firearms, and Explosives (ATF) to expand multijurisdictional gun trafficking strike forces with additional personnel, increase regulation of the firearms industry, enhance ATF's National Integrated Ballistic Information Network, and modernize the National Tracing Center. The Budget includes $1.8 billion for the U.S. Marshals Service to support personnel dedicated to fighting violent crime, including through fugitive apprehension and enforcement operations. The Budget also provides the Federal Bureau of Investigation (FBI) with an additional $69 million to address violent crime, including violent crimes against children and crime in Indian Country. In addition, the Budget provides the U.S. Attorneys with $72.1 million to prosecute violent crimes.

- **Supports State and Local Law Enforcement and Community Violence Prevention and Intervention Programs to Make Our Neighborhoods Safer.** The Budget provides $3.2 billion in discretionary resources for State and local grants and $30 billion in mandatory resources to support law enforcement, crime prevention, and community violence intervention.

- **Reinvigorates Federal Civil Rights Enforcement.** In order to address longstanding inequities and strengthen civil rights protections, the Budget invests $367 million, an increase of $101 million over the 2021 enacted level, in civil rights protection across DOJ. These resources would support police reform, the prosecution of hate crimes, enforcement of voting rights, and efforts to provide equitable access to justice. Investments also provide mediation and conciliation services through the Community Relations Service. The Budget also continues investments in civil rights enforcement at the FBI by providing $18 million to expand civil rights investigations across the Nation, $8 million to the U.S. Attorneys to expand prosecutions of violations of civil rights, and nearly $1 million to the Criminal Division to expand investigations of election-related crimes, including voter suppression.

- **Reforms the Federal Criminal Justice System.** The Budget leverages the capacity of the Federal justice system to advance innovative criminal justice reform initiatives and serve as a model for reform that is not only comprehensive in scope, but evidence-informed and high-impact. The Budget supports key investments in First Step Act (FSA) implementation, including $100 million for a historic collaboration between the Bureau of Prisons (BOP) and the Department of Labor (DOL) for a national initiative to provide comprehensive workforce development services to people in the Federal prison system, both during their time in BOP facilities and after they are transferred to community placement. Thousands of incarcerated people would have access to a wide variety of evidence-informed models and practices, and in service of continuing to build the evidence base, DOL and BOP would oversee a ground-breaking, large-scale evaluation that assesses the impact of these programs on recidivism, labor market outcomes, and other key metrics. To support rehabilitative programming, improve conditions of confinement, and address augmentation in BOP facilities, the Budget proposes $151 million to hire additional staff, including $72 million for FSA-dedicated programmatic staff and $79 million for front-line correctional officers. In support of Federal law enforcement reform and oversight, the Budget also proposes $106 million to support the deployment of body-worn cameras (BWC) to DOJ's law enforcement officers, as well as an impact evaluation to assess the role of BWC in advancing criminal justice reform.

- **Reforms the Juvenile Justice System and Supports Existing Criminal Justice Reform Programs.** The Budget proposes $760 million for juvenile justice programs, an increase of $414 million over the 2021 enacted level, to bolster diversionary juvenile justice strategies. In addition to these resources, funding is provided to support existing reform programs such as the Second Chance Act of 2007, research and innovation programs, and alternative court systems.

- **Addresses Terrorism**. The Budget invests resources to address the threats of both foreign and domestic terrorism while respecting civil rights and civil liberties. The FBI is provided an increase of $33 million for domestic terrorism investigations.

- **Prioritizes Efforts to End Gender-Based Violence.** The Budget proposes a historic investment of $1 billion to support Violence Against Women Act of 1994 (VAWA) programs, a $487 million or 95-percent increase over the 2021 enacted level. The Budget supports substantial increases for longstanding VAWA programs, including key investments in legal assistance for victims, transitional housing, and sexual assault services. Resources are also provided for new programs to support transgender survivors, build community-based organizational capacity, combat online harassment and abuse, support community-based restorative practices, and address emerging issues in gender-based violence, including a new financial assistance program for survivors. The Budget strongly supports underserved and tribal communities by providing $35 million for culturally-specific services, $10 million for underserved populations, $5.5 million to assist enforcement of tribal special domestic violence jurisdiction, and $3 million to support tribal Special Assistant U.S. Attorneys. In addition, the Budget provides $120 million, an increase of $72 million above the 2021 enacted level, to the Office of Justice Programs for the Sexual Assault Kit Initiative to address the rape kit backlog, and for a new Regional Sexual Assault Investigative Training Academies Program.

- **Counters Cyber Threats.** The Budget expands DOJ's ability to pursue cyber threats through investments that support a multiyear effort to build cyber investigative capabilities at FBI field divisions nationwide. These investments include an additional $52 million for more agents, enhanced response capabilities, and strengthened intelligence collection and analysis capabilities. These investments are in line with the Administration's counter-ransomware strategy that emphasizes disruptive activity and combatting the misuse of cryptocurrency.

- **Improves Immigration Courts.** The Budget invests $1.4 billion, an increase of $621 million above the 2021 enacted level, in the Executive Office for Immigration Review (EOIR) to continue addressing the backlog of over 1.5 million cases that are currently pending in the immigration courts. This funding supports 100 new immigration judges, including the support personnel required to create maximum efficiencies in the court systems, as well as an expansion of EOIR's virtual court initiative. The Budget would also invest new resources in legal access programming, including $150 million in discretionary resources to provide access to representation for adults and families in the immigration proceedings. Complementing this new program is a proposal for $4.5 billion in mandatory resources to expand these efforts over a ten-year period. Providing resources to support legal representation in the immigration system would create greater efficiencies in processing cases while making the system fairer and more equitable.

- **Bolsters Antitrust Enforcement.** The Budget reflects the Administration's commitment to vigorous marketplace competition through robust enforcement of antitrust law by including a historic increase of $88 million over the 2021 enacted level for the Antitrust Division.

- **Supports Environmental Justice.** The Budget expands DOJ's work in environmental justice, providing $1.4 million to launch an Office for Environmental Justice. An additional $6.5 million funds the Environment and Natural Resources Division's work in securing environmental justice and combatting the climate crisis. These resources would be central to the Division and DOJ's execution of a comprehensive environmental justice strategy in support of the President's Executive Order 14008, "Tackling the Climate Crisis at Home and Abroad."

# DEPARTMENT OF LABOR

The Department of Labor (DOL) is responsible for protecting the health, safety, wages, and income security of workers and retirees. The President's 2023 Budget for DOL invests in: building the skills of America's workers; protecting workers' rights, health and safety, and wages; strengthening the integrity and accessibility of the Unemployment Insurance (UI) program; and creating good, middle-class jobs that are safe, equitable, pay fair wages and benefits, empower workers, and offer opportunities for advancement.

The Budget requests $14.6 billion in discretionary funding for DOL, a $2.2 billion or 18-percent increase from the 2021 enacted level.

## The President's 2023 Budget:

- **Empowers and Protects Workers.** To ensure workers are treated with dignity and respect in the workplace, the Budget invests $2.2 billion, an increase of $397 million above the 2021 enacted level, in the Department's worker protection agencies. Between 2016 and 2020, DOL worker protection agencies lost approximately 14 percent of their staff, limiting their ability to perform inspections and conduct investigations. The Budget would enable DOL to conduct the enforcement and regulatory work needed to ensure workers' wages and benefits are protected, address the misclassification of workers as independent contractors, and improve workplace health and safety. The Budget also ensures fair treatment for millions of workers by restoring resources to oversee and enforce the equal employment obligations of Federal contractors, including protections against discrimination based on race, gender, disability, gender identity, and sexual orientation.

- **Equips Workers with Skills They Need to Obtain High-Quality Jobs.** The Budget invests in effective, evidence-based training models to equip workers with the skills they need to obtain high-quality jobs. Community colleges play a critical role in providing accessible, low-cost, and high-quality training, and the Budget invests $100 million to build their capacity to work with the public workforce development system and employers to design and deliver high-quality workforce programs. The Budget also provides $100 million for a new Sectoral Employment through Career Training for Occupational Readiness program, which would support training programs focused on growing industries, enabling underserved and underrepresented workers to access good jobs and creating the skilled workforce the economy needs to thrive.

- **Expands Access to Registered Apprenticeships (RA).** RA is a proven earn-and-learn model that raises participants' wages and places them on a reliable path to the middle class.

The Budget invests $303 million, a $118 million increase above the 2021 enacted level, to expand RA opportunities in high-growth fields, such as technology, advanced manufacturing, healthcare, and transportation, while increasing access for historically underrepresented groups, including people of color and women, and diversifying the industry sectors involved. To improve access to RAs for women, the Budget doubles DOL's investment in its Women in Apprenticeship and Nontraditional Occupations grants, which provide pre-apprenticeship opportunities to boost women's participation in RA.

- **Provides Training and Employment Pathways for Youth.** The Budget invests in programs that provide youth with equitable access to high-quality training and career opportunities. The Budget invests $75 million for a new National Youth Employment Program, which would create high-quality summer and year-round job opportunities for underserved youth. The Budget also provides $145 million for YouthBuild, $48 million above the 2021 enacted level, to enable more at-risk youth to gain both the education and occupational skills they need to obtain good jobs. To further advance equity and inclusion, the Budget provides $15 million to test new ways to enable low-income youth with disabilities, including youth who are in foster care, involved in the justice system, or who are experiencing homelessness, to successfully transition to employment.

- **Supports Legacy Energy Communities.** In order to address changes in the energy economy, the Budget continues to invest in strategic planning, partnership development, and training and reemployment activities for displaced workers. The Budget provides $100 million to support DOL's role in the multi-agency POWER+ Initiative, which aims to assist displaced workers and transform local economies and communities transitioning away from fossil fuel production to new, sustainable industries. The Budget also includes $35 million, administered in partnership with the Appalachian Regional Commission and the Delta Regional Authority, to help Appalachian and Delta communities develop local and regional workforce development strategies that promote long-term economic stability and opportunities for workers, especially those connected to the energy industry. Further, the Budget provides $20 million for DOL to partner with AmeriCorps and other agencies to establish a Civilian Climate Corps program to help communities address the climate crisis by creating service opportunities and job training programs in emerging industries.

- **Modernizes, Protects, and Strengthens the UI Safety Net.** The UI program has helped millions of Americans through periods of unemployment during the COVID-19 pandemic. The Budget invests $3.4 billion, an increase of $769 million above the 2021 enacted level, to modernize, protect, and strengthen this critical program. This includes several investments aimed at tackling fraud in the UI program, including funding to support more robust identity verification for UI applicants, help States develop and test fraud-prevention tools and strategies, and allow the DOL Office of Inspector General to increase its investigations into fraud rings targeting the UI program. To allow States to serve claimants more quickly and effectively while strengthening program integrity, the Budget also updates the formula for determining the amount States receive to administer UI, the first comprehensive update in decades. The Budget also proposes principles to guide future efforts to reform the UI system, including improving benefit levels and access, scaling UI benefits automatically during recessions, expanding eligibility to reflect the modern labor force, improving State and Federal solvency through more equitable and progressive financing, expanding reemployment services, and safeguarding the program from fraud.

- **Strengthens Mental Health Parity Protections.** The Budget requires all health plans to cover mental health benefits, ensures that plans have an adequate network of behavioral health providers, and improves DOL's ability to enforce the law. In addition, the Budget includes $275 million over 10 years to increase the Department's capacity to ensure that large group market health plans and issuers comply with mental health and substance use disorder requirements, and expand the Agency's capacity to take action against plans and issuers that do not comply.

# DEPARTMENT OF STATE AND OTHER INTERNATIONAL PROGRAMS

The Department of State (State), U.S. Agency for International Development (USAID), and other international programs advance the interests and security of the American people by using diplomatic and development tools to address global challenges and advance a free, peaceful, and prosperous world. The President's 2023 Budget for State, USAID, and other international programs strengthens American power and influence by working with allies and partners to solve global challenges including through the launch of the President's Build Back Better World Initiative. These investments would position the United States to compete with China, and any other nation, from a position of strength.

The Budget requests $67.6 billion in discretionary funding for the Department of State and other international programs, a $10.2 billion or 18-percent increase from the 2021 enacted level, excluding emergency funding. Within this total, the Budget includes $60.4 billion for the Department of State and USAID, an increase of $7.4 billion or 14 percent above the 2021 enacted levels. This Budget also includes $4.4 billion for the international programs at the Department of the Treasury, an increase of $2.5 billion or 131 percent above the 2021 enacted level.

## The President's 2023 Budget:

- **Advances the President's Historic Climate Finance Pledge.** The Budget includes over $11 billion in international climate finance, meeting the President's pledge to quadruple international climate finance, a year early. This includes $5.3 billion in appropriations, including a $1.6 billion contribution to the Green Climate Fund, a critical multilateral tool for financing climate adaptation and mitigation projects in developing countries. The Budget also supports a $3.2 billion loan to the Clean Technology Fund to finance clean energy projects in developing countries. U.S. international climate assistance and financing would: accelerate the global energy transition to net zero emissions by 2050; help developing countries build resilience to the growing impacts of climate change, including through the *President's Emergency Plan for Adaptation and Resilience (PREPARE)* and other programs; and support the implementation of the President's *Plan to Conserve Global Forests: Critical Carbon Sinks*–while increasing energy independence by decreasing reliance on producers of non-renewable resources.

- **Advances American Leadership in Global Health, Including Global Health Security and Pandemic Preparedness.** The Budget includes $10.6 billion to bolster U.S. leadership in addressing global health and health security challenges, a $1.4 billion increase above the 2021 enacted level. Within this total, the Budget demonstrates U.S. leadership by supporting a $2 billion contribution for the Global Fund's seventh replenishment, for an intended pledge of $6 billion over three years, to save lives and continue the fight against HIV/AIDS, tuberculosis, and malaria, and to support the Global Fund's expanded response to COVID-19 and global health strengthening. This total also includes $1 billion to prevent, prepare for, and respond to infectious disease outbreaks, including the continued expansion of Global Health Security Agenda capacity-building programs and a multilateral financial intermediary fund for health security and pandemic preparedness. The Budget also invests in the global health workforce and systems to enhance countries' abilities to provide core health services, improve health systems resiliency, and respond to crises while mitigating the impacts of crises on routine health services. In addition, the Budget includes $6.5 billion in mandatory funding for State and USAID over five years to make transformative investments in pandemic and other biological threat preparedness globally in support of U.S. biodefense and pandemic preparedness strategies and plans. The pandemic preparedness funding would strengthen the global health workforce, support pandemic preparedness research and development (R&D), advance global R&D capacity, and support health security capacity and financing to strengthen global capacity to prevent, detect, and respond to future COVID-19 variants and other infectious disease outbreaks.

- **Revitalizes Alliances and Partnerships in the Indo-Pacific and Europe.** To strengthen and modernize America's alliances and partnerships in vital global regions and assert U.S. leadership in strategic competition, the Budget includes nearly $1.8 billion to support a free and open, connected, secure, and resilient Indo-Pacific Region and the Indo-Pacific Strategy, and $400 million for the Countering the People's Republic of China Malign Influence Fund. In addition, the Budget provides $682 million for Ukraine, an increase of $219 million above the 2021 enacted level, to continue to counter Russian malign influence and to meet emerging needs related to security, energy, cyber security issues, disinformation, macroeconomic stabilization, and civil society resilience.

- **Champions an Open and Secure Digital and Technological Ecosystem.** The Budget invests more than $350 million to expand reliable and affordable internet access through the development and deployment of secure digital and technological infrastructure. The Budget would improve international cybersecurity practices and promote the adoption of policies that support an open, interoperable, secure, and reliable internet. These resources would further development programming across sectors in line with the State's cyberspace and emerging technology diplomacy and USAID's digital development strategy. State and USAID will also seek to close the digital gender gap in low- and middle-income countries by increasing women and girls' access to information communication technologies and addressing online harassment and abuse globally.

- **Renews America's Leadership in International Institutions.** The Budget continues the Administration's efforts to lead through international organizations by meeting the Nation's commitments to fully fund U.S. contributions and to pay United Nations peacekeeping dues on time and in full. Strengthening the Nation's international partnerships is critical to meeting the Sustainable Development Goals, including global education, ending hunger and malnutrition, building more sustainable, equitable, and resilient food systems and addressing other global challenges.

- **Supports Democracy Globally.** In response to political fragility and increasing authoritarianism around the world, the Budget provides more than $3.2 billion to support global democracy, human rights, anti-corruption, and good governance programming, consistent with the commitments made during the President's Summit for Democracy. The Budget advances the Presidential Memorandum on Advancing the Human Rights of Lesbian, Gay, Bisexual, Transgender, Queer, and Intersex Persons Around the World, the U.S. Strategy on Countering Corruption, and the Presidential Initiative on Democratic Renewal.

- **Restores U.S. Leadership in International Development.** The Budget provides $1.4 billion for the World Bank's International Development Association (IDA). This investment restores the United States' historical role as the largest World Bank donor to support the development of low- and middle-income countries, which benefits the American people by increasing global stability, mitigating climate and health risks, and developing new markets for U.S exports. The U.S. contribution would also support the United States' $3.5 billion pledge to the next replenishment of the IDA, a critical component of the global response to the devastating impacts of the COVID-19 pandemic on developing countries. The Budget also funds bilateral partner capacity building efforts in key areas such as judicial sector strengthening, countering and preventing terrorism, and provision of basic services.

- **Continues Collaborative U.S. Leadership in Central America and Haiti.** As part of a comprehensive strategy to advance systemic reform while addressing the root causes of irregular migration from Central America to the United States, the Budget invests $987 million in the region to continue meeting the President's four-year commitment of $4 billion. Further, in response to deteriorating conditions and widespread violence in Haiti, the Budget invests $275 million to strengthen Haiti's recovery from political and economic shocks, such as strengthening the capacity of the Haitian National Police, combating corruption, strengthening the capacity of civil society, and supporting services for marginalized populations. These investments would ensure that the United States is able to revitalize partnerships that build economic resilience, democratic stability, and citizen security in the region.

- **Supports America's Allies in the Middle East.** The Budget fully supports the U.S.-Israel Memorandum of Understanding, provides $1.4 billion in economic and security assistance for Jordan, and includes $1.4 billion to support the U.S. diplomatic and security partnership with Egypt. As part of the Administration's commitment to advancing security, prosperity, and freedom for both Israelis and Palestinians, the Budget also provides $219 million for critical assistance to the Palestinian people in the West Bank and Gaza, as well as across the region, in support of a two-state solution with Israel.

- **Strengthens African Engagement.** The Budget includes more than $7.7 billion for sub-Saharan Africa, including more than $250 million to support the second United States-Africa Leaders' Summit to strengthen ties with African partners based on principles of mutual respect and shared interests and values. These investments would strengthen collaboration, trade and investment, electrification, ecosystems for mutual growth and prosperity, and the promotion of digital transformation in Africa.

- **Strengthens U.S. Leadership on Refugee and Humanitarian Issues.** The Budget provides more than $10 billion to respond to the unprecedented need arising from conflict and natural disasters around the world to serve over 70 countries and approximately 240 million people. The Budget continues rebuilding the Nation's refugee admissions program and supports up to 125,000 admissions in 2023.

- **Advances Equity and Equality Globally.** The Budget provides $2.6 billion to advance gender equity and equality across a broad range of sectors, more than doubling the gender attributions of the policies of this Administration. This includes $200 million for the Gender

Equity and Equality Action Fund to advance the economic security of women and girls. This total also includes funding to strengthen the participation of women in conflict prevention, resolution, and recovery through the implementation of the Women, Peace, and Security Act of 2017. To further implement the President's Executive Order 13985, "Advancing Racial Equity and Support for Underserved Communities," the Budget would better integrate equity through more inclusive policies, strategies, and practice including enhancing the ability of potential non-traditional partners to pursue Federal opportunities and address the barriers they face in the Federal award process, and new efforts to identify spaces to support and advance underserved population appropriate to the country context.

- **Addresses Food Insecurity and Fosters Inclusive and Sustainable Agriculture-led Economic Growth.** The Budget supports the President's pledge to alleviate global food insecurity by providing over $1 billion in bilateral agriculture and food security programming, and continuing robust support for the International Fund for Agricultural Development. These investments are key to increasing communities' access to nutritious food, strengthening their resilience to shocks and stresses, and lifting them from entrenched poverty.

- **Revitalizes and Expands the Diplomatic and Development Workforce.** Strengthening American diplomacy and development requires rebuilding and modernizing the State and USAID workforce. The 2023 Budget provides $7.6 billion to recruit, retain, and develop the diverse, highly capable workforce needed to support efforts around the world and manage increasingly complex national security issues, particularly in the Indo-Pacific region. The Budget also increases investments to diversify the workforce of foreign affairs agencies to reflect and draw on the richness and diversity of the United States, including through paid internships and targeted fellowship programs, and strengthening partnerships with Minority Serving Institutions, and expanded professional development opportunities.

# DEPARTMENT OF TRANSPORTATION

The Department of Transportation (DOT) is responsible for ensuring that the United States has the safest, most equitable, reliable, and modern transportation system in the world. The President's 2023 Budget for DOT supports the historic investments in surface transportation, aviation, and maritime made by the Infrastructure and Investment Jobs Act (Bipartisan Infrastructure Law), which will strengthen the Nation's transportation system while tackling climate change and protecting environmental resources, addressing inequities and advancing environmental justice, and promoting good-paying jobs and economic vitality.

The Budget requests $26.8 billion in discretionary budget authority for 2023, a $1.5 billion or six-percent increase from the 2021 enacted level. Consistent with the Bipartisan Infrastructure Law, the Budget also includes $78.4 billion in mandatory funds, including contract authority and obligation limitations, and $36.8 billion in emergency-designated advance budget authority, for transportation infrastructure investments in 2023.

**The President's 2023 Budget:**

- **Modernizes and Upgrades Roads and Bridges.** To modernize, repair, and improve the safety and efficiency of the Nation's network of roads and bridges, the Budget provides $68.9 billion for the Federal-aid Highway program, a $19.8 billion increase from the 2021 enacted level. This includes $9.4 billion provided by the Bipartisan Infrastructure Law for 2023 and which also supports: $8 billion for new competitive and formula grant programs to rebuild the Nation's bridges; $1.4 billion to deploy a nationwide, publicly-accessible network of electric vehicle chargers and other alternative fueling infrastructure; $1.3 billion for a new carbon reduction grant program; and $1.7 billion for a new resiliency grant program to enhance the resilience of surface transportation infrastructure to hazards and climate change.

- **Improves Highway Safety.** The Budget provides more than $2.5 billion for the Federal Motor Carrier Safety Administration and the National Highway Traffic Safety Administration (NHTSA), an $857 million increase above the 2021 enacted level. The Budget also provides critical resources to support NHTSA's rulemaking efforts including those to address climate change and emerging technologies. This builds on the Agency's National Roadway Safety Strategy, which uses a safe system approach to address the crisis of roadway fatalities.

- **Provides High-Quality Transit Options to More Americans.** To strengthen the Nation's transit systems, reduce emissions, and improve transportation access for people with disabilities and historically disadvantaged communities, the Budget provides the Federal Transit Administration with $21.1 billion, an $8.2 billion increase over the 2021 enacted level. This includes $3.2 billion in additional funding on top of the $4.3 billion already provided by the Bipartisan Infrastructure Law for 2023.  The Budget includes $4.5 billion for the Capital Investment Grant program, which would advance the construction of new, high-quality transit corridors to reduce travel time and increase economic development.

- **Invests in Reliable Passenger and Freight Rail.**  To ensure the safety and performance of the rail industry today and deliver the passenger rail network of the future, the Budget provides the Federal Railroad Administration  a historic investment of $17.9 billion, a $15 billion increase over the 2021 enacted level.  This includes $4.7 billion in additional funding on top of $13.2 billion already provided by the Bipartisan Infrastructure Law for 2023.  These resources would provide $7.4 billion to significantly improve Amtrak's rolling stock and facilities and $10.1 billion for existing and new competitive grant programs to support passenger rail modernization and expansion, address critical safety needs, and support the vitality of the freight rail network.

- **Reduces Bottlenecks and Commute Times through Investments in Competitive Programs.**  The Budget provides robust support for transportation projects that reduce commute times, improve safety, reduce freight bottlenecks, better connect communities, and reduce transportation-related greenhouse gas emissions.  Investments include $4 billion, $3 billion above the 2021 enacted level, for National Infrastructure Investments grant programs to support transportation projects with significant benefits across multiple modes, and $1.64 billion, a $640 million increase above the 2021 enacted level for the Infrastructure for Rebuilding America grants program which focuses on reducing freight and highway bottlenecks.

- **Advances Racial Equity and Supports Underserved Communities.**  The Budget requests an additional $20 million above the 2021 enacted level for the Office of the Secretary to lead DOT's efforts to promote equity and inclusion.  With these resources, DOT would better ensure that historic investments under the Bipartisan Infrastructure Law  deliver resources and benefits equitably, including communities that have been historically underserved and adversely affected by persistent poverty or income inequality.  DOT actions include workforce development, disadvantaged business enterprise procurement, data collection, reporting, public participation, and assistance measures mitigating or negating the effects of structural obstacles to building wealth.

- **Prioritizes Aviation Safety and Infrastructure.**  The Budget provides $15.2 billion in discretionary budget authority for the Federal Aviation Administration (FAA) to improve aviation safety, transform the Nation's aviation infrastructure, and improve cybersecurity.  These investments also promote environmental justice and climate change mitigation by prioritizing sustainable design and construction, and enhancing equity through more inclusive contracting and workforce development.  The resources provided through the Budget complement the $5 billion already provided by the Bipartisan Infrastructure Law for 2023 to upgrade the FAA's air traffic control facilities and to improve the safety, capacity, accessibility, and efficiency of the Nation's airports.

- **Accelerates Efforts to Move More Goods Faster through the Nation's Ports and Waterways.**  The Budget continues support for the historic levels of Federal investment to modernize America's port and waterway infrastructure initiated under the Bipartisan Infrastructure Law.  The Budget includes $230 million for the Port Infrastructure Development Program to strengthen maritime freight capacity.  In addition to keeping the Nation's supply chain moving by improving efficiency, DOT would prioritize projects that also lower emissions—reducing environmental impact in and around the Nation's ports.

- **Supports Pipeline and Hazardous Materials Safety.** The Budget improves pipeline and hazardous material transportation safety through new investments to hire additional safety inspectors and engineers, and for robust data collection to inform safety standards. The Budget would help reduce methane emissions and preserve the climate, with investments in new safety standards for pipelines and continued safety checks on underground natural gas storage facilities. The Budget also increases hazardous materials staffing for accident investigations and additional outreach and training to improve compliance with safety requirements.

# DEPARTMENT OF THE TREASURY

The Department of the Treasury (Treasury) is responsible for maintaining a strong economy, promoting conditions that enable economic growth and stability, protecting the integrity of the financial system, combating global financial crime and corruption, and managing the U.S. Government's finances and resources effectively. The President's 2023 Budget for Treasury invests in: a fair and robust tax system; enforcing the tax code and ensuring compliance by the wealthy and corporations; improving the taxpayer experience and customer service; providing resources to expand job-creating investments and access to credit in disadvantaged communities; and enhancing cybersecurity.

The Budget requests $16.2 billion in discretionary funding for Treasury, a $2.7 billion or 20-percent increase from the 2021 enacted level.

## The President's 2023 Budget:

- **Improves Taxpayer Experience and Supports a Fair and Equitable Tax System.** Last year, the IRS delivered more than $600 billion in direct economic relief to American households and businesses through Economic Impact Payments, monthly advance child tax credit payments, and more. Yet the agency's funding and staffing levels have not kept pace with its expanding scope. To ensure that taxpayers receive the highest quality customer service and that all Americans are treated fairly by the U.S. tax system, the Budget provides a total of $14.1 billion for the Internal Revenue Service (IRS), $2.2 billion, or 18 percent, above the 2021 enacted level. This includes an increase of $798 million to improve the taxpayer experience and expand customer service outreach to underserved communities and the tax-paying public at large. The Budget also provides $310 million for IRS Business Systems Modernization, which is 39 percent above the 2021 enacted level, to accelerate the development of new digital tools to enable better communication between taxpayers and the IRS. Increased funding for the IRS would also facilitate more effective oversight of high-income and corporate tax returns. In addition to these resources, the Administration continues to support multiyear investments in IRS tax enforcement to increase tax compliance and revenues that the President has previously proposed. This investment reflects decades of analysis demonstrating that program integrity investments to enforce existing tax laws increase revenues in a progressive way by closing the tax gap—the difference between taxes owed and taxes paid.

- **Expands Lending in Disadvantaged Communities and Increases Affordable Housing Supply.** The Budget provides $331 million for the Community Development Financial Institutions (CDFI) Fund, an increase of $61 million, or 23 percent, above the

97

2021 enacted level. To address the critical shortage of affordable housing in communities, the Budget also proposes $5 billion in long-term mandatory funding for CDFI financing of new construction and substantial rehabilitation that creates net new units of affordable rental and for sale housing. CDFIs provide historically underserved and often low-income communities access to credit, capital, and financial support to grow businesses, increase affordable housing, and reinforce healthy neighborhood development.

- **Increases Corporate Transparency and Safeguards the Financial System.** Treasury plays a leading role in monitoring and disrupting corruption, money laundering, terrorist financing, and the use of the financial system by malicious actors domestically and abroad. Investment in Treasury staff and technical capabilities is critical to these efforts, including closing financial reporting loopholes that allow illicit actors to evade scrutiny, mask their dealings, and undermine corporate accountability. The Budget provides $210 million for the Financial Crimes Enforcement Network, $83 million above the 2021 enacted level, to increase oversight of the financial sector, strengthen corporate accountability, and provide adequate support to law enforcement and investigative entities. In addition, the Budget provides $212 million to the Office of Terrorism and Financial Intelligence, $37 million above the 2021 enacted level, to modernize and update the sanctions process consistent with the findings of the Treasury 2021 Sanctions Review.

- **Strengthens Enterprise Cybersecurity.** The Budget provides $215 million, an increase of $197 million above the 2021 enacted level, to protect and defend sensitive agency systems and information, including those designated as high-value assets. The Budget increases centralized funding to strengthen Treasury's overall cybersecurity efforts and establish a Zero Trust Architecture. These investments would protect Treasury systems from future attacks and accelerate Treasury's response to the SolarWinds incident and Log4j vulnerabilities.

- **Restores Critical Agency Capacity.** The Budget provides $293 million for Treasury's Departmental Offices, a 26-percent increase over the 2021 enacted level, to rebuild institutional capacity and strengthen the role of Treasury policy offices. Additional funding for Treasury's Climate Hub would support a sustainable economic recovery and advance climate goals both domestically and internationally, including domestic coal transition and engagement with international financial institutions. Increased staffing would also support assessments of climate-related financial risk arising from private insurance coverage gaps in regions of the Nation particularly vulnerable to climate change impacts. The Budget also builds institutional capacity to expand engagement with historically underrepresented and underserved groups and develop actionable goals to advance equity across all Treasury programs.

# DEPARTMENT OF VETERANS AFFAIRS

The Department of Veterans Affairs (VA) is responsible for providing military veterans and VA survivors with the benefits, care, and support they have earned through sacrifice and service to the Nation. The President's 2023 Budget for VA honors the Nation's sacred obligation to veterans by investing in: world-class healthcare, including mental health, and enhancing veterans' general well-being; benefits delivery, including disability claims processing; education; employment training; and insurance, burial, and other benefits to enhance veterans' prosperity. The Budget ensures that all veterans, including women veterans, veterans of color, and Lesbian, Gay, Bisexual, Transgender, Queer, and Intersex veterans receive the care they have earned, and prioritizes addressing veteran homelessness, suicide prevention, and caregiver support.

The Budget requests $135 billion in discretionary funding for VA, a $31 billion or 29-percent increase, from the 2021 enacted level. The Budget also includes $128 billion in advance appropriations for VA medical care programs in 2024.

## The President's 2023 Budget:

- **Prioritizes VA Medical Care.** The Budget provides $119 billion—a historic 32-percent increase above the 2021 enacted level for VA. In addition to fully funding inpatient, outpatient, mental health, and long-term care services, the Budget supports programs that improve VA healthcare quality and delivery, including investments in training programs for clinicians, health professionals, and medical students. The Budget also further supports VA's preparedness for regional and national public health emergencies.

- **Prioritizes Veteran Suicide Prevention.** The Budget provides $497 million to support the Administration's veteran suicide prevention initiatives, including implementation of: the Veterans Crisis Line's 988 expansion initiative; the suicide prevention 2.0 program to grow public health efforts in communities; a lethal means safety campaign in partnership with other agencies; and the Staff Sergeant Parker Gordon Fox Suicide Prevention Grant Program to enhance community-based prevention strategies.

- **Improves Veterans' Mental Healthcare Services.** The Budget provides $13.9 billion for VA mental healthcare, which offers a system of comprehensive treatments and services to meet the needs of each veteran and the family members involved in the veteran's care. The Budget focuses on increasing access to quality mental healthcare and lowering the cost of mental health services for veterans, with the goal of helping veterans take charge of their treatment and live full and meaningful lives.

- **Supports Women Veterans' Healthcare.** The Budget invests $9.8 billion for all of women veterans' healthcare, including $767 million toward women's gender specific care. More women are choosing VA healthcare than ever before, with women accounting for over 30 percent of the increase in veterans enrolled over the past five years. Investments support comprehensive specialty medical and surgical services for women veterans at a VA facility or through referrals to the community. The Budget proposes to increase access to infertility counseling and assisted reproductive technology and to eliminate copayments for contraceptive coverage. The Budget also improves the safety of women veterans seeking healthcare at VA facilities by supporting implementation of the zero-tolerance policy for sexual harassment and assault.

- **Bolsters Efforts to End Veteran Homelessness.** The Budget increases resources for veterans' homelessness programs to $2.7 billion, with the goal of ensuring every veteran has permanent, sustainable housing with access to healthcare and other supportive services to prevent and end veteran homelessness.

- **Invests in Caregivers Support Program.** The Budget recognizes the important role of family caregivers in supporting the health and wellness of veterans. The Budget provides funding for the Program of General Caregivers Support Services. The Budget also provides $1.8 billion for the Program of Comprehensive Assistance for Family Caregivers, which includes stipend payments and support services to help empower family caregivers of eligible veterans.

- **Invests in Overdose Prevention and Treatment Programs.** The Budget provides $663 million toward opioid use disorder prevention and treatment programs, including programs authorized in the Jason Simcakoski Memorial and Promise Act.

- **Supports Research Critical to Veterans' Health Needs.** VA conducts thousands of studies at VA medical centers, outpatient clinics, and nursing homes each year. This research has significantly contributed to advancements in healthcare for veterans and other Americans from every walk of life. The Budget provides $916 million to continue the development of VA's research enterprise, including research in support of *American Pandemic Preparedness: Transforming Our Capabilities* plan goals.

- **Addresses Environmental Exposures.** The Budget increases resources for new presumptive disability compensation claims related to environmental exposures from military service. The Budget also invests $51 million within VA research programs and $63 million within the VA medical care program for Health Outcomes Military Exposures to increase scientific understanding of and clinical support for veterans and healthcare providers regarding the potential adverse impacts from environmental exposures during military service.

- **Supports Cancer Moonshot and Precision Oncology.** The Budget invests $81 million within VA research programs, together with $167 million within the VA medical care program, for precision oncology to provide access to the best possible cancer care for veterans. Funds support research and programs that address cancer care, rare cancers, and cancers in women, as well as genetic counseling and consultation that advance tele-oncology and precision oncology care.

- **Provides Claims Processing Automation.** The Budget provides $120 million for VA to support automating the disability compensation claims process from submission to authorization. Investments in automation would increase VA's ability to deliver faster and more accurate claim decisions for veterans.

- **Supports VA Home Loan Programs.** The Budget provides $284 million for VA housing program administration to ensure that all eligible veterans receive maximum benefits and protections as new or existing homeowners, and enable VA to manage record growth in its home loan guaranty volume, which exceeded $860 billion in outstanding principal in 2021. In addition, in accordance with the President's Executive Order 14030, "Climate-Related Financial Risk," the VA housing program is working with the Departments of Agriculture and Housing and Urban Development to consider approaches to better integrate climate-related financial risk into Federal credit programs. Efforts to date include contracting for additional expert analytical support, identifying and sharing initial risk assessments in working groups comprised of credit representatives of these agencies, and exploring the financial sensitivity of proposed 2023 activity to adverse movements in default and recovery performance that could be related to climate-change risks.

- **Modernizes VA Information Technology.** The Budget includes $5.8 billion for VA's Office of Information Technology to prioritize cybersecurity, financial management business transformation, claims automation, and the Infrastructure Readiness program, with the mission to ensure a seamless customer experience for veterans. The Budget also provides $1.8 billion to continue modernizing VA's Electronic Health Record to ensure veterans receive world-class healthcare well into the future.

- **Invests in New and Replacement Medical and Cemetery Facilities.** The Budget includes $3 billion for construction and expansion of critical infrastructure and facilities. This funding supports seven major investments in new and replacement medical facilities and new or expanded cemeteries in three locations. In addition, VA would make improvements and alterations to existing medical facilities, further expanding healthcare capacities. These capital investments enable the delivery of high-quality healthcare, benefits, and services for veterans.

- **Honors the Memory of All Veterans.** The Budget includes $430 million to ensure veterans and their families have access to exceptional memorial benefits including two new and replacement national cemeteries. These funds maintain national shrine standards at the 158 VA managed cemeteries and provide the initial operational investment required to open new cemeteries.

# CORPS OF ENGINEERS—CIVIL WORKS

The Army Corps of Engineers—Civil Works program (Corps) is responsible for: developing, managing, restoring, and protecting water resources primarily through the construction, operation and maintenance, and study of water-related infrastructure projects; regulating development in waters of the United States; and working with other Federal agencies to help communities respond to and recover from floods and other natural disasters. The President's 2023 Budget for the Corps invests in modernizing the Nation's water infrastructure, including U.S. coastal ports, increasing climate resilience, and advancing environmental justice.

The Budget requests $6.6 billion in discretionary funding for the Corps. Resources provided through the 2023 Budget complement historic investments in modernizing the Nation's ports and waterways and improving resilience of water resources infrastructure to climate change through the Infrastructure Investment and Jobs Act (Bipartisan Infrastructure Law).

**The President's 2023 Budget:**

- **Restores Aquatic Ecosystems.** The Budget invests in the restoration of some of the Nation's most unique aquatic ecosystems, such as the Chesapeake Bay, Great Lakes, Upper Mississippi, and Columbia River. For Florida's Everglades restoration project, the Budget invests $407 million—building on the Bipartisan Infrastructure Law's single largest investment in history for Everglades restorations. This iconic American landscape provides drinking water supply for more than 8 million Floridians, supports the State's $90 billion tourism economy, and is home to dozens of endangered or threatened species.

- **Increases Resilience to Climate Change.** The Budget invests in programs and projects that would reduce the risk of damages from floods and storms and restore the Nation's aquatic ecosystems. The Budget also invests in helping local communities identify and address their risks associated with climate change and improve resilience of Corps' infrastructure to climate change, including taking climate resilience into account in developing options and selecting projects.

- **Facilitates Safe, Reliable, and Sustainable Commercial Navigation.** The Budget includes $1.7 billion for the Harbor Maintenance Trust Fund to facilitate safe, reliable, and environmentally sustainable navigation at the Nation's coastal ports.

- **Advances Equity and Environmental Justice.** The Budget invests in technical assistance, studies, and the construction of projects to address water resources challenges in disadvantaged and tribal communities in line with the President's Justice40 Initiative. For example, the Budget includes funding for remedial clean-up of the Bradford Island site on the Columbia River to address decades of contamination, including in important tribal fishing areas.

- **Invests in High Return Projects.** The Budget invests in projects that would provide a high economic or environmental return or address a significant risk to public safety. For example, the Budget prioritizes funding to address the highest dam safety risks the Corps has identified at its dams, and to facilitate safe and efficient navigation on the highest use inland waterways.

# ENVIRONMENTAL PROTECTION AGENCY

The Environmental Protection Agency (EPA) is responsible for protecting human health and the environment. The President's 2023 Budget for EPA: restores the Agency's capacity to carry out its mission; implements the President's historic Justice40 commitment; and funds a broad suite of recently authorized programs to improve the Nation's water infrastructure.

The Budget requests $11.9 billion in discretionary funding for EPA, a $2.6 billion or 29-percent increase from the 2021 enacted level. Resources provided through the 2023 Budget complement investments in water infrastructure, including lead pipe replacements, and in the remediation of contaminated and idle land provided in the Infrastructure Investment and Jobs Act (Bipartisan Infrastructure Law).

**The President's 2023 Budget:**

- **Tackles the Climate Crisis with Urgency.** To help address greenhouse gas emissions and make the Nation's infrastructure more resilient, the Budget invests $100 million in grants to States and Tribes that would support the implementation of on-the-ground efforts in communities across the Nation, such as reducing methane emissions. The Budget proposes an additional $35 million over the 2021 enacted level to implement the recently enacted American Innovation and Manufacturing Act to continue phasing out potent greenhouse gases known as hydrofluorocarbons (HFCs). The Budget also invests an additional $13 million over the 2021 enacted level in wildfire prevention and readiness to bolster EPA's abilities to forecast where smoke will harm people and better communicate where smoke events are occurring.

- **Restores Critical Capacity to Carry Out EPA's Core Mission.** Staffing reductions under the previous administration continue to impact the Agency's ability to carry out its mission to protect human health and the environment. The Budget adds more than 1,900 Full Time Equivalents (FTEs) relative to 2021 levels, for a total of more than 16,200 FTEs, to help rebuild the Agency's capacity. Restoring staffing capacity across the Agency would allow EPA to help cut air, water, and climate pollution, and advance environmental justice. Staffing resources would also fund a significant expansion of EPA's paid student internship program to develop a pipeline of qualified staff.

- **Advances Environmental Justice.** The Administration continues to prioritize efforts to deliver environmental justice in communities across the United States, including meeting the President's Justice40 commitment to ensure at least 40 percent of the benefits of Federal investments in climate and clean energy reach disadvantaged communities. The Budget bolsters these efforts by investing nearly $1.5 billion across numerous programs that would help create good-paying jobs, clean up pollution, implement Justice40, advance racial equity, and secure environmental justice for communities that too often have been left behind, including rural and tribal communities. This funding includes $100 million for support of a new community air quality monitoring and notification program and additional investments in protection for fenceline communities, civil rights compliance, and environmental permitting.

- **Upgrades Drinking Water and Wastewater Infrastructure Nationwide.** The Budget provides roughly $4 billion for water infrastructure, an increase of $1 billion over the 2021 enacted level. These resources would advance efforts to upgrade drinking water and wastewater infrastructure nationwide, with a focus on underserved communities that have historically been overlooked. The Budget funds all of the authorizations in the original Drinking Water and Wastewater Infrastructure Act of 2021, including the creation of 20 new targeted water grant programs and an increase of over $160 million above 2021 enacted levels for the Reducing Lead in Drinking Water grant program. The Budget also maintains funding for EPA's State Revolving Funds (SRF) at 2021 enacted levels, which would complement the $23.4 billion provided for the traditional SRF programs in the Bipartisan Infrastructure Law.

- **Protects Communities from Hazardous Waste and Environmental Damage.** Preventing and cleaning up environmental damage that harms communities and poses a risk to public health and safety continues to be a top priority for the Administration. The Budget provides nearly $1.2 billion for the Superfund program for EPA to continue cleaning up some of the Nation's most contaminated land and respond to environmental emergencies and natural disasters, and begins to adjust for revenue from the Superfund tax. The Budget also provides $215 million for EPA's Brownfields program to enable EPA to provide technical assistance and grants to communities, including disadvantaged communities, so they can safely clean up and reuse contaminated properties. These funds complement Brownfields funding provided in the Bipartisan Infrastructure Law. These programs also support presidential priorities such as the Cancer Moonshot initiative, by addressing contaminants that lead to greater cancer risk.

- **Strengthens the Administration's Commitment to Successfully Implement the Toxic Substances Control Act (TSCA) and Transform the Science of New Chemical Reviews.** The Budget provides $124 million and 449 FTE for TSCA efforts to deliver on the promises made to the American people by the Frank R. Lautenberg Chemical Safety for the 21st Century Act. These resources would provide resources to complete EPA-initiated chemical risk evaluations, issue protective regulations in accordance with statutory timelines and establish a pipeline of prioritized chemicals for risk evaluation.

- **Tackles Per- and Polyfluoroalkyl Substances (PFAS) Pollution.** PFAS are a set of man-made chemicals that threaten the health and safety of communities across the Nation, disproportionately impacting historically disadvantaged communities. As part of the President's commitment to tackling PFAS pollution, the Budget provides approximately $126 million, $57 million over the 2021 enacted level, for EPA to: increase the understanding of PFAS impacts to human health, as well as its ecological effects; restrict use to prevent PFAS from entering the air, land, and water; and remediate PFAS that have been released into the environment.

- **Enforces and Assures Compliance with the Nation's Environmental Laws.** The Budget provides $213 million for civil enforcement efforts, which includes funding to increase enforcement efforts in communities with high pollution exposure and to prevent the illegal importations and use of HFCs in the United States. The Budget also includes: $7 million to operate a coal combustion residuals compliance program; $148 million for compliance monitoring efforts, including funds to conduct inspections in underserved and overburdened communities; and $69 million for criminal enforcement efforts, which includes funding to increase outreach to victims of environmental crimes and to develop a specialized criminal enforcement task force to address environmental justice issues in partnership with the Department of Justice.

# NATIONAL AERONAUTICS AND SPACE ADMINISTRATION

The National Aeronautics and Space Administration (NASA) inspires the Nation by sending astronauts and robotic missions to explore the solar system, advances the Nation's understanding of the Earth and space, and develops new technologies and approaches to improve aviation and space activities. The President's 2023 Budget for NASA invests in: human and robotic exploration of the Moon; new technologies to improve the Nation's space capabilities; and addressing the climate crisis through cutting-edge research satellites and green aviation research.

The Budget requests $26 billion in discretionary funding for NASA, a $2.7 billion or 11.6-percent increase from the 2021 enacted level.

**The President's 2023 Budget:**

- **Enhances U.S. Human Spaceflight Leadership.** The Budget provides $7.5 billion, $1.1 billion above the 2021 enacted level, for Artemis lunar exploration. Artemis would return American astronauts to the Moon as early as 2025, land the first woman and person of color on the Moon, deepen the Nation's scientific understanding of the Moon, and test technologies that would allow humans to safely and sustainably explore Mars. Lunar landing missions would also include astronauts from international partners.

- **Addresses the Climate Crisis.** The Budget invests $2.4 billion in Earth-observing satellites and related research to improve the Nation's understanding of climate change. The new satellite missions would form an Earth System Observatory that would provide a three-dimensional, holistic view of Earth that is needed to better understand natural hazards and climate change. In addition, NASA would collaborate with other agencies to enhance greenhouse gas monitoring and make greenhouse gas data more accessible to a broad range of users. The Budget also provides more than $500 million to reduce the climate impacts of the aviation industry as part of a $972 million request for NASA's Aeronautics program. This includes the Sustainable Flight National Partnership, through which NASA and U.S. companies would develop and fly a highly-efficient, next-generation airliner prototype as early as 2026.

- **Supports the Development of Commercial Space Stations.** The Budget supports operations of the International Space Station, paving the way for its continued operation through 2030, and allocates $224 million to support the development of commercial space stations that NASA, other Government agencies, the Nation's international partners, and the private sector can use after the International Space Station is retired.

- **Advances Robotic Exploration of the Moon and Mars.** The Budget invests over $480 million in lunar robotic missions, including a rover to investigate ice deposits that could provide future astronauts with fuel and oxygen and the Commercial Lunar Payload Services initiative that supports low-cost deliveries to the Moon. The Budget also provides $822 million for the Mars Sample Return mission, which would return Martian rock and soil samples to Earth.

- **Spurs Research and Development.** The Budget increases funding for NASA's Space Technology research and development portfolio to more than $1.4 billion, a $338 million increase above the 2021 enacted level. This investment would support new technologies to help the commercial space industry grow, enhance mission capabilities, and reduce costs. NASA has a key role in better understanding the worsening orbital debris environment and supporting the development of innovative approaches to help protect the Nation's satellites and reduce the risk posed by space debris. The Budget provides over $30 million for orbital debris research, early-stage technology, and measurement technologies.

- **Broadens Participation in Science, Technology, Engineering, and Mathematics (STEM).** The Budget provides $150 million, $23 million above the 2021 enacted level, for NASA's Office of STEM Engagement in order to attract diverse groups of students to STEM through learning opportunities that spark interest and provide connections to NASA's mission and work. This effort includes targeted engagement of underserved populations, including underserved students and people of color.

# NATIONAL SCIENCE FOUNDATION

The National Science Foundation (NSF) is responsible for promoting the progress of science and for science education. The President's 2023 Budget for NSF invests in combatting the climate crisis, strengthening U.S. leadership in emerging technologies, boosting research and development, and advancing equity.

The Budget requests $10.5 billion in discretionary funding for NSF, a $2 billion or 24-percent increase from the 2021 enacted level.

**The President's 2023 Budget:**

- **Spurs Climate Research and Development.** The Budget provides $1.6 billion for research and development, an increase of more than $500 million above the 2021 enacted level, to better understand and prepare for the adverse impacts of climate change. This robust investment would support research in atmospheric composition, water and carbon cycles, modeling climate systems, renewable energy technologies, materials sciences, plant genomics, climate resilience technologies for communities heavily affected by climate change, and social, behavioral, and economic research on human responses to climate change.

- **Strengthens U.S. Leadership in Emerging Technologies.** The Budget provides $880 million for the Directorate for Technology, Innovation, and Partnerships within NSF to help translate research into practical applications. The Directorate will work with programs across the Agency and with other Federal and non-Federal entities to expedite technology development in emerging areas that are crucial for U.S. technological leadership, including trustworthy artificial intelligence, high performance computing, disaster response and resilience, quantum information systems, robotics, advanced communications technologies, biotechnology, cybersecurity, advanced energy technologies, and materials science. The Budget provides an additional $10 million to build and strengthen the national cybersecurity workforce pipeline through education, K-12 programs, and funding to universities and colleges. These investments would help improve U.S. competitiveness in emerging technologies.

- **Advances Racial Equity in Science and Engineering.** The Budget provides $393 million, an increase of $172 million or 78 percent above the 2021 enacted level, for programs to increase the participation of historically underrepresented communities in science and engineering fields. Funding would support: curriculum design; research on successful recruitment and retention methods; development of outreach or mentorship programs; fellowships; and building science and engineering research and education capacity at Historically Black Colleges

and Universities and other Minority-Serving Institutions. These investments would help ensure the U.S. science and technology workforce reflects the Nation as a whole.

- **Fosters Scientific and Technological Advances.** The Budget provides $2 billion for re-
search infrastructure at NSF, an increase of $65 million above the 2021 enacted level. Funding
would support the construction and procurement of research facilities and instrumentation
across the Nation to enable scientific and technological advances. The Budget also supports
major NSF research facilities, including long-term upgrades of NSF's major Antarctic infrastructure, construction of the Vera C. Rubin Observatory to support astronomy research, and
upgrades to the Large Hadron Collider, the world's largest particle accelerator.

# SMALL BUSINESS ADMINISTRATION

The Small Business Administration (SBA) helps to ensure that small businesses and entrepreneurs have access to the information and resources they need to start, grow, or recover their business. The President's 2023 Budget for SBA makes historic investments in counseling and training programs, expanding access to capital, supporting domestic manufacturing and innovation, and promoting access to Government contracting opportunities.

The Budget requests $914 million in discretionary funding for SBA, a $159 million or 21-percent increase from the 2021 enacted level.

**The President's 2023 Budget:**

- **Supports Underserved Entrepreneurs.** The Budget provides a $31 million increase over the 2021 enacted level to support women, people of color, veterans, and other underserved entrepreneurs through SBA's Entrepreneurial Development programs. This bold commitment ensures entrepreneurs have access to counseling, training, and mentoring services. Access to these services is essential to addressing inequities, expanding economic opportunity, and ensuring small businesses have the tools to succeed.

- **Expands Access to Capital for Small Businesses.** The Budget addresses the need for greater access to affordable capital, particularly in underserved communities. The Budget increases the authorized lending levels in SBA's flagship 7(a) loan guarantee program, the 504 loan program for fixed assets, Small Business Investment Companies, and the Secondary Market Guarantee program by a total of $9.5 billion. Increasing these lending levels would drive economic growth by significantly expanding the availability of working capital, fixed capital, and venture capital funding for small businesses.

- **Strengthens Domestic Manufacturing.** Investing in Growth Accelerators, Regional Innovation Clusters, as well as the Federal and State Technology Partnership Program is key to ensuring entrepreneurs have access to the tools, networks, and services they need to bring cutting-edge innovation to the market. The Budget provides $30 million, an $18 million increase over the 2021 enacted level, to build and strengthen these innovation ecosystems. The Budget also provides $4 million for the creation of a Manufacturing Hub to expand SBA's capacity to support domestic manufacturing by helping small businesses connect with service providers to commercialize innovation, automate processes, enter new markets, expand capacity, and strengthen their resiliency.

- **Implements a Government-Wide Certification Program for Veterans.** The Budget provides $20 million for a uniform certification process to enable veteran and service-disabled veteran-owned small businesses to access business opportunities across the Federal Government.

- **Engages Small Businesses in Combatting Climate Change.** The Budget provides $10 million to facilitate access to capital for investments to help small businesses become more resilient to climate change or support the clean energy economy.

# SOCIAL SECURITY ADMINISTRATION

The Social Security Administration (SSA) provides essential benefits to retirees, survivors, individuals with disabilities, and older Americans with limited income and resources. The President's 2023 Budget for SSA invests in improving service delivery, advancing equity, and promoting program integrity.

The Budget requests $14.8 billion in discretionary funding for SSA, a $1.8 billion or 14-percent increase from the 2021 enacted level, including funding for program integrity activities.

**The President's 2023 Budget:**

- **Improves Service Delivery.** Each year, SSA processes more than six million retirement, survivors, and Medicare claims, as well as more than two million disability and Supplemental Security Income claims. The Budget provides an increase of $1.6 billion, or 14 percent over the 2021 enacted level, to improve services at SSA's field offices, State disability determination services, and teleservice centers for retirees, individuals with disabilities, and their families who rely on the Agency. The Budget also improves access to SSA's services by adding staff to speed disability claims processing and reduce wait times.

- **Advances Equity and Accessibility.** SSA remains committed to breaking down barriers to access experienced by people who rely on its services, including individuals experiencing homelessness, children with disabilities, and people with mental and intellectual disabilities. The Budget makes investments to decrease customer wait times, simplify application processes, and increase outreach to people who are difficult to reach. SSA will also continue to modernize its information technology systems to make more services available online and improve 800 Number access.

- **Promotes Program Integrity.** The Budget includes $1.8 billion, $224 million above the 2021 enacted level, for dedicated program integrity activities to promote responsible spending of Social Security funds and ensure that the Agency is providing the correct benefit amounts only to those who qualify. These funds also support actions to investigate and help prosecute fraud.

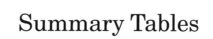

# Summary Tables

## Table S–1. Budget Totals[1]

(In billions of dollars and as a percent of GDP)

| | 2021 | 2022 | 2023 | 2024 | 2025 | 2026 | 2027 | 2028 | 2029 | 2030 | 2031 | 2032 | Totals 2023–2027 | Totals 2023–2032 |
|---|---|---|---|---|---|---|---|---|---|---|---|---|---|---|
| **Budget totals in billions of dollars:** | | | | | | | | | | | | | | |
| Receipts | 4,047 | 4,437 | 4,638 | 4,874 | 5,076 | 5,406 | 5,696 | 5,969 | 6,227 | 6,500 | 6,795 | 7,083 | 25,690 | 58,264 |
| Outlays | 6,822 | 5,852 | 5,792 | 6,075 | 6,406 | 6,734 | 7,048 | 7,502 | 7,670 | 8,114 | 8,477 | 8,867 | 32,055 | 72,685 |
| Deficit[2] | 2,775 | 1,415 | 1,154 | 1,201 | 1,330 | 1,328 | 1,352 | 1,533 | 1,443 | 1,614 | 1,682 | 1,784 | 6,364 | 14,421 |
| Debt held by the public | 22,284 | 24,836 | 26,033 | 27,271 | 28,644 | 29,988 | 31,368 | 32,923 | 34,388 | 36,022 | 37,727 | 39,542 | | |
| Debt held by the public net of financial assets | 20,673 | 22,085 | 23,238 | 24,439 | 25,769 | 27,097 | 28,449 | 29,982 | 31,425 | 33,045 | 34,732 | 36,516 | | |
| Gross domestic product (GDP) | 22,358 | 24,256 | 25,567 | 26,694 | 27,787 | 28,912 | 30,080 | 31,307 | 32,615 | 34,018 | 35,498 | 37,041 | | |
| **Budget totals as a percent of GDP:** | | | | | | | | | | | | | | |
| Receipts | 18.1% | 18.3% | 18.1% | 18.3% | 18.3% | 18.7% | 18.9% | 19.1% | 19.1% | 19.1% | 19.1% | 19.1% | 18.5% | 18.8% |
| Outlays | 30.5% | 24.1% | 22.7% | 22.8% | 23.1% | 23.3% | 23.4% | 24.0% | 23.5% | 23.9% | 23.9% | 23.9% | 23.0% | 23.4% |
| Deficit | 12.4% | 5.8% | 4.5% | 4.5% | 4.8% | 4.6% | 4.5% | 4.9% | 4.4% | 4.7% | 4.7% | 4.8% | 4.6% | 4.7% |
| Debt held by the public | 99.7% | 102.4% | 101.8% | 102.2% | 103.1% | 103.7% | 104.3% | 105.2% | 105.4% | 105.9% | 106.3% | 106.7% | | |
| Debt held by the public net of financial assets | 92.5% | 91.0% | 90.9% | 91.6% | 92.7% | 93.7% | 94.6% | 95.8% | 96.4% | 97.1% | 97.8% | 98.6% | | |
| **Memorandum, real net interest:** | | | | | | | | | | | | | | |
| Real net interest in billions of dollars | –291 | –514 | –146 | –48 | 20 | 73 | 129 | 181 | 221 | 254 | 298 | 337 | 29 | 1,319 |
| Real net interest as a percent of GDP | –1.3% | –2.1% | –0.6% | –0.2% | 0.1% | 0.3% | 0.4% | 0.6% | 0.7% | 0.7% | 0.8% | 0.9% | 0.0% | 0.4% |

[1] The Budget includes a reserve for legislation that reduces costs, expands productive capacity, and reforms the tax system. While the President is committed to reducing the deficit with this legislation, this allowance is shown as deficit neutral to be conservative for purposes of the budget totals. Because discussions with Congress continue, the Budget does not break down the reserve among specific policies or between revenues and outlays.

[2] The estimated deficit for 2022 is based on partial year actual data and generally incorporates actuals through February. At the time the 2023 Budget was prepared, 2022 appropriations remained incomplete. The baseline reflects annualized continuing appropriations for 2022.

## Table S–2. Effect of Budget Proposals on Projected Deficits

(Deficit increases (+) or decreases (−) in billions of dollars)

| | 2021 | 2022 | 2023 | 2024 | 2025 | 2026 | 2027 | 2028 | 2029 | 2030 | 2031 | 2032 | Totals 2023–2027 | Totals 2023–2032 |
|---|---|---|---|---|---|---|---|---|---|---|---|---|---|---|
| **Projected deficits in the baseline[1]** | 2,775 | 1,421 | 1,176 | 1,279 | 1,422 | 1,399 | 1,419 | 1,630 | 1,562 | 1,748 | 1,818 | 2,014 | 6,694 | 15,466 |
| Percent of GDP | 12.4% | 5.9% | 4.6% | 4.8% | 5.1% | 4.8% | 4.7% | 5.2% | 4.8% | 5.1% | 5.1% | 5.4% | | |
| **Proposals in the 2023 Budget:** | | | | | | | | | | | | | | |
| Reserve for legislation that reduces costs, expands productive capacity, and reforms the tax system[2] | …… | …… | …… | …… | …… | …… | …… | …… | …… | …… | …… | …… | …… | 383 |
| Invest in K–12 education and college affordability | | | 3 | 22 | 28 | 33 | 38 | 44 | 50 | 54 | 55 | 56 | 125 | 383 |
| Improve public health by investing in preparedness, mental health, tribal health, and other areas | | | 22 | 44 | 38 | 36 | 37 | 37 | 35 | 37 | 39 | 41 | 177 | 365 |
| Increase affordable housing supply | | | 1 | 3 | 6 | 7 | 8 | 8 | 6 | 4 | 3 | 2 | 25 | 48 |
| Combat and prevent crime | | | 1 | 2 | 3 | 4 | 5 | 4 | 3 | 2 | 2 | 2 | 15 | 28 |
| Minimum tax on billionaires | | | | −36 | −40 | −43 | −43 | −43 | −43 | −38 | −36 | −38 | −163 | −361 |
| Additional investments and reforms | | −6 | −50 | −112 | −124 | −103 | −104 | −137 | −158 | −176 | −180 | −269 | −493 | −1,413 |
| Debt service and other interest effects | | −* | −* | −1 | −3 | −5 | −7 | −9 | −12 | −15 | −19 | −24 | −16 | −95 |
| **Total proposals in the 2023 Budget[3]** | | −6 | −22 | −78 | −93 | −70 | −67 | −97 | −119 | −133 | −136 | −229 | −330 | −1,045 |
| **Resulting deficits in the 2023 Budget** | 2,775 | 1,415 | 1,154 | 1,201 | 1,330 | 1,328 | 1,352 | 1,533 | 1,443 | 1,614 | 1,682 | 1,784 | 6,364 | 14,421 |
| Percent of GDP | 12.4% | 5.8% | 4.5% | 4.5% | 4.8% | 4.6% | 4.5% | 4.9% | 4.4% | 4.7% | 4.7% | 4.8% | | |

\* $500 million or less

[1] At the time the 2023 Budget was prepared, 2022 appropriations remained incomplete. The baseline reflects annualized continuing appropriations for 2022.

[2] The Budget includes a reserve for legislation that reduces costs, expands productive capacity, and reforms the tax system. While the President is committed to reducing the deficit with this legislation, this allowance is shown as deficit neutral to be conservative for purposes of the budget totals. Because discussions with Congress continue, the Budget does not break down the reserve among specific policies or between revenues and outlays.

[3] Reflects budget deficit reduction compared to a baseline that does not include the Consolidated Appropriations Act, 2022 (Public Law 117–103), which was enacted after the baseline was finalized. Deficit reduction relative to a baseline that incorporated that legislation would be significantly greater.

## Table S–3. Baseline by Category[1]

(In billions of dollars)

| | 2021 | 2022 | 2023 | 2024 | 2025 | 2026 | 2027 | 2028 | 2029 | 2030 | 2031 | 2032 | Totals 2023–2027 | Totals 2023–2032 |
|---|---|---|---|---|---|---|---|---|---|---|---|---|---|---|
| **Outlays:** | | | | | | | | | | | | | | |
| Discretionary programs: | | | | | | | | | | | | | | |
| Defense | 742 | 766 | 766 | 784 | 802 | 815 | 828 | 847 | 866 | 886 | 906 | 927 | 3,995 | 8,426 |
| Non-defense | 895 | 928 | 873 | 949 | 931 | 935 | 952 | 974 | 994 | 1,013 | 1,033 | 1,055 | 4,641 | 9,710 |
| Subtotal, discretionary programs | 1,636 | 1,694 | 1,639 | 1,733 | 1,733 | 1,750 | 1,781 | 1,822 | 1,860 | 1,899 | 1,939 | 1,981 | 8,636 | 18,137 |
| Mandatory programs: | | | | | | | | | | | | | | |
| Social Security | 1,129 | 1,214 | 1,313 | 1,398 | 1,482 | 1,571 | 1,663 | 1,760 | 1,858 | 1,958 | 2,061 | 2,167 | 7,427 | 17,231 |
| Medicare | 689 | 753 | 847 | 853 | 972 | 1,071 | 1,158 | 1,311 | 1,261 | 1,420 | 1,492 | 1,645 | 4,901 | 12,031 |
| Medicaid | 521 | 562 | 536 | 566 | 595 | 627 | 661 | 703 | 749 | 796 | 844 | 896 | 2,984 | 6,972 |
| Other mandatory programs | 2,495 | 1,272 | 954 | 852 | 854 | 870 | 862 | 929 | 915 | 962 | 989 | 1,035 | 4,393 | 9,222 |
| Subtotal, mandatory programs | 4,834 | 3,800 | 3,650 | 3,670 | 3,904 | 4,138 | 4,344 | 4,703 | 4,783 | 5,136 | 5,386 | 5,743 | 19,705 | 45,456 |
| Net interest | 352 | 357 | 396 | 477 | 567 | 653 | 736 | 818 | 891 | 963 | 1,038 | 1,116 | 2,829 | 7,655 |
| Total outlays | 6,822 | 5,852 | 5,685 | 5,880 | 6,204 | 6,540 | 6,861 | 7,342 | 7,534 | 7,998 | 8,363 | 8,840 | 31,171 | 71,248 |
| **Receipts:** | | | | | | | | | | | | | | |
| Individual income taxes | 2,044 | 2,257 | 2,305 | 2,319 | 2,431 | 2,727 | 2,926 | 3,074 | 3,241 | 3,420 | 3,610 | 3,789 | 12,708 | 29,843 |
| Corporation income taxes | 372 | 383 | 412 | 447 | 454 | 437 | 445 | 468 | 465 | 457 | 454 | 455 | 2,196 | 4,495 |
| Social insurance and retirement receipts: | | | | | | | | | | | | | | |
| Social Security payroll taxes | 952 | 1,047 | 1,101 | 1,158 | 1,208 | 1,264 | 1,315 | 1,381 | 1,439 | 1,505 | 1,575 | 1,644 | 6,046 | 13,590 |
| Medicare payroll taxes | 295 | 329 | 343 | 361 | 376 | 393 | 409 | 430 | 448 | 469 | 491 | 514 | 1,883 | 4,233 |
| Unemployment insurance | 57 | 58 | 55 | 55 | 55 | 55 | 56 | 56 | 60 | 62 | 62 | 64 | 275 | 580 |
| Other retirement | 10 | 12 | 12 | 13 | 13 | 14 | 15 | 15 | 16 | 16 | 17 | 18 | 67 | 149 |
| Excise taxes | 75 | 84 | 90 | 95 | 95 | 96 | 96 | 96 | 98 | 100 | 101 | 103 | 473 | 971 |
| Estate and gift taxes | 27 | 26 | 25 | 25 | 26 | 27 | 41 | 42 | 44 | 47 | 50 | 53 | 144 | 380 |
| Customs duties | 80 | 93 | 54 | 46 | 47 | 49 | 51 | 53 | 55 | 58 | 60 | 53 | 247 | 526 |
| Deposits of earnings, Federal Reserve System | 100 | 108 | 76 | 43 | 34 | 35 | 39 | 45 | 50 | 57 | 65 | 73 | 227 | 516 |
| Other miscellaneous receipts | 34 | 35 | 36 | 39 | 42 | 45 | 49 | 52 | 56 | 58 | 60 | 62 | 211 | 499 |
| Total receipts | 4,047 | 4,431 | 4,509 | 4,601 | 4,782 | 5,142 | 5,442 | 5,712 | 5,972 | 6,250 | 6,545 | 6,826 | 24,476 | 55,781 |
| **Deficit** | **2,775** | **1,421** | **1,176** | **1,279** | **1,422** | **1,399** | **1,419** | **1,630** | **1,562** | **1,748** | **1,818** | **2,014** | **6,694** | **15,466** |
| Net interest | 352 | 357 | 396 | 477 | 567 | 653 | 736 | 818 | 891 | 963 | 1,038 | 1,116 | 2,829 | 7,655 |
| Primary deficit | 2,423 | 1,064 | 780 | 801 | 855 | 746 | 683 | 813 | 672 | 784 | 780 | 898 | 3,865 | 7,812 |
| On-budget deficit | 2,724 | 1,381 | 1,090 | 1,164 | 1,277 | 1,224 | 1,220 | 1,406 | 1,300 | 1,456 | 1,495 | 1,656 | 5,976 | 13,289 |
| Off-budget deficit/surplus (–) | 52 | 41 | 86 | 115 | 145 | 174 | 198 | 225 | 262 | 292 | 323 | 357 | 718 | 2,178 |

[1] Baseline estimates are on the basis of the economic assumptions shown in Table S–9, which incorporate the effects of the Administration's fiscal policies and incorporate certain adjustments described in the "Current Services" chapter of the *Analytical Perspectives* volume. At the time the 2023 Budget was prepared, 2022 appropriations remained incomplete. The baseline reflects annualized continuing appropriations for 2022. See Tables S–7 and S–8 for more information about discretionary funding levels.

## Table S–4. Proposed Budget by Category [1]

(In billions of dollars)

| | 2021 | 2022 | 2023 | 2024 | 2025 | 2026 | 2027 | 2028 | 2029 | 2030 | 2031 | 2032 | Totals 2023–2027 | Totals 2023–2032 |
|---|---|---|---|---|---|---|---|---|---|---|---|---|---|---|
| **Outlays:** | | | | | | | | | | | | | | |
| Discretionary programs: | | | | | | | | | | | | | | |
| Defense | 742 | 766 | 795 | 822 | 837 | 843 | 853 | 864 | 872 | 879 | 885 | 891 | 4,150 | 8,541 |
| Non-defense | 895 | 928 | 915 | 1,022 | 1,012 | 1,019 | 1,026 | 1,030 | 1,039 | 1,051 | 1,065 | 1,083 | 4,993 | 10,261 |
| Subtotal, discretionary programs | 1,636 | 1,694 | 1,709 | 1,844 | 1,848 | 1,862 | 1,879 | 1,894 | 1,911 | 1,930 | 1,950 | 1,974 | 9,142 | 18,802 |
| Mandatory programs: | | | | | | | | | | | | | | |
| Social Security | 1,129 | 1,214 | 1,313 | 1,398 | 1,482 | 1,570 | 1,662 | 1,759 | 1,857 | 1,957 | 2,059 | 2,165 | 7,425 | 17,222 |
| Medicare | 689 | 753 | 846 | 853 | 971 | 1,070 | 1,157 | 1,310 | 1,260 | 1,420 | 1,513 | 1,612 | 4,898 | 12,013 |
| Medicaid | 521 | 562 | 536 | 567 | 599 | 631 | 666 | 706 | 752 | 799 | 847 | 898 | 2,999 | 7,001 |
| Other mandatory programs | 2,495 | 1,272 | 993 | 937 | 942 | 953 | 954 | 1,024 | 1,012 | 1,060 | 1,088 | 1,126 | 4,778 | 10,089 |
| Subtotal, mandatory programs | 4,834 | 3,800 | 3,687 | 3,755 | 3,994 | 4,224 | 4,439 | 4,800 | 4,880 | 5,236 | 5,508 | 5,801 | 20,099 | 46,324 |
| Net interest | 352 | 357 | 396 | 476 | 564 | 648 | 729 | 808 | 879 | 948 | 1,019 | 1,092 | 2,813 | 7,559 |
| Total outlays | 6,822 | 5,852 | 5,792 | 6,075 | 6,406 | 6,734 | 7,048 | 7,502 | 7,670 | 8,114 | 8,477 | 8,867 | 32,055 | 72,685 |
| **Receipts:** | | | | | | | | | | | | | | |
| Individual income taxes | 2,044 | 2,263 | 2,345 | 2,427 | 2,549 | 2,819 | 3,007 | 3,156 | 3,324 | 3,502 | 3,692 | 3,876 | 13,147 | 30,698 |
| Corporation income taxes | 372 | 383 | 501 | 616 | 633 | 612 | 620 | 644 | 638 | 627 | 623 | 625 | 2,982 | 6,139 |
| Social insurance and retirement receipts: | | | | | | | | | | | | | | |
| Social Security payroll taxes | 952 | 1,047 | 1,101 | 1,158 | 1,208 | 1,264 | 1,315 | 1,381 | 1,439 | 1,505 | 1,575 | 1,644 | 6,046 | 13,590 |
| Medicare payroll taxes | 295 | 329 | 342 | 360 | 375 | 392 | 408 | 428 | 446 | 467 | 489 | 512 | 1,876 | 4,218 |
| Unemployment insurance | 57 | 58 | 55 | 55 | 55 | 55 | 56 | 56 | 60 | 62 | 62 | 64 | 275 | 579 |
| Other retirement | 10 | 12 | 12 | 13 | 13 | 14 | 15 | 15 | 16 | 16 | 17 | 18 | 67 | 149 |
| Excise taxes | 75 | 84 | 91 | 96 | 95 | 96 | 97 | 96 | 99 | 101 | 101 | 103 | 474 | 974 |
| Estate and gift taxes | 27 | 26 | 25 | 23 | 25 | 25 | 40 | 42 | 45 | 47 | 51 | 54 | 138 | 376 |
| Customs duties | 80 | 93 | 54 | 46 | 47 | 49 | 51 | 53 | 55 | 58 | 60 | 53 | 247 | 526 |
| Deposits of earnings, Federal Reserve System | 100 | 108 | 76 | 43 | 34 | 35 | 39 | 45 | 50 | 57 | 65 | 73 | 227 | 516 |
| Other miscellaneous receipts | 34 | 35 | 36 | 39 | 42 | 45 | 49 | 52 | 56 | 58 | 60 | 62 | 211 | 499 |
| Total receipts | 4,047 | 4,437 | 4,638 | 4,874 | 5,076 | 5,406 | 5,696 | 5,969 | 6,227 | 6,500 | 6,795 | 7,083 | 25,690 | 58,264 |
| **Deficit** | 2,775 | 1,415 | 1,154 | 1,201 | 1,330 | 1,328 | 1,352 | 1,533 | 1,443 | 1,614 | 1,682 | 1,784 | 6,364 | 14,421 |
| Net interest | 352 | 357 | 396 | 476 | 564 | 648 | 729 | 808 | 879 | 948 | 1,019 | 1,092 | 2,813 | 7,559 |
| Primary deficit | 2,423 | 1,058 | 758 | 724 | 766 | 680 | 622 | 725 | 565 | 667 | 663 | 692 | 3,551 | 6,862 |
| On-budget deficit | 2,724 | 1,374 | 1,068 | 1,085 | 1,184 | 1,153 | 1,153 | 1,308 | 1,181 | 1,323 | 1,360 | 1,428 | 5,643 | 12,243 |
| Off-budget deficit/surplus (−) | 52 | 41 | 86 | 116 | 146 | 175 | 199 | 225 | 262 | 292 | 322 | 356 | 721 | 2,178 |

[1] The Budget includes a reserve for legislation that reduces costs, expands productive capacity, and reforms the tax system. While the President is committed to reducing the deficit with this legislation, this allowance is shown as deficit neutral to be conservative for purposes of the budget totals. Because discussions with Congress continue, the Budget does not break down the reserve among specific policies or between revenues and outlays.

## Table S-5. Proposed Budget by Category as a Percent of GDP[1]

(As a percent of GDP)

| | 2021 | 2022 | 2023 | 2024 | 2025 | 2026 | 2027 | 2028 | 2029 | 2030 | 2031 | 2032 | Averages 2023-2027 | Averages 2023-2032 |
|---|---|---|---|---|---|---|---|---|---|---|---|---|---|---|
| **Outlays:** | | | | | | | | | | | | | | |
| Discretionary programs: | | | | | | | | | | | | | | |
| Defense | 3.3 | 3.2 | 3.1 | 3.1 | 3.0 | 2.9 | 2.8 | 2.8 | 2.7 | 2.6 | 2.5 | 2.4 | 3.0 | 2.8 |
| Non-defense | 4.0 | 3.8 | 3.6 | 3.8 | 3.6 | 3.5 | 3.4 | 3.3 | 3.2 | 3.1 | 3.0 | 2.9 | 3.6 | 3.3 |
| Subtotal, discretionary programs | 7.3 | 7.0 | 6.7 | 6.9 | 6.7 | 6.4 | 6.2 | 6.0 | 5.9 | 5.7 | 5.5 | 5.3 | 6.6 | 6.1 |
| Mandatory programs: | | | | | | | | | | | | | | |
| Social Security | 5.0 | 5.0 | 5.1 | 5.2 | 5.3 | 5.4 | 5.5 | 5.6 | 5.7 | 5.8 | 5.8 | 5.8 | 5.3 | 5.5 |
| Medicare | 3.1 | 3.1 | 3.3 | 3.2 | 3.5 | 3.7 | 3.8 | 4.2 | 3.9 | 4.2 | 4.3 | 4.4 | 3.5 | 3.8 |
| Medicaid | 2.3 | 2.3 | 2.1 | 2.1 | 2.2 | 2.2 | 2.2 | 2.3 | 2.3 | 2.3 | 2.4 | 2.4 | 2.2 | 2.2 |
| Other mandatory programs | 11.2 | 5.2 | 3.9 | 3.5 | 3.4 | 3.3 | 3.2 | 3.3 | 3.1 | 3.1 | 3.1 | 3.0 | 3.5 | 3.3 |
| Subtotal, mandatory programs | 21.6 | 15.7 | 14.4 | 14.1 | 14.4 | 14.6 | 14.8 | 15.3 | 15.0 | 15.4 | 15.5 | 15.7 | 14.4 | 14.9 |
| Net interest | 1.6 | 1.5 | 1.5 | 1.8 | 2.0 | 2.2 | 2.4 | 2.6 | 2.7 | 2.8 | 2.9 | 2.9 | 2.0 | 2.4 |
| Total outlays | 30.5 | 24.1 | 22.7 | 22.8 | 23.1 | 23.3 | 23.4 | 24.0 | 23.5 | 23.9 | 23.9 | 23.9 | 23.0 | 23.4 |
| **Receipts:** | | | | | | | | | | | | | | |
| Individual income taxes | 9.1 | 9.3 | 9.2 | 9.1 | 9.2 | 9.8 | 10.0 | 10.1 | 10.2 | 10.3 | 10.4 | 10.5 | 9.4 | 9.9 |
| Corporation income taxes | 1.7 | 1.6 | 2.0 | 2.3 | 2.3 | 2.1 | 2.1 | 2.1 | 2.0 | 1.8 | 1.8 | 1.7 | 2.1 | 2.0 |
| Social insurance and retirement receipts: | | | | | | | | | | | | | | |
| Social Security payroll taxes | 4.3 | 4.3 | 4.3 | 4.3 | 4.3 | 4.4 | 4.4 | 4.4 | 4.4 | 4.4 | 4.4 | 4.4 | 4.3 | 4.4 |
| Medicare payroll taxes | 1.3 | 1.4 | 1.3 | 1.3 | 1.3 | 1.4 | 1.4 | 1.4 | 1.4 | 1.4 | 1.4 | 1.4 | 1.3 | 1.4 |
| Unemployment insurance | 0.3 | 0.2 | 0.2 | 0.2 | 0.2 | 0.2 | 0.2 | 0.2 | 0.2 | 0.2 | 0.2 | 0.2 | 0.2 | 0.2 |
| Other retirement | * | * | * | * | * | * | * | * | * | * | * | * | * | * |
| Excise taxes | 0.3 | 0.3 | 0.4 | 0.4 | 0.3 | 0.3 | 0.3 | 0.3 | 0.3 | 0.3 | 0.3 | 0.3 | 0.3 | 0.3 |
| Estate and gift taxes | 0.1 | 0.1 | 0.1 | 0.1 | 0.1 | 0.1 | 0.1 | 0.1 | 0.1 | 0.1 | 0.1 | 0.1 | 0.1 | 0.1 |
| Customs duties | 0.4 | 0.4 | 0.2 | 0.2 | 0.2 | 0.2 | 0.2 | 0.2 | 0.2 | 0.2 | 0.2 | 0.1 | 0.2 | 0.2 |
| Deposits of earnings, Federal Reserve System | 0.4 | 0.4 | 0.3 | 0.2 | 0.1 | 0.1 | 0.1 | 0.1 | 0.2 | 0.2 | 0.2 | 0.2 | 0.2 | 0.2 |
| Other miscellaneous receipts | 0.2 | 0.1 | 0.1 | 0.1 | 0.2 | 0.2 | 0.2 | 0.2 | 0.2 | 0.2 | 0.2 | 0.2 | 0.2 | 0.2 |
| Total receipts | 18.1 | 18.3 | 18.1 | 18.3 | 18.3 | 18.7 | 18.9 | 19.1 | 19.1 | 19.1 | 19.1 | 19.1 | 18.5 | 18.8 |
| **Deficit** | 12.4 | 5.8 | 4.5 | 4.5 | 4.8 | 4.6 | 4.5 | 4.9 | 4.4 | 4.7 | 4.7 | 4.8 | 4.6 | 4.7 |
| Net interest | 1.6 | 1.5 | 1.5 | 1.8 | 2.0 | 2.2 | 2.4 | 2.6 | 2.7 | 2.8 | 2.9 | 2.9 | 2.0 | 2.4 |
| Primary deficit | 10.8 | 4.4 | 3.0 | 2.7 | 2.8 | 2.4 | 2.1 | 2.3 | 1.7 | 2.0 | 1.9 | 1.9 | 2.6 | 2.3 |
| On-budget deficit | 12.2 | 5.7 | 4.2 | 4.1 | 4.3 | 4.0 | 3.8 | 4.2 | 3.6 | 3.9 | 3.8 | 3.9 | 4.1 | 4.0 |
| Off-budget deficit/surplus (−) | 0.2 | 0.2 | 0.3 | 0.4 | 0.5 | 0.6 | 0.7 | 0.7 | 0.8 | 0.9 | 0.9 | 1.0 | 0.5 | 0.7 |

*0.05 percent of GDP or less

[1] The Budget includes a reserve for legislation that reduces costs, expands productive capacity, and reforms the tax system. While the President is committed to reducing the deficit with this legislation, this allowance is shown as deficit neutral to be conservative for purposes of the budget totals. Because discussions with Congress continue, the Budget does not break down the reserve among specific policies or between revenues and outlays.

## Table S–6.  Mandatory and Receipt Proposals

(Deficit increases (+) or decreases (−) in millions of dollars)

| | 2022 | 2023 | 2024 | 2025 | 2026 | 2027 | 2028 | 2029 | 2030 | 2031 | 2032 | Totals 2023–2027 | Totals 2023–2032 |
|---|---|---|---|---|---|---|---|---|---|---|---|---|---|
| **Mandatory initiatives and savings:** | | | | | | | | | | | | | |
| Multi-agency proposals: | | | | | | | | | | | | | |
| Reserve for legislation that reduces costs, expands productive capacity, and reforms the tax system ..... | ...... | ...... | ...... | ...... | ...... | ...... | ...... | ...... | ...... | ...... | ...... | ...... | ...... |
| Transform mental health & substance use disorder coverage and infrastructure: | | | | | | | | | | | | | |
| Department of Health and Human Services: | | | | | | | | | | | | | |
| Invest in behavioral health workforce and delivery ..... | ...... | 750 | 750 | 750 | 750 | 750 | 750 | 750 | 750 | 750 | 750 | 3,750 | 7,500 |
| Expand and convert Medicaid demonstration programs to improve community behavioral health services into a permanent program ..... | ...... | 45 | 1,430 | 1,960 | 2,430 | 2,560 | 2,750 | 2,930 | 3,120 | 3,320 | 3,520 | 8,425 | 24,065 |
| Establish Medicaid provider capacity grants for mental health & substance use disorder treatment ..... | ...... | 40 | 170 | 1,640 | 2,340 | 2,600 | 710 | ...... | ...... | ...... | ...... | 6,790 | 7,500 |
| Utilize clinically appropriate criteria for Medicaid behavioral health services ..... | ...... | 190 | 200 | 210 | 220 | 230 | 240 | 250 | 270 | 280 | 290 | 1,050 | 2,380 |
| Establish performance bonus fund to improve behavioral health in Medicaid ..... | ...... | 500 | 500 | 500 | 500 | 500 | ...... | ...... | ...... | ...... | ...... | 2,500 | 2,500 |
| Apply the Mental Health Parity and Addiction Equity Act (MHPAEA) to Medicare ..... | ...... | ...... | ...... | ...... | ...... | ...... | ...... | ...... | ...... | ...... | ...... | ...... | ...... |
| Eliminate the 190-day lifetime limit on psychiatric hospital services ..... | ...... | 30 | 90 | 110 | 110 | 120 | 120 | 130 | 140 | 140 | 150 | 460 | 1,140 |
| Revise criteria for psychiatric hospital terminations from Medicare ..... | ...... | ...... | ...... | ...... | ...... | ...... | ...... | ...... | ...... | ...... | ...... | ...... | ...... |
| Modernize Medicare mental health benefits[1] ..... | ...... | ...... | ...... | ...... | ...... | ...... | ...... | ...... | ...... | ...... | ...... | ...... | ...... |
| Require Medicare to cover three behavioral health visits without cost-sharing ..... | ...... | ...... | 100 | 130 | 140 | 150 | 160 | 150 | 170 | 170 | 180 | 520 | 1,350 |
| Increase access to consumer protections in self-insured non-federal governmental plans ..... | ...... | ...... | ...... | ...... | ...... | ...... | ...... | ...... | ...... | ...... | ...... | ...... | ...... |
| Provide mandatory funding for state enforcement of mental health parity requirements ..... | ...... | 10 | 40 | 25 | 25 | 25 | 25 | ...... | ...... | ...... | ...... | 125 | 125 |
| Permanently extend funding for Community Mental Health Centers (CMHCs) ..... | ...... | 124 | 289 | 372 | 413 | 413 | 413 | 413 | 413 | 413 | 413 | 1,611 | 3,676 |
| Department of Labor: | | | | | | | | | | | | | |
| Authorize the Department of Labor (DOL) to pursue parity violations by entities that provide administrative services to Employee Retirement Income Security Act (ERISA) group health plans ..... | ...... | ...... | ...... | ...... | ...... | ...... | ...... | ...... | ...... | ...... | ...... | ...... | ...... |
| Amend ERISA to allow participants and beneficiaries to recover losses due to parity violations ..... | ...... | ...... | ...... | ...... | ...... | ...... | ...... | ...... | ...... | ...... | ...... | ...... | ...... |
| Authorize DOL to impose civil monetary penalties for MHPAEA noncompliance ..... | ...... | ...... | −3 | −4 | −4 | −4 | −4 | −4 | −4 | −4 | −4 | −15 | −35 |

## Table S–6. Mandatory and Receipt Proposals—Continued

(Deficit increases (+) or decreases (−) in millions of dollars)

| | 2022 | 2023 | 2024 | 2025 | 2026 | 2027 | 2028 | 2029 | 2030 | 2031 | 2032 | Totals 2023–2027 | Totals 2023–2032 |
|---|---|---|---|---|---|---|---|---|---|---|---|---|---|
| Provide mandatory funding for DOL to perform additional Non-Quantitative Treatment Limitations (NQTL) audits | ........ | 2 | 5 | 25 | 25 | 34 | 35 | 36 | 37 | 38 | 38 | 91 | 275 |
| Cross-Cutting proposals: | | | | | | | | | | | | | |
| Improve access to behavioral healthcare in the private insurance market[2] | ........ | 1,881 | 2,664 | 2,842 | 2,933 | 3,052 | 3,184 | 3,354 | 3,503 | 3,661 | 3,847 | 13,371 | 30,920 |
| Require coverage of three behavioral health visits and three primary care visits without cost-sharing[2] | ........ | 1,202 | 1,740 | 1,823 | 1,937 | 2,025 | 2,117 | 2,229 | 2,316 | 2,388 | 2,506 | 8,728 | 20,284 |
| Subtotal, transform mental health & substance use disorder coverage and infrastructure | ........ | 4,774 | 7,975 | 10,383 | 11,819 | 12,455 | 10,475 | 10,238 | 10,715 | 11,156 | 11,690 | 47,406 | 101,680 |
| Increase affordable housing supply: | | | | | | | | | | | | | |
| Department of Housing and Urban Development: | | | | | | | | | | | | | |
| Fund affordable housing production grants | ........ | 500 | 2,000 | 3,500 | 4,500 | 5,000 | 4,500 | 3,000 | 1,500 | 500 | ........ | 15,500 | 25,000 |
| Reduce affordable housing barriers | ........ | 200 | 800 | 1,400 | 1,800 | 2,000 | 1,800 | 1,200 | 600 | 200 | ........ | 6,200 | 10,000 |
| Department of the Treasury: | | | | | | | | | | | | | |
| Establish Community Development Financial Institutions Affordable Housing Supply Fund | ........ | 500 | 500 | 500 | 500 | 500 | 500 | 500 | 500 | 500 | 500 | 2,500 | 5,000 |
| Allow selective basis boosts for bond-financed Low-Income Housing Credit projects[2] | ........ | 2 | 29 | 140 | 354 | 617 | 895 | 1,148 | 1,359 | 1,561 | 1,769 | 1,142 | 7,874 |
| Subtotal, increase affordable housing supply | ........ | 1,202 | 3,329 | 5,540 | 7,154 | 8,117 | 7,695 | 5,848 | 3,959 | 2,761 | 2,269 | 25,342 | 47,874 |
| Protect our elections and the right to vote: | | | | | | | | | | | | | |
| Election Assistance Commission: | | | | | | | | | | | | | |
| Fund election grants to increase access and security | ........ | 2,040 | 810 | 830 | 840 | 860 | 880 | 900 | 920 | 950 | 970 | 5,380 | 10,000 |
| Postal Service: | | | | | | | | | | | | | |
| Expand affordability and reliability of election-related mail service | ........ | 500 | 500 | 500 | 500 | 500 | 500 | 500 | 500 | 500 | 500 | 2,500 | 5,000 |
| Subtotal, protect our elections and the right to vote | ........ | 2,540 | 1,310 | 1,330 | 1,340 | 1,360 | 1,380 | 1,400 | 1,420 | 1,450 | 1,470 | 7,880 | 15,000 |
| Expand legal representation for asylum seekers: | | | | | | | | | | | | | |
| Department of Health and Human Services: | | | | | | | | | | | | | |
| Provide unaccompanied children with legal representation | ........ | 120 | 302 | 470 | 644 | 892 | 1,063 | 1,121 | 1,161 | 1,194 | 1,223 | 2,428 | 8,190 |
| Department of Justice: | | | | | | | | | | | | | |
| Provide representation in the immigration court system | ........ | 68 | 248 | 428 | 450 | 450 | 450 | 450 | 450 | 450 | 450 | 1,644 | 3,894 |
| Subtotal, expand legal representation for asylum seekers | ........ | 188 | 550 | 898 | 1,094 | 1,342 | 1,513 | 1,571 | 1,611 | 1,644 | 1,673 | 4,072 | 12,084 |
| Advance child welfare: | | | | | | | | | | | | | |
| Department of Health and Human Services: | | | | | | | | | | | | | |

# Table S-6. Mandatory and Receipt Proposals—Continued

(Deficit increases (+) or decreases (−) in millions of dollars)

| | 2022 | 2023 | 2024 | 2025 | 2026 | 2027 | 2028 | 2029 | 2030 | 2031 | 2032 | Totals 2023–2027 | Totals 2023–2032 |
|---|---|---|---|---|---|---|---|---|---|---|---|---|---|
| Create new flexibilities and support in the Chafee program for youth who experienced foster care | ..... | 100 | 100 | 100 | 100 | 100 | 100 | 100 | 100 | 100 | 100 | 500 | 1,000 |
| Prevent and combat religious, sexual orientation, gender identity, gender expression, or sex discrimination in the child welfare system | ..... | ..... | ..... | ..... | ..... | ..... | ..... | ..... | ..... | ..... | ..... | ..... | ..... |
| Expand and encourage participation in the title IV-E Prevention Services and Kinship Navigator programs | 161 | 280 | 318 | 376 | 445 | 389 | 457 | 539 | 628 | 701 | 767 | 1,808 | 4,900 |
| Reauthorize, increase funding for, and amend the Promoting Safe and Stable Families program | ..... | 78 | 250 | 292 | 295 | 300 | 300 | 300 | 300 | 300 | 300 | 1,215 | 2,715 |
| Increase support for foster care placements with kin caregivers | ..... | 91 | 100 | 108 | 116 | 126 | 136 | 145 | 155 | 162 | 169 | 541 | 1,308 |
| Reduce reimbursement rates for foster care congregate care placements | ..... | −27 | −24 | −21 | −18 | −17 | −16 | −15 | −14 | −14 | −14 | −107 | −180 |
| Department of the Treasury: | | | | | | | | | | | | | |
| Make the adoption tax credit refundable and allow certain guardianship arrangements to qualify[2] | ..... | 11 | 2,037 | 1,244 | 1,015 | 1,038 | 1,009 | 1,016 | 1,031 | 1,043 | 1,050 | 5,345 | 10,494 |
| Subtotal, advance child welfare | 161 | 533 | 2,781 | 2,099 | 1,953 | 1,936 | 1,986 | 2,085 | 2,200 | 2,292 | 2,372 | 9,302 | 20,237 |
| Ensure future pandemic and public health preparedness: | | | | | | | | | | | | | |
| Department of Health and Human Services: | | | | | | | | | | | | | |
| Invest in development of medical countermeasures, surge capacity, and public health systems | ..... | 13,509 | 28,734 | 17,183 | 10,354 | 6,627 | 4,449 | 723 | 120 | ..... | ..... | 76,407 | 81,699 |
| Establish the Vaccines for Adults program | ..... | 1,712 | 2,155 | 2,238 | 2,326 | 2,416 | 2,511 | 2,608 | 2,711 | 2,816 | 2,926 | 10,847 | 24,419 |
| Expand Vaccines for Children (VFC) program to all Children's Health Insurance Program (CHIP) children and make program improvements | ..... | 20 | 30 | 30 | 30 | 20 | 40 | 30 | 30 | 20 | 30 | 130 | 280 |
| Authorize coverage for drugs and devices authorized for emergency use[1] | ..... | ..... | ..... | ..... | ..... | ..... | ..... | ..... | ..... | ..... | ..... | ..... | ..... |
| Encourage development of innovative antimicrobial drugs[1] | ..... | ..... | ..... | ..... | ..... | ..... | ..... | ..... | ..... | ..... | ..... | ..... | ..... |
| Consolidate all vaccine coverage under Medicare Part B | ..... | ..... | 400 | 460 | 450 | 440 | 420 | 400 | 370 | 350 | 290 | 1,750 | 3,580 |
| Ensure consistency and clarity of data reporting requirements for Medicare providers, suppliers, and contractors during public health emergencies | ..... | ..... | ..... | ..... | ..... | ..... | ..... | ..... | ..... | ..... | ..... | ..... | ..... |
| Enable the Secretary to temporarily modify or waive the application of specific requirements of the Clinical Laboratory Improvement Amendments of 1988 (CLIA) Act[1] | ..... | ..... | ..... | ..... | ..... | ..... | ..... | ..... | ..... | ..... | ..... | ..... | ..... |
| Department of State and United States Agency for International Development (USAID) | | | | | | | | | | | | | |

## Table S-6. Mandatory and Receipt Proposals—Continued

(Deficit increases (+) or decreases (–) in millions of dollars)

| | 2022 | 2023 | 2024 | 2025 | 2026 | 2027 | 2028 | 2029 | 2030 | 2031 | 2032 | Totals 2023–2027 | Totals 2023–2032 |
|---|---|---|---|---|---|---|---|---|---|---|---|---|---|
| Strengthen the global health workforce, advance research and development capacity, and increase health security financing | ...... | 2,275 | 1,950 | 1,625 | 325 | 325 | ...... | ...... | ...... | ...... | ...... | 6,500 | 6,500 |
| Subtotal, ensure future pandemic and public health preparedness | ...... | 17,516 | 33,269 | 21,536 | 13,485 | 9,828 | 7,420 | 3,761 | 3,231 | 3,186 | 3,246 | 95,634 | 116,478 |
| **Reclassifications:** | | | | | | | | | | | | | |
| Shift the Indian Health Service from discretionary to mandatory funding | | | | | | | | | | | | | |
| Technical Reclassification: | | | | | | | | | | | | | |
| Reduction in discretionary spending (non-add) | ...... | –7,398 | –8,977 | –9,498 | –9,716 | –9,939 | –10,170 | –10,402 | –10,641 | –10,886 | –11,136 | –45,528 | –98,763 |
| Shift to mandatory spending | ...... | 7,398 | 8,977 | 9,498 | 9,716 | 9,939 | 10,170 | 10,402 | 10,641 | 10,886 | 11,136 | 45,528 | 98,763 |
| Provide adequate funding and close service gaps | ...... | ...... | 2,721 | 6,272 | 10,022 | 13,986 | 18,178 | 20,207 | 21,762 | 23,421 | 25,191 | 33,001 | 141,760 |
| Total IHS Request (Budget authority) (non-add) | ...... | 9,121 | 12,731 | 16,535 | 20,545 | 24,777 | 29,246 | 30,956 | 32,771 | 34,697 | 36,741 | 83,709 | 248,120 |
| End Deficit Reduction Contributions from Passenger Security Fee | ...... | 1,520 | 1,560 | 1,600 | 1,640 | 1,680 | ...... | ...... | ...... | ...... | ...... | 8,000 | 8,000 |
| Discretionary effects (non-add) | ...... | –1,520 | –1,560 | –1,600 | –1,640 | –1,680 | ...... | ...... | ...... | ...... | ...... | –8,000 | –8,000 |
| Provide mandatory funding for previously enacted Tribal Water Settlements Operations and Maintenance | ...... | 20 | 34 | 34 | 34 | 34 | 34 | 34 | 34 | 34 | 34 | 156 | 326 |
| Discretionary effects (non-add) | ...... | –20 | –34 | –34 | –34 | –34 | –34 | –34 | –34 | –34 | –34 | –156 | –326 |
| Reclassify Tribal Lease Payments | ...... | 55 | 56 | 57 | 58 | 60 | 61 | 62 | 63 | 64 | 66 | 286 | 602 |
| Discretionary effects (non-add) | ...... | –55 | –56 | –57 | –58 | –60 | –61 | –62 | –63 | –64 | –66 | –286 | –602 |
| Reclassify Contract Support Costs | ...... | 237 | 397 | 410 | 422 | 434 | 447 | 456 | 466 | 474 | 484 | 1,900 | 4,227 |
| Discretionary effects (non-add) | ...... | –237 | –397 | –410 | –422 | –434 | –447 | –456 | –466 | –474 | –484 | –1,900 | –4,227 |
| Subtotal, reclassifications | ...... | 9,230 | 13,745 | 17,871 | 21,892 | 26,133 | 28,890 | 31,161 | 32,966 | 34,879 | 36,911 | 88,871 | 253,678 |
| **Program integrity proposals:** | | | | | | | | | | | | | |
| Capture savings to Medicare and Medicaid from Health Care Fraud and Abuse Control (HCFAC) allocation adjustment | ...... | –1,119 | –1,181 | –1,246 | –1,315 | –1,354 | –1,393 | –1,435 | –1,479 | –1,523 | –1,569 | –6,215 | –13,614 |
| Implement HCFAC allocation adjustment, discretionary outlays (non-add) | ...... | 576 | 593 | 611 | 629 | 648 | 667 | 687 | 708 | 729 | 751 | 3,057 | 6,599 |
| Net effect of HCFAC allocation adjustment (non-add) | ...... | –543 | –588 | –635 | –686 | –706 | –726 | –748 | –771 | –794 | –818 | –3,158 | –7,015 |
| Capture savings to Unemployment Insurance (UI) from Reemployment Services and Eligibility Assessments (RESEA) allocation adjustment[2] | –290 | –474 | –684 | –701 | –630 | –618 | –597 | –583 | –574 | –851 | –911 | –3,107 | –6,623 |
| Implement RESEA allocation adjustment, discretionary outlays (non-add) | 79 | 249 | 424 | 528 | 605 | 631 | 648 | 661 | 677 | 692 | 709 | 2,437 | 5,824 |
| Net effect of RESEA allocation adjustment (non-add) | –211 | –225 | –260 | –173 | –25 | 13 | 51 | 78 | 103 | –159 | –202 | –670 | –799 |
| Capture savings from the Social Security Administration (SSA) allocation adjustments[3] | ...... | –112 | –1,776 | –3,142 | –3,992 | –4,885 | –6,021 | –6,289 | –7,440 | –8,242 | –8,981 | –13,907 | –50,880 |
| Implement SSA allocation adjustments, discretionary outlays (non-add) | ...... | 1,516 | 1,579 | 1,405 | 1,502 | 1,577 | 1,626 | 1,683 | 1,765 | 1,801 | 1,834 | 7,579 | 16,288 |

## Table S-6. Mandatory and Receipt Proposals—Continued

(Deficit increases (+) or decreases (−) in millions of dollars)

| | 2022 | 2023 | 2024 | 2025 | 2026 | 2027 | 2028 | 2029 | 2030 | 2031 | 2032 | Totals 2023–2027 | Totals 2023–2032 |
|---|---|---|---|---|---|---|---|---|---|---|---|---|---|
| *Net effect of SSA allocation adjustments (non-add)* | ...... | *1,404* | *−197* | *−1,737* | *−2,490* | *−3,308* | *−4,395* | *−4,606* | *−5,675* | *−6,441* | *−7,147* | *−6,328* | *−34,592* |
| Subtotal, program integrity proposals | −290 | −1,705 | −3,641 | −5,089 | −5,937 | −6,857 | −8,011 | −8,307 | −9,493 | −10,616 | −11,461 | −23,229 | −71,117 |
| Increase Afghan Special Immigrant Visas | ...... | 52 | 81 | 80 | 72 | 66 | 64 | 58 | 52 | 53 | 54 | 351 | 632 |
| Smooth and extend BBEDCA Section 251A sequestration | ...... | ...... | ...... | ...... | ...... | ...... | ...... | ...... | 1,730 | 22,450 | −36,537 | ...... | −12,357 |
| **Proposals by Agency:** | | | | | | | | | | | | | |
| **Department of Defense--Military Programs:** | | | | | | | | | | | | | |
| Extend authority to provide increased voluntary separation incentive pay for civilian employees of the Department of Defense | ...... | ...... | 1 | 1 | 1 | ...... | ...... | ...... | ...... | ...... | ...... | 3 | 3 |
| Authorize mandatory collection of Survivor Benefit Plan premiums from Veterans Disability Compensation | ...... | ...... | ...... | ...... | ...... | ...... | ...... | ...... | ...... | ...... | ...... | ...... | ...... |
| Expand the current Medicare Eligible Retiree Health Care Fund to include all uniformed services retiree health care costs | ...... | ...... | 464 | 462 | 406 | 351 | 209 | 52 | −99 | −235 | −355 | 1,683 | 1,255 |
| Establish reserve component duty status reform | ...... | ...... | ...... | ...... | ...... | ...... | ...... | ...... | ...... | ...... | ...... | ...... | ...... |
| **Department of Education** | | | | | | | | | | | | | |
| Double the maximum Pell Grant by 2029 | ...... | 2,847 | 8,442 | 12,710 | 16,988 | 21,428 | 26,563 | 32,148 | 35,348 | 36,010 | 36,671 | 62,415 | 229,155 |
| Increase the Pell Grant discretionary award (effect on mandatory costs) | ...... | ...... | 54 | 125 | 125 | 126 | 135 | 148 | 148 | 149 | 150 | 430 | 1,160 |
| Shift mandatory funds to support Pell award increase | ...... | ...... | −54 | −125 | −125 | −126 | −135 | −148 | −148 | −149 | −150 | −430 | −1,160 |
| Increase Title I funding | ...... | 640 | 13,455 | 15,205 | 16,354 | 17,050 | 17,442 | 17,844 | 18,252 | 18,674 | 19,102 | 62,704 | 154,018 |
| *Title I Mandatory Request (Budget authority) (non-add)* | ...... | *16,000* | *16,368* | *16,745* | *17,130* | *17,523* | *17,927* | *18,338* | *18,761* | *19,192* | *19,634* | *83,766* | *177,618* |
| **Department of Energy:** | | | | | | | | | | | | | |
| Strengthen clean energy manufacturing | ...... | 40 | 100 | 160 | 180 | 190 | 160 | 100 | 40 | 20 | 10 | 670 | 1,000 |
| **Department of Health and Human Services:** | | | | | | | | | | | | | |
| Fund the Administration's HIV/AIDS strategy: | | | | | | | | | | | | | |
| Eliminate barriers to pre-exposure prophylaxis (PrEP) under Medicaid | ...... | −290 | −310 | −340 | −370 | −390 | −430 | −460 | −500 | −530 | −580 | −1,700 | −4,200 |
| Establish PrEP Delivery Program to end the HIV epidemic | ...... | 213 | 371 | 526 | 687 | 853 | 1,027 | 1,206 | 1,394 | 1,587 | 1,789 | 2,650 | 9,653 |
| Extend and expand the Maternal Infant Early Childhood Home Visiting (MIECHV) program | ...... | 19 | 142 | 415 | 532 | 611 | 646 | 502 | 116 | 22 | ...... | 1,719 | 3,005 |
| Provide CMS Program Management Implementation Funding | ...... | 50 | 150 | 100 | ...... | ...... | ...... | ...... | ...... | ...... | ...... | 300 | 300 |
| Standardize data collection to improve quality and promote equitable care | ...... | ...... | ...... | ...... | ...... | ...... | ...... | ...... | ...... | ...... | ...... | ...... | ...... |
| Add Medicare coverage of services furnished by community health workers[1] | ...... | ...... | ...... | ...... | ...... | ...... | ...... | ...... | ...... | ...... | ...... | ...... | ...... |
| Establish a Contingency Fund for the Unaccompanied Children Program | ...... | 696 | 1,315 | 1,439 | 789 | 201 | 108 | 62 | 31 | ...... | ...... | 4,440 | 4,641 |

## Table S–6. Mandatory and Receipt Proposals—Continued

(Deficit increases (+) or decreases (–) in millions of dollars)

| | 2022 | 2023 | 2024 | 2025 | 2026 | 2027 | 2028 | 2029 | 2030 | 2031 | 2032 | Totals 2023–2027 | Totals 2023–2032 |
|---|---|---|---|---|---|---|---|---|---|---|---|---|---|
| Treat certain populations as refugees for public benefit purposes | ...... | 111 | 122 | 127 | 132 | 138 | 133 | 11 | 4 | 4 | 4 | 630 | 786 |
| Prohibit unsolicited Medicare beneficiary contacts[1] | ...... | ...... | ...... | ...... | ...... | ...... | ...... | ...... | ...... | ...... | ...... | ...... | ...... |
| Expand tools to identify and investigate fraud in the Medicare Advantage program[1] | ...... | ...... | ...... | ...... | ...... | ...... | ...... | ...... | ...... | ...... | ...... | ...... | ...... |
| Hold long-term care facility owners accountable for noncompliant closures and substandard care | ...... | ...... | ...... | ...... | ...... | ...... | ...... | ...... | ...... | ...... | ...... | ...... | ...... |
| Increase transparency by disclosing accreditation surveys | ...... | ...... | ...... | ...... | ...... | ...... | ...... | ...... | ...... | ...... | ...... | ...... | ...... |
| Remove restrictions on the certification of new entities as Organ Procurement Organizations and increase enforcement flexibility | ...... | ...... | ...... | ...... | ...... | ...... | ...... | ...... | ...... | ...... | ...... | ...... | ...... |
| Enhance the physician fee schedule conversion factor update in CY 2025 | ...... | ...... | ...... | 250 | 380 | 410 | 430 | 460 | 480 | 500 | 540 | 1,040 | 3,450 |
| Modify the Medicaid Drug Rebate Program in the Territories | ...... | ...... | ...... | ...... | ...... | ...... | ...... | ...... | ...... | ...... | ...... | ...... | ...... |
| Enhance Medicaid managed care enforcement | ...... | –100 | –200 | –200 | –200 | –200 | –200 | –200 | –200 | –300 | –300 | –900 | –2,100 |
| Medicaid interactions | ...... | ...... | ...... | 60 | 100 | 100 | 30 | ...... | ...... | ...... | ...... | 260 | 290 |
| **Department of Homeland Security:** | | | | | | | | | | | | | |
| Establish Electronic Visa Update System user fee[2] | ...... | ...... | ...... | ...... | ...... | ...... | ...... | ...... | ...... | ...... | ...... | ...... | ...... |
| Extend expiring Customs and Border Protection (CBP) user fees | ...... | ...... | ...... | ...... | ...... | ...... | ...... | ...... | ...... | ...... | –5,939 | ...... | –5,939 |
| Establish an affordability program for the National Flood Insurance Program | ...... | 43 | 328 | 375 | 427 | 480 | 534 | 580 | 630 | 676 | 720 | 1,653 | 4,793 |
| **Department of Justice:** | | | | | | | | | | | | | |
| Combat and prevent crime | ...... | 1,064 | 2,055 | 3,289 | 4,157 | 4,535 | 3,551 | 2,875 | 2,249 | 1,992 | 1,892 | 15,100 | 27,662 |
| **Department of Labor:** | | | | | | | | | | | | | |
| Shift timing of Pension Benefit Guarantee Corporation's Single Employer premiums | ...... | ...... | ...... | 3,314 | –3,314 | ...... | ...... | ...... | ...... | ...... | ...... | ...... | ...... |
| Expand Foreign Labor Certification Fees | ...... | 4 | 5 | –40 | –2 | 4 | 4 | 5 | 6 | 6 | 7 | –29 | –1 |
| **Department of the Treasury:** | | | | | | | | | | | | | |
| Reduce paperwork burden by permanently authorizing current home to work transportation for the IRS Commissioner | ...... | ...... | ...... | ...... | ...... | ...... | ...... | ...... | ...... | ...... | ...... | ...... | ...... |
| Amend the Bank Merger Act to allow for the transition of Treasury-sponsored debit cards accounts | ...... | ...... | ...... | ...... | ...... | ...... | ...... | ...... | ...... | ...... | ...... | ...... | ...... |
| Fund the Federal Payment Levy Program via collections[2] | ...... | 22 | 22 | 22 | 22 | 22 | 22 | 22 | 22 | 22 | 22 | 110 | 220 |
| **Department of Veterans Affairs:** | | | | | | | | | | | | | |
| Modernize records management program | ...... | ...... | ...... | ...... | ...... | ...... | ...... | ...... | ...... | ...... | ...... | ...... | ...... |
| Extend authority for the Specially Adapted Housing Assistive Technology Grant Program | ...... | ...... | ...... | ...... | ...... | ...... | ...... | ...... | ...... | ...... | ...... | 5 | 5 |
| Extend authority for Specially Adapted Housing Temporary Residence Adaptation grant | ...... | 1 | 1 | 1 | 1 | 1 | 1 | 1 | 1 | 1 | 1 | 5 | 10 |

## Table S–6. Mandatory and Receipt Proposals—Continued

(Deficit increases (+) or decreases (−) in millions of dollars)

| | 2022 | 2023 | 2024 | 2025 | 2026 | 2027 | 2028 | 2029 | 2030 | 2031 | 2032 | Totals 2023–2027 | Totals 2023–2032 |
|---|---|---|---|---|---|---|---|---|---|---|---|---|---|
| Environmental Protection Agency: | | | | | | | | | | | | | |
| Expand use of pesticide licensing user fees | ........ | 2 | 2 | 2 | 2 | 1 | 1 | 1 | ........ | ........ | ........ | 9 | 11 |
| General Services Administration: | | | | | | | | | | | | | |
| Establish and capitalize the Federal Capital Revolving Fund[4] | ........ | 966 | 2,264 | 1,132 | 133 | −133 | 83 | −183 | 33 | −47 | −123 | 4,362 | 4,125 |
| Expand the Disposal Fund authorities | ........ | 1 | 1 | 1 | 1 | 1 | 1 | 1 | 1 | 1 | 1 | 5 | 10 |
| International Assistance Programs: | | | | | | | | | | | | | |
| Fund renegotiated Compacts of Free Association[1] | ........ | ........ | ........ | ........ | ........ | ........ | ........ | ........ | ........ | ........ | ........ | ........ | ........ |
| National Aeronautics and Space Administration: | | | | | | | | | | | | | |
| Distribute the Science, Space, and Technology Education Trust Fund | ........ | 16 | ........ | ........ | ........ | ........ | ........ | ........ | ........ | ........ | ........ | 16 | 16 |
| Office of Personnel Management: | | | | | | | | | | | | | |
| Amend Administration of Tribal Federal Employees Health Benefits Program (FEHBP) Enrollment System | ........ | 2 | 2 | 2 | 2 | 2 | 2 | 2 | 2 | 2 | 2 | 10 | 20 |
| Expand Family Member Eligibility under the Federal Employees Dental and Vision Insurance Program (FEDVIP) | ........ | ........ | ........ | ........ | ........ | ........ | ........ | ........ | ........ | ........ | ........ | ........ | ........ |
| Expand FEDVIP to Tribal Employers | ........ | ........ | ........ | ........ | ........ | ........ | ........ | ........ | ........ | ........ | ........ | ........ | ........ |
| Expand FEHBP to Tribal Colleges and Universities | ........ | ........ | ........ | ........ | ........ | ........ | ........ | ........ | ........ | ........ | ........ | ........ | ........ |
| Small Business Administration: | | | | | | | | | | | | | |
| Support SBA COVID programs' oversight and servicing | ........ | ........ | ........ | ........ | ........ | ........ | ........ | ........ | ........ | ........ | ........ | ........ | ........ |
| Consumer Product Safety Commission: | | | | | | | | | | | | | |
| Strengthen mandatory recall authorities | ........ | ........ | ........ | ........ | ........ | ........ | ........ | ........ | ........ | ........ | ........ | ........ | ........ |
| **Total, mandatory initiatives and savings** | **−129** | **40,679** | **88,132** | **93,662** | **90,280** | **100,036** | **101,729** | **102,844** | **106,201** | **127,660** | **65,151** | **412,789** | **916,374** |
| **Tax proposals:** | | | | | | | | | | | | | |
| Reform business and international taxation: | | | | | | | | | | | | | |
| Raise the corporate income tax rate to 28 percent | ........ | −83,500 | −138,893 | −136,355 | −134,942 | −137,761 | −139,987 | −137,573 | −135,244 | −134,857 | −135,448 | −631,451 | −1,314,560 |
| Adopt the Undertaxed Profits Rule | ........ | ........ | −20,427 | −33,464 | −29,329 | −26,655 | −26,170 | −25,638 | −25,109 | −25,665 | −27,006 | −109,875 | −239,463 |
| Provide tax incentives for locating jobs and business activity in the United States and remove tax deductions for shipping jobs overseas: | | | | | | | | | | | | | |
| Provide tax credit for inshoring jobs to the United States | ........ | 8 | 13 | 14 | 14 | 15 | 16 | 16 | 17 | 18 | 18 | 64 | 149 |
| Remove tax deductions for shipping jobs overseas | ........ | −8 | −13 | −14 | −14 | −15 | −16 | −16 | −17 | −18 | −18 | −64 | −149 |
| Subtotal, provide tax incentives for locating jobs and business activity in the United States and remove tax deductions for shipping jobs overseas | ........ | ........ | ........ | ........ | ........ | ........ | ........ | ........ | ........ | ........ | ........ | ........ | ........ |
| Prevent basis shifting by related parties through partnerships | ........ | −3,320 | −5,676 | −5,912 | −6,153 | −6,401 | −6,621 | −6,785 | −6,887 | −6,959 | −7,025 | −27,462 | −61,739 |

## Table S-6. Mandatory and Receipt Proposals—Continued

(Deficit increases (+) or decreases (−) in millions of dollars)

| | 2022 | 2023 | 2024 | 2025 | 2026 | 2027 | 2028 | 2029 | 2030 | 2031 | 2032 | Totals 2023–2027 | Totals 2023–2032 |
|---|---|---|---|---|---|---|---|---|---|---|---|---|---|
| Conform definition of "control" with corporate affiliation test | ...... | −761 | −1,104 | −1,125 | −1,143 | −1,158 | −1,170 | −1,179 | −1,182 | −1,182 | −1,176 | −5,291 | −11,180 |
| Expand access to retroactive qualified electing fund elections | ...... | ...... | −1 | −2 | −2 | −3 | −4 | −5 | −6 | −7 | −9 | −8 | −39 |
| Expand the definition of foreign business entity to include taxable units | ...... | −300 | −324 | −290 | −193 | −89 | −96 | −103 | −112 | −120 | −130 | −1,196 | −1,757 |
| Subtotal, reform business and international taxation | −87,881 | −166,425 | −177,148 | −171,762 | −172,067 | −174,048 | −171,283 | −168,540 | −168,790 | −170,794 | | −775,283 | −1,628,738 |
| **Support housing and urban development:** | | | | | | | | | | | | | |
| Make permanent the New Markets Tax Credit | ...... | ...... | ...... | ...... | 97 | 278 | 483 | 716 | 990 | 1,290 | 1,602 | 375 | 5,456 |
| Subtotal, support housing and urban development | ...... | ...... | ...... | ...... | 97 | 278 | 483 | 716 | 990 | 1,290 | 1,602 | 375 | 5,456 |
| **Modify fossil fuel taxation:** | | | | | | | | | | | | | |
| **Eliminate fossil fuel tax preferences:** | | | | | | | | | | | | | |
| Repeal the enhanced oil recovery credit | ...... | ...... | ...... | −31 | −80 | −130 | −186 | −237 | −271 | −301 | −330 | −241 | −1,566 |
| Repeal the deduction for costs paid or incurred for any tertiary injectant used as part of tertiary recovery method[5] | ...... | ...... | ...... | ...... | ...... | ...... | ...... | ...... | ...... | ...... | ...... | ...... | ...... |
| Repeal credit for oil and gas produced from marginal wells | ...... | ...... | −3 | −52 | −144 | −219 | −265 | −288 | −301 | −317 | −333 | −418 | −1,922 |
| Repeal expensing of intangible drilling costs | ...... | −1,508 | −2,231 | −1,806 | −1,401 | −847 | −600 | −597 | −601 | −590 | −561 | −7,793 | −10,742 |
| Repeal exception to passive loss limitation provided to working interests in oil and natural gas properties | ...... | −10 | −9 | −9 | −9 | −8 | −8 | −8 | −8 | −7 | −7 | −45 | −83 |
| Repeal the use of percentage depletion with respect to oil and natural gas wells | ...... | −925 | −1,037 | −1,085 | −1,178 | −1,267 | −1,351 | −1,433 | −1,510 | −1,579 | −1,649 | −5,492 | −13,014 |
| Increase geological and geophysical amortization period for independent producers | ...... | −631 | −831 | −930 | −1,008 | −1,045 | −1,086 | −1,128 | −1,158 | −1,193 | −1,218 | −4,445 | −10,228 |
| Repeal expensing of mine exploration and development costs | ...... | −131 | −194 | −156 | −122 | −74 | −52 | −52 | −52 | −50 | −49 | −677 | −932 |
| Repeal percentage depletion for hard mineral fossil fuels | ...... | −163 | −183 | −191 | −208 | −224 | −239 | −253 | −267 | −279 | −291 | −969 | −2,298 |
| Repeal capital gains treatment for royalties | ...... | −27 | −52 | −54 | −57 | −62 | −64 | −66 | −69 | −71 | −73 | −252 | −595 |
| Repeal the exemption from the corporate income tax for fossil fuel publicly traded partnerships | ...... | ...... | ...... | ...... | ...... | ...... | −90 | −176 | −216 | −253 | −288 | ...... | −1,023 |
| Eliminate the Oil Spill Liability Trust Fund (OSLTF) excise tax exemption for crude oil derived from bitumen and kerogen-rich rock | ...... | −29 | −38 | −39 | −40 | −41 | −41 | −42 | −43 | −45 | −46 | −187 | −404 |
| Repeal accelerated amortization of air pollution control equipment | ...... | −14 | −34 | −54 | −71 | −88 | −103 | −117 | −115 | −103 | −92 | −261 | −791 |
| Subtotal, eliminate fossil fuel tax preferences | ...... | −3,438 | −4,612 | −4,407 | −4,318 | −4,005 | −4,085 | −4,397 | −4,611 | −4,788 | −4,937 | −20,780 | −43,598 |
| **Modify OSLTF financing and Superfund excise taxes:** | | | | | | | | | | | | | |
| Eliminate the tax exemption for crude oil from bitumen and kerogen-rich rock for the Superfund | ...... | −64 | −85 | −87 | −88 | −88 | −89 | −90 | −92 | −95 | −95 | −412 | −873 |
| Eliminate drawback for the OSLTF | ...... | −53 | −70 | −71 | −72 | −72 | −72 | −72 | −72 | −72 | −72 | −338 | −698 |
| Subtotal, modify OSLTF financing and Superfund excise taxes | ...... | −117 | −155 | −158 | −160 | −160 | −161 | −162 | −164 | −167 | −167 | −750 | −1,571 |
| Subtotal, modify fossil fuel taxation | ...... | −3,555 | −4,767 | −4,565 | −4,478 | −4,165 | −4,246 | −4,559 | −4,775 | −4,955 | −5,104 | −21,530 | −45,169 |

# Table S-6. Mandatory and Receipt Proposals—Continued

(Deficit increases (+) or decreases (−) in millions of dollars)

| | 2022 | 2023 | 2024 | 2025 | 2026 | 2027 | 2028 | 2029 | 2030 | 2031 | 2032 | Totals 2023–2027 | Totals 2023–2032 |
|---|---|---|---|---|---|---|---|---|---|---|---|---|---|
| **Strengthen taxation of high-income taxpayers:** | | | | | | | | | | | | | |
| Increase the top marginal income tax rate for high earners | −5,861 | −23,895 | −39,877 | −46,351 | −19,648 | −7,909 | −8,573 | −9,153 | −9,796 | −10,451 | −11,156 | −137,680 | −186,809 |
| Reform the taxation of capital income | −263 | −5,464 | −15,229 | −17,487 | −17,979 | −17,969 | −18,452 | −19,224 | −20,025 | −20,885 | −21,774 | −74,128 | −174,488 |
| Impose a minimum income tax on the wealthiest taxpayers | ......... | ......... | −36,115 | −40,478 | −42,662 | −43,395 | −43,053 | −42,591 | −38,087 | −36,047 | −38,415 | −162,650 | −360,843 |
| Subtotal, strengthen taxation of high-income taxpayers | −6,124 | −29,359 | −91,221 | −104,316 | −80,289 | −69,273 | −70,078 | −70,968 | −67,908 | −67,383 | −71,345 | −374,458 | −722,140 |
| **Support families and students:** | | | | | | | | | | | | | |
| Provide income exclusion for student debt relief [6] | ......... | ......... | ......... | ......... | 2 | 17 | 41 | 266 | 292 | 320 | 351 | 19 | 1,289 |
| Subtotal, support families and students | ......... | ......... | ......... | ......... | 2 | 17 | 41 | 266 | 292 | 320 | 351 | 19 | 1,289 |
| **Modify estate and gift taxation:** | | | | | | | | | | | | | |
| Modify income, estate, and gift tax rules for certain grantor trusts | ......... | −452 | −1,699 | −2,405 | −2,349 | −3,950 | −4,949 | −5,504 | −6,049 | −6,912 | −7,261 | −10,855 | −41,530 |
| Require consistent valuation of promissory notes | ......... | −342 | −716 | −747 | −697 | −695 | −658 | −649 | −637 | −619 | −601 | −3,197 | −6,361 |
| Improve tax administration for trusts and decedents' estates | ......... | 15 | 23 | 24 | 25 | 30 | 34 | 38 | 43 | 45 | 49 | 117 | 326 |
| Limit duration of generation-skipping transfer tax exemption | ......... | | | | | | | | | | | | |
| Subtotal, modify estate and gift taxation | ......... | −779 | −2,392 | −3,128 | −3,021 | −4,615 | −5,573 | −6,115 | −6,643 | −7,486 | −7,813 | −13,935 | −47,565 |
| **Close loopholes:** | | | | | | | | | | | | | |
| Tax carried (profits) interests as ordinary income | ......... | −406 | −677 | −675 | −674 | −672 | −679 | −692 | −706 | −720 | −735 | −3,104 | −6,636 |
| Repeal deferral of gain from like-kind exchanges | ......... | −676 | −1,857 | −1,914 | −1,971 | −2,030 | −2,091 | −2,154 | −2,218 | −2,285 | −2,354 | −8,448 | −19,550 |
| Require 100 percent recapture of depreciation deductions as ordinary income for certain depreciable real property | ......... | −35 | −113 | −233 | −364 | −505 | −657 | −821 | −1,000 | −1,192 | −1,400 | −1,250 | −6,320 |
| Limit a partner's deduction in certain syndicated conservation easement transactions | ......... | −925 | −4,689 | −2,739 | −2,114 | −1,488 | −1,261 | −1,299 | −1,337 | −1,377 | −1,419 | −11,955 | −18,648 |
| Limit use of donor advised funds to avoid private foundation payout requirement | ......... | −16 | −15 | −10 | −6 | −3 | −2 | −3 | −3 | −3 | −3 | −50 | −64 |
| Extend the period for assessment of tax for certain Qualified Opportunity Fund investors | ......... | −4 | −13 | −15 | −15 | −13 | −10 | −9 | −8 | −6 | −2 | −60 | −95 |
| Establish an untaxed income account regime for certain small insurance companies | ......... | −908 | −2,241 | −1,017 | −865 | −795 | −764 | −757 | −748 | −739 | −730 | −5,826 | −9,564 |
| Expand pro rata interest expense disallowance for business-owned life insurance | ......... | −530 | −540 | −582 | −619 | −665 | −704 | −739 | −774 | −812 | −850 | −2,936 | −6,815 |
| Correct drafting errors in the taxation of insurance companies under the Tax Cuts and Jobs Act of 2017 | ......... | −86 | −112 | −116 | −100 | −75 | −70 | −63 | −59 | −55 | −51 | −489 | −787 |
| Define the term "ultimate purchaser" for purposes of diesel fuel exportation | ......... | −4 | −6 | −9 | −10 | −13 | −14 | −17 | −20 | −22 | −24 | −42 | −139 |
| Subtotal, close loopholes | ......... | −3,590 | −10,263 | −7,310 | −6,738 | −6,259 | −6,252 | −6,554 | −6,873 | −7,211 | −7,568 | −34,160 | −68,618 |
| **Improve tax administration and compliance:** | | | | | | | | | | | | | |
| Enhance accuracy of tax information: | | | | | | | | | | | | | |

## Table S–6. Mandatory and Receipt Proposals—Continued

(Deficit increases (+) or decreases (–) in millions of dollars)

| | 2022 | 2023 | 2024 | 2025 | 2026 | 2027 | 2028 | 2029 | 2030 | 2031 | 2032 | Totals 2023–2027 | Totals 2023–2032 |
|---|---|---|---|---|---|---|---|---|---|---|---|---|---|
| Expand the Secretary's authority to require electroning filing for forms and returns | ........ | ........ | ........ | ........ | ........ | ........ | ........ | ........ | ........ | ........ | ........ | ........ | ........ |
| Improve information reporting for reportable payments subject to backup withholding | ........ | –38 | –87 | –148 | –202 | –211 | –221 | –231 | –241 | –252 | –276 | –686 | –1,907 |
| Subtotal, enhance accuracy of tax information | ........ | –38 | –87 | –148 | –202 | –211 | –221 | –231 | –241 | –252 | –276 | –686 | –1,907 |
| Address taxpayer noncompliance with listed transactions: | | | | | | | | | | | | | |
| Extend statute of limitations for listed transactions | ........ | –23 | –51 | –64 | –78 | –76 | –74 | –73 | –72 | –70 | –69 | –292 | –650 |
| Impose liability on shareholders to collect unpaid income taxes of applicable corporations | ........ | –430 | –448 | –466 | –485 | –505 | –525 | –548 | –571 | –596 | –622 | –2,334 | –5,196 |
| Subtotal, address taxpayer noncompliance | ........ | –453 | –499 | –530 | –563 | –581 | –599 | –621 | –643 | –666 | –691 | –2,626 | –5,846 |
| Amend the centralized partnership audit regime to permit the carryover of a reduction in tax that exceeds a partner's tax liability | ........ | 5 | 5 | 5 | 5 | 6 | 6 | 7 | 7 | 7 | 7 | 26 | 60 |
| Incorporate Chapters 2/2A in centralized partnership audit regime proceedings | ........ | ........ | ........ | ........ | ........ | ........ | ........ | ........ | ........ | ........ | ........ | ........ | ........ |
| Authorize limited sharing of business tax return information to measure the economy more accurately | ........ | ........ | ........ | ........ | ........ | ........ | ........ | ........ | ........ | ........ | ........ | ........ | ........ |
| Require employers to withhold tax on failed nonqualified deferred compensation plans | ........ | –555 | –580 | –605 | –631 | –658 | –687 | –718 | –752 | –787 | –824 | –3,029 | –6,797 |
| Impose an affirmative requirement to disclose a position contrary to a regulation | ........ | –5 | –7 | –11 | –11 | –12 | –12 | –14 | –14 | –15 | –15 | –46 | –116 |
| Extend to six years the statute of limitations for certain tax assessments | ........ | ........ | ........ | ........ | ........ | ........ | ........ | ........ | ........ | ........ | ........ | ........ | ........ |
| Expand and increase penalties for noncompliant return preparation and e-filing and authorize IRS oversight of paid preparers: | | | | | | | | | | | | | |
| Expand and increase penalties for noncompliant return preparation and e-filing [6] | ........ | –14 | –31 | –38 | –45 | –51 | –53 | –55 | –58 | –60 | –63 | –179 | –468 |
| Grant authority to IRS for oversight of all paid preparers [6] | ........ | –25 | –34 | –45 | –51 | –50 | –54 | –58 | –64 | –70 | –76 | –205 | –527 |
| Subtotal, expand and increase penalties for noncompliant return preparation and e-filing and authorize IRS oversight of paid preparers | ........ | –39 | –65 | –83 | –96 | –101 | –107 | –113 | –122 | –130 | –139 | –384 | –995 |
| Address compliance in connection with tax responsibilities of expatriates | ........ | ........ | –1 | –1 | –1 | –1 | –1 | –2 | –2 | –2 | –2 | –4 | –13 |
| Simplify foreign exchange gain or loss rules and exchange rate rules for individuals | ........ | 1 | 2 | 2 | 2 | 3 | 3 | 3 | 3 | 3 | 3 | 10 | 25 |
| Increase threshold for simplified foreign tax credit rules and reporting | ........ | 14 | 25 | 27 | 29 | 31 | 31 | 32 | 32 | 32 | 34 | 126 | 287 |
| Subtotal, improve tax administration and compliance | ........ | –1,070 | –1,207 | –1,344 | –1,468 | –1,524 | –1,587 | –1,657 | –1,732 | –1,810 | –1,903 | –6,613 | –15,302 |

# Table S–6. Mandatory and Receipt Proposals—Continued

(Deficit increases (+) or decreases (−) in millions of dollars)

| | 2022 | 2023 | 2024 | 2025 | 2026 | 2027 | 2028 | 2029 | 2030 | 2031 | 2032 | Totals 2023–2027 | Totals 2023–2032 |
|---|---|---|---|---|---|---|---|---|---|---|---|---|---|
| Modernize rules, including those for digital assets: | | | | | | | | | | | | | |
| Modernize rules treating loans of securities as tax-free to include other asset classes and address income inclusion | ........ | ........ | ........ | ........ | ........ | ........ | ........ | ........ | ........ | ........ | ........ | ........ | ........ |
| Provide for information reporting by certain financial institutions and digital asset brokers for purposes of exchange of information | ........ | −48 | −95 | −179 | −209 | −222 | −237 | −251 | −267 | −287 | −303 | −753 | −2,098 |
| Require reporting by certain taxpayers of foreign digital asset accounts | ........ | −50 | −100 | −188 | −220 | −234 | −250 | −264 | −282 | −302 | −319 | −792 | −2,209 |
| Amend the mark-to-market rules to include digital assets | ........ | −4,846 | −133 | −146 | −161 | −177 | −194 | −214 | −235 | −259 | −284 | −5,463 | −6,649 |
| Subtotal, modernize rules, including those for digital assets | ........ | −4,944 | −328 | −513 | −590 | −633 | −681 | −729 | −784 | −848 | −906 | −7,008 | −10,956 |
| Improve benefits tax administration: | | | | | | | | | | | | | |
| Clarify tax treatment of fixed indemnity health policies | ........ | ........ | ........ | ........ | ........ | ........ | ........ | ........ | ........ | ........ | ........ | ........ | ........ |
| Clarify tax treatment of on-demand pay arrangements | ........ | ........ | ........ | ........ | ........ | ........ | ........ | ........ | ........ | ........ | ........ | ........ | ........ |
| Rationalize funding for post-retirement medical and life insurance benefits | ........ | ........ | ........ | ........ | ........ | ........ | ........ | ........ | ........ | ........ | ........ | ........ | ........ |
| Subtotal, improve benefits tax administration | ........ | ........ | ........ | ........ | ........ | ........ | ........ | ........ | ........ | ........ | ........ | ........ | ........ |
| **Total, receipt proposals** | −6,124 | −131,178 | −276,603 | −298,324 | −268,247 | −258,241 | −261,941 | −260,883 | −255,973 | −256,873 | −263,480 | −1,232,593 | −2,531,743 |
| **Grand total, mandatory and receipt proposals** | −6,253 | −90,499 | −188,471 | −204,662 | −177,967 | −158,205 | −160,212 | −158,039 | −149,772 | −129,213 | −198,329 | −819,804 | −1,615,369 |

[1] Estimates were not available at the time of Budget publication.

[2] The estimates for this proposal include effects on receipts. The receipt effects included in the totals above are as follows:

| | 2022 | 2023 | 2024 | 2025 | 2026 | 2027 | 2028 | 2029 | 2030 | 2031 | 2032 | Totals 2023–2027 | Totals 2023–2032 |
|---|---|---|---|---|---|---|---|---|---|---|---|---|---|
| Improve access to behavioral healthcare in the private insurance market | ........ | 1,435 | 1,991 | 2,089 | 2,305 | 2,449 | 2,564 | 2,683 | 2,812 | 2,948 | 3,093 | 10,269 | 24,369 |
| Require coverage of three primary care visits and three behavioral health visits without cost-sharing | ........ | 916 | 1,271 | 1,335 | 1,490 | 1,585 | 1,657 | 1,738 | 1,822 | 1,909 | 2,005 | 6,597 | 15,728 |
| Allow selective basis boosts for bond-financed Low-Income Housing Credit projects | ........ | 2 | 29 | 140 | 354 | 617 | 895 | 1,148 | 1,359 | 1,561 | 1,769 | 1,142 | 7,874 |
| Make adoption tax credit refundable and allow certain guardianship arrangements to qualify | ........ | 11 | 42 | 42 | 42 | 42 | 42 | 42 | 42 | 42 | 42 | 179 | 389 |
| Capture savings to UI from RESEA allocation adjustment | ........ | ........ | 24 | 62 | 115 | 158 | 195 | 225 | 250 | −12 | −54 | 359 | 963 |
| Establish user fee for Electronic Visa Update System | ........ | −47 | −52 | −58 | −64 | −72 | −79 | −88 | −108 | −118 | −130 | −293 | −816 |
| Fund the Federal Payment Levy Program via collections | ........ | 22 | 22 | 22 | 22 | 22 | 22 | 22 | 22 | 22 | 22 | 110 | 220 |
| Total, receipt effects of mandatory proposals | ........ | 2,339 | 3,327 | 3,632 | 4,264 | 4,801 | 5,296 | 5,770 | 6,199 | 6,352 | 6,747 | 18,363 | 48,727 |

[3] Represents the savings associated with continuing to provide dedicated funding, through a discretionary allocation adjustment, for program integrity activities to confirm program participants remain eligible to receive benefits.

[4] This proposal includes an intragovernmental transfer between the Federal Capital Revolving Fund (FCRF) and the Federal Building Fund (FBF). The collections and spending in the FBF, the receiving account, are not counted for PAYGO purposes because the proposal expects the PAYGO cost to be recorded in the FCRF. The intragovernmental transfers net to zero and are as follows:

## Table S–6. Mandatory and Receipt Proposals—Continued

(Deficit increases (+) or decreases (−) in millions of dollars)

| | 2022 | 2023 | 2024 | 2025 | 2026 | 2027 | 2028 | 2029 | 2030 | 2031 | 2032 | Totals 2023–2027 | Totals 2023–2032 |
|---|---|---|---|---|---|---|---|---|---|---|---|---|---|
| Establish and capitalize the Federal Capital Revolving Fund | ......... | −1,004 | 104 | 217 | 321 | 259 | 103 | ......... | ......... | ......... | ......... | ......... | ......... |
| Provide income exclusion for student debt relief | ......... | ......... | ......... | ......... | ......... | 1 | 1 | 21 | 24 | 27 | 29 | 1 | 103 |
| Expand and increase penalties for noncompliant return preparation and e-filing | ......... | ......... | −6 | −6 | −6 | −7 | −7 | −7 | −8 | −8 | −8 | −25 | −63 |
| Grant authority to IRS for oversight of all paid preparers | ......... | −12 | −14 | −21 | −23 | −19 | −20 | −21 | −23 | −25 | −27 | −89 | −205 |
| Total, outlay effects of receipt proposals | ......... | −12 | −20 | −27 | −29 | −25 | −26 | −7 | −7 | −6 | −6 | −113 | −165 |

[5] Effects are included in the estimate of "Repeal the enhanced oil recovery credit."

[6] The estimates for this proposal includes effects on outlays. The outlay effects included in the totals above are as follows:

# Table S–7. Funding Levels for Appropriated ("Discretionary") Programs by Category

(Budget authority in billions of dollars)

| | Actual[1] 2021 | CR[2] 2022 | CAA[3] 2022 | Request 2023 | Outyears 2024 | 2025 | 2026 | 2027 | 2028 | 2029 | 2030 | 2031 | 2032 | Totals 2023–2027 | 2023–2032 |
|---|---|---|---|---|---|---|---|---|---|---|---|---|---|---|---|
| **Base Discretionary Funding Allocation** | 1,374 | 1,393 | 1,473 | 1,582 | 1,643 | 1,670 | 1,703 | 1,728 | 1,754 | 1,780 | 1,807 | 1,834 | 1,862 | 8,326 | 17,362 |
| **Non-Defense Shifts to Mandatory[4]** | ...... | ...... | ...... | –10 | –10 | –10 | –10 | –10 | –11 | –11 | –11 | –11 | –12 | –50 | –106 |
| Bureau of Indian Affairs | ...... | ...... | ...... | –* | –* | –* | –* | –1 | –1 | –1 | –1 | –1 | –1 | –2 | –5 |
| Indian Health Service | ...... | ...... | ...... | –9 | –9 | –10 | –10 | –10 | –10 | –10 | –11 | –11 | –11 | –48 | –101 |
| **Non-Base Discretionary Funding (not included above):[5]** | | | | | | | | | | | | | | | |
| Emergency and COVID–19 Supplemental Funding | 198 | 45 | 58 | ...... | | | | | | | | | | | |
| Program Integrity | 2 | 2 | 2 | 2 | 3 | 3 | 3 | 3 | 3 | 3 | 3 | 3 | 3 | 13 | 29 |
| Disaster Relief | 17 | 17 | 19 | 20 | 11 | 11 | 11 | 11 | 11 | 11 | 11 | 11 | 11 | 64 | 119 |
| Wildfire Suppression | 2 | 2 | 2 | 3 | 3 | 3 | 3 | 3 | 3 | 3 | 3 | 3 | 3 | 13 | 26 |
| 21st Century Cures Appropriations | * | * | 1 | 1 | * | * | * | * | ...... | ...... | ...... | ...... | ...... | 2 | 2 |
| **Total, Non-Base Funding** | 220 | 67 | 82 | 26 | 17 | 16 | 17 | 16 | 17 | 17 | 17 | 17 | 17 | 92 | 175 |
| **Grand Total, Discretionary Budget Authority** | 1,594 | 1,461 | 1,555 | 1,598 | 1,650 | 1,676 | 1,709 | 1,734 | 1,759 | 1,786 | 1,812 | 1,839 | 1,867 | 8,367 | 17,431 |
| *Memorandum: Presentation of base discretionary by defense and non-defense:[6]* | | | | | | | | | | | | | | | |
| Defense Allocation[7] | 741 | 746 | 782 | 813 | 843 | 851 | 865 | 871 | 877 | 883 | 889 | 895 | 902 | 4,242 | 8,688 |
| Non-Defense Allocation | 544 | 551 | 594 | 650 | 665 | 680 | 696 | 712 | 728 | 745 | 762 | 780 | 797 | 3,402 | 7,215 |
| Veterans Affairs Medical Care Program | 90 | 96 | 97 | 119 | 136 | 139 | 142 | 145 | 149 | 152 | 156 | 159 | 163 | 681 | 1,459 |
| *Memorandum: Presentation of base discretionary by security and nonsecurity:[6]* | | | | | | | | | | | | | | | |
| Security Allocation | 850 | 855 | 894 | 936 | 968 | 979 | 996 | 1,005 | 1,016 | 1,026 | 1,035 | 1,045 | 1,055 | 4,884 | 10,062 |
| Nonsecurity Allocation | 434 | 442 | 482 | 527 | 540 | 552 | 565 | 578 | 589 | 602 | 616 | 630 | 644 | 2,761 | 5,841 |
| Veterans Affairs Medical Care Program | 90 | 96 | 97 | 119 | 136 | 139 | 142 | 145 | 149 | 152 | 156 | 159 | 163 | 681 | 1,459 |
| *Memorandum: Discretionary appropriations provided in the Infrastructure, Investment, and Jobs Act[8]* | ...... | 174 | N/A | 69 | 69 | 68 | 66 | 2 | 2 | 2 | 2 | 2 | 2 | 273 | 283 |

\* Less than $500 million.

1 The 2021 actual level includes changes that occur after appropriations are enacted that are part of budget execution such as transfers, reestimates, and the rebasing as mandatory any changes in mandatory programs (CHIMPs) enacted in appropriations bills. The 2021 levels are adjusted to add back OMB's scoring of CHIMPs enacted in 2021 appropriations Acts for a better illustrative comparison with the 2023 request.

2 At the time the 2023 Budget was prepared, 2022 appropriations remained incomplete and the 2022 column reflects at the account level annualized continuing appropriations provided under the Continuing Appropriations Act, 2022 (division A of Public Law 117–70, division A of Public Law 117–86, and Public Law 117–95; CR). The 2022 column also reflects enacted full-year emergency appropriations enacted in the Disaster Relief Supplemental Appropriations Act, 2022, the Afghanistan Supplemental Appropriations Act, 2022, and the Additional Afghanistan Supplemental Appropriations Act, 2022 (divisions B and C of Public Law 117–43 and division B of Public Law 117–70, respectively).

3 The 2023 Budget was finalized before 2022 appropriations were completed. To allow a high-level comparison of the 2023 Budget with enacted appropriations, this column provides a preliminary summary of 2022 enacted appropriations in the Consolidated Appropriations Act, 2022 (Public Law 117–103; CAA), using the Congressional Budget Office (CBO) estimate of the legislation (see CBO estimate for H.R. 2471, the Consolidated Appropriations Act, 2022 on CBO's website). CBO estimates of IIJA appropriations are not included since OMB includes its own estimate for 2022.

## Table S–7. Funding Levels for Appropriated ("Discretionary") Programs by Category—Continued

(Budget authority in billions of dollars)

[4] The 2023 Budget proposes to shift the Indian Health Service (IHS) in HHS as well as contract support costs and 105(l) leases within the Bureau of Indian Programs (BIA) in the Department of the Interior to the mandatory side of the Budget starting in 2023. See the "Budget Process" chapter of the *Analytical Perspectives* volume of the Budget for more information on these proposals.

[5] The 2023 Budget presents funding for anomalous or above-base activities such as emergency requirements, program integrity, disaster relief, wildfire suppression, and 21st Century Cures appropriations outside of base allocations, which is largely consistent with allocation adjustments in the FY 2022 Congressional Budget Resolution (H.Con.Res. 14).

[6] The section presents base discretionary funding by both defense and non-defense and by security and nonsecurity allocations. The definition of security and nonsecurity is the same as the definition specified in the Budget Control Act of 2011 with security including the Departments of Defense, Homeland Security, Veterans Affairs, the National Nuclear Security Administration, the International Budget Function (150), and the Intelligence Community Management Account and with all other discretionary programs in the nonsecurity category. This presentation of discretionary excludes the proposed shifts to mandatory.

[7] The amounts in the 2023 Budget are based on the forthcoming National Security and National Defense strategies and the Department of Defense Future Years Defense Program, which includes a five-year appropriations plan and estimated expenditures necessary to support the programs, projects, and activities of the Department of Defense. After 2027, the Budget mechanically extrapolates the growth rate from the final year of the five-year appropriations plan.

[8] Section 905(c) of division J of the Infrastructure Investment and Jobs Act (Public Law 117-58; IIJA) specified that amounts provided in division J and certain rescissions in section 90007 of IIJA should be considered as emergency discretionary appropriations. The amounts provided as discretionary appropriations in IIJA are summarized here, however, these amounts are kept separate from other discretionary amounts included above that are considered during the regular appropriations process.

# Table S–8. 2023 Discretionary Request by Major Agency

(Budget authority in billions of dollars)

| | 2021 Actual[1] | 2022 CR[2] | 2023 Request | 2023 Request Less 2021 Enacted | |
|---|---|---|---|---|---|
| | | | | Dollar | Percent |
| **Base Discretionary Funding:** | | | | | |
| **Cabinet Departments:** | | | | | |
| Agriculture[3] | 24.4 | 23.7 | 28.5 | +4.2 | +17.1% |
| Commerce | 8.9 | 8.9 | 11.7 | +2.8 | +31.2% |
| Defense | 703.7 | 709.2 | 773.0 | +69.3 | +9.8% |
| Education | 73.0 | 73.0 | 88.3 | +15.3 | +20.9% |
| Energy (DOE)[4] | 41.9 | 41.8 | 48.2 | +6.3 | +15.1% |
| Health and Human Services (HHS)[5] | 108.6 | 110.4 | 138.0 | +29.4 | +27.1% |
| *Proposed IHS Shift to Mandatory (non-add)[6]* | *(6.5)* | *(6.6)* | *(9.1)* | *(+2.6)* | *N/A* |
| *HHS, BA excluding IHS (non-add)* | *(102.0)* | *(103.9)* | *(128.9)* | *(+26.9)* | *(+26.3%)* |
| Homeland Security (DHS) | 53.8 | 52.7 | 56.7 | +2.9 | +5.4% |
| Housing and Urban Development (HUD): | | | | | |
| *HUD program level* | *59.6* | *60.3* | *71.9* | *+12.3* | *+20.5%* |
| *HUD receipts* | *–16.1* | *–13.1* | *–11.1* | *+5.0* | *N/A* |
| Interior (DOI) | 14.9 | 15.1 | 17.9 | +3.0 | +20.5% |
| *Proposed BIA Shift to Mandatory (non-add)[6]* | *(0.2)* | *(0.4)* | *(0.5)* | *(+0.2)* | *N/A* |
| *DOI, BA excluding BIA (non-add)* | *(14.6)* | *(14.7)* | *(17.5)* | *(+2.8)* | *(+19.3%)* |
| Justice | 33.5 | 33.6 | 37.7 | +4.2 | +12.5% |
| Labor | 12.5 | 12.5 | 14.6 | +2.2 | +17.6% |
| State and International Programs[3,7] | 57.5 | 57.9 | 67.6 | +10.2 | +17.7% |
| Transportation (DOT) | 25.3 | 25.5 | 26.8 | +1.5 | +6.0% |
| Treasury[7] | 13.5 | 13.5 | 16.2 | +2.7 | +19.9% |
| Veterans Affairs | 104.5 | 111.1 | 135.2 | +30.7 | +29.4% |
| **Major Agencies:** | | | | | |
| Corps of Engineers (Corps) | 7.8 | 7.8 | 6.6 | –1.2 | –15.3% |
| Environmental Protection Agency | 9.2 | 9.2 | 11.9 | +2.6 | +28.6% |
| General Services Administration | –0.9 | –1.3 | 1.3 | +2.2 | N/A |
| National Aeronautics and Space Administration | 23.3 | 23.3 | 26.0 | +2.7 | +11.6% |
| National Science Foundation | 8.5 | 8.5 | 10.5 | +2.0 | +23.6% |
| Small Business Administration | 0.8 | 0.8 | 0.9 | +0.2 | +21.0% |
| Social Security Administration[5] | 9.0 | 8.9 | 10.1 | +1.1 | +12.8% |
| Other Agencies | 23.3 | 23.3 | 28.1 | +4.8 | +20.7% |
| Changes in mandatory program offsets[8] | –26.0 | –23.3 | –34.7 | –8.7 | +33.5% |
| **Subtotal, Base Discretionary Budget Authority (BA)** | **1,374.2** | **1,393.5** | **1,582.0** | **+207.8** | **+15.1%** |
| *Subtotal, BA excluding programs shifted to mandatory* | *1,367.5* | *1,386.5* | *1,572.4* | *+205.0* | *+15.0%* |

## Table S–8. 2023 Discretionary Request by Major Agency—Continued

(Budget authority in billions of dollars)

| | 2021 Actual[1] | 2022 CR[2] | 2023 Request | 2023 Request Less 2021 Enacted — Dollar | 2023 Request Less 2021 Enacted — Percent |
|---|---|---|---|---|---|
| **Non-Base Discretionary Funding:** | | | | | |
| Emergency Requirements and COVID-19 Supplemental Funding: | | | | | |
| Agriculture | 1.0 | 11.6 | ...... | –1.0 | N/A |
| Commerce | 0.3 | 0.4 | ...... | –0.3 | N/A |
| Defense | 1.0 | 7.4 | ...... | –1.0 | N/A |
| Education | 81.6 | ...... | ...... | –81.6 | N/A |
| Energy | –2.3 | 0.0 | ...... | +2.3 | N/A |
| Health and Human Services | 73.8 | 5.5 | ...... | –73.8 | N/A |
| Homeland Security | 2.8 | 1.0 | ...... | –2.8 | N/A |
| Housing and Urban Development | 0.7 | 5.0 | ...... | –0.7 | N/A |
| Interior | 0.4 | 0.6 | ...... | –0.4 | N/A |
| Justice | 0.6 | 0.1 | ...... | –0.6 | N/A |
| Labor | 1.5 | ...... | ...... | –1.5 | N/A |
| State and International Programs | 5.9 | 3.4 | ...... | –5.9 | N/A |
| Transportation | 27.0 | 2.7 | ...... | –27.0 | N/A |
| Treasury | 0.5 | ...... | ...... | –0.5 | N/A |
| Corps of Engineers (Corps) | ...... | 5.7 | ...... | ...... | N/A |
| Small Business Administration | 2.0 | 1.2 | ...... | –2.0 | N/A |
| Other Agencies | 0.9 | 0.4 | ...... | –0.9 | N/A |
| Subtotal, Emergency Requirements | 197.8 | 45.1 | ...... | –197.8 | N/A |
| Program Integrity: | | | | | |
| Health and Human Services | 0.5 | 0.5 | 0.6 | +0.1 | +16.1% |
| Labor | 0.1 | 0.1 | 0.3 | +0.2 | +210.8% |
| Social Security Administration | 1.3 | 1.3 | 1.5 | +0.2 | +16.1% |
| Subtotal, Program Integrity | 1.9 | 1.9 | 2.3 | +0.5 | +24.7% |
| Disaster Relief: | | | | | |
| Homeland Security | 17.1 | 17.1 | 19.7 | +2.6 | +15.2% |
| Small Business Administration | 0.1 | 0.1 | 0.1 | ...... | N/A |
| Subtotal, Disaster Relief | 17.3 | 17.3 | 19.9 | +2.6 | +15.0% |
| Wildfire Suppression: | | | | | |
| Agriculture | 2.0 | 2.0 | 2.2 | +0.2 | +8.3% |
| Interior | 0.3 | 0.3 | 0.3 | +* | +9.7% |
| Subtotal, Wildfire Suppression | 2.4 | 2.4 | 2.6 | +0.2 | +8.5% |
| 21st Century Cures appropriations: | | | | | |
| Health and Human Services | 0.5 | 0.5 | 1.1 | +0.7 | +139.5% |
| **Subtotal, Non-Base Discretionary Funding** | **219.8** | **67.1** | **25.9** | **–193.9** | **–88.2%** |

## Table S–8.    2023 Discretionary Request by Major Agency—Continued

(Budget authority in billions of dollars)

| | 2021 Actual[1] | 2022 CR[2] | 2023 Request | 2023 Request Less 2021 Enacted Dollar | 2023 Request Less 2021 Enacted Percent |
|---|---|---|---|---|---|
| **Total, Discretionary BA** | **1,594.0** | **1,460.5** | **1,607.9** | **+13.9** | **+0.9%** |
| *Total, BA excluding programs shifted to mandatory* | *1,587.2* | *1,453.6* | *1,598.3* | *+11.1* | *+0.7%* |
| | | 2022 CAA | 2023 Request | 2023 Request Less 2022 CAA | |
| *Memorandum - Comparison of 2022 Omnibus to 2023 Request:*[9] | | | | | |
| *Total, Base Discretionary Funding* | | *1,472.9* | *1,582.0* | *+109.0* | *+7.4%* |
| *Base Discretionary by Defense and Non-Defense:* | | | | | |
| *Defense* | | *782.2* | *813.3* | *+31.2* | *+4.0%* |
| *Non-Defense* | | *593.6* | *649.9* | *+56.3* | *+9.5%* |
| *Veterans Affairs Medical Care Program*[10] | | *97.2* | *118.7* | *+21.5* | *+22.2%* |
| *Base Discretionary by Security and Nonsecurity:*[10] | | | | | |
| *Security* | | *894.2* | *935.9* | *+41.7* | *+4.7%* |
| *Nonsecurity* | | *481.6* | *527.3* | *+45.8* | *+9.5%* |
| *Veterans Affairs Medical Care Program* | | *97.2* | *118.7* | *+21.5* | *+22.2%* |

\* Less than $50 million.

[1] The 2021 actual level includes changes that occur after appropriations are enacted that are part of budget execution such as transfers, reestimates, and the rebasing as mandatory any changes in mandatory programs (CHIMPs) enacted in appropriations bills. The 2021 levels are adjusted to add back OMB's scoring of CHIMPs enacted in 2021 appropriations Acts for a better illustrative comparison with the 2023 request.

[2] At the time the 2023 Budget was prepared, 2022 appropriations remained incomplete and the 2022 column reflects at the account level annualized continuing appropriations provided under the Continuing Appropriations Act, 2022 (division A of Public Law 117–70, division A of Public Law 117–86, and Public Law 117–95; CR). The 2022 column also reflects enacted full-year emergency appropriations enacted in the Disaster Relief Supplemental Appropriations Act, 2022, the Afghanistan Supplemental Appropriations Act, 2022, and the Additional Afghanistan Supplemental Appropriations Act, 2022 (divisions B and C of Public Law 117–43 and division B of Public Law 117–70, respectively).

[3] Funding for Food for Peace Title II Grants is included in the State and International Programs total. Although the funds are appropriated to the Department of Agriculture, the funds are administered by the U.S. Agency for International Development (USAID).

[4] The Department of Energy base total in 2021 includes an appropriation of $2.3 billion that had been designated as emergency in Public Law 116–260 since the activities were for regular operations and not emergency purposes.

[5] Funding from the Hospital Insurance and Supplementary Medical Insurance trust funds for administrative expenses incurred by the Social Security Administration that support the Medicare program are included in the Health and Human Services total and not in the Social Security Administration total.

[6] The 2023 Budget proposes to shift the Indian Health Service (IHS) in HHS as well as contract support costs and 105(l) leases within the Bureau of Indian Programs (BIA) in DOI to the mandatory side of the Budget starting in 2023. See the "Budget Process" chapter of the *Analytical Perspectives* volume of the Budget for more information on these proposals.

[7] The State and International Programs total includes funding for the Department of State, USAID, Treasury International, and 11 international agencies while the Treasury total excludes Treasury's International Programs.

[8] The limitation enacted and proposed in the Justice Department's Crime Victims Fund program and cancellations in the Children's Health Insurance Program in HHS make up the bulk of these offsets.

[9] The 2023 Budget was finalized before 2022 appropriations were completed. To allow a high-level comparison of the 2023 Budget with enacted appropriations, this memorandum section provides a preliminary summary of 2022 enacted base appropriations in the Consolidated Appropriations Act, 2022 (Public Law 117–103; CAA), using the Congressional Budget Office (CBO) estimate of the legislation (see CBO estimate for H.R. 2471, the Consolidated Appropriations Act, 2022 on CBO's website). This presentation of discretionary excludes the proposed shifts to mandatory.

[10] The definition of security and nonsecurity is the same as the definition specified in the Budget Control Act of 2011 with security including the Departments of Defense, Homeland Security, Veterans Affairs, the National Nuclear Security Administration, the International Budget Function (150), and the Intelligence Community Management Account and with all other discretionary programs in the nonsecurity category.

## Table S–9. Economic Assumptions[1]

(Calendar years)

| | Actual 2020 | 2021 | Projections | | | | | | | | | | |
| --- | --- | --- | --- | --- | --- | --- | --- | --- | --- | --- | --- | --- | --- |
| | | | 2022 | 2023 | 2024 | 2025 | 2026 | 2027 | 2028 | 2029 | 2030 | 2031 | 2032 |
| **Gross Domestic Product (GDP):** | | | | | | | | | | | | | |
| Nominal level, billions of dollars | 20,894 | 22,899 | 24,631 | 25,853 | 26,966 | 28,064 | 29,200 | 30,380 | 31,626 | 32,957 | 34,382 | 35,877 | 37,437 |
| Percent change, nominal GDP, year/year | –2.2 | 9.6 | 7.6 | 5.0 | 4.3 | 4.1 | 4.0 | 4.0 | 4.1 | 4.2 | 4.3 | 4.3 | 4.3 |
| Real GDP, percent change, year/year | –3.4 | 5.5 | 4.2 | 2.8 | 2.2 | 2.0 | 2.0 | 2.0 | 2.1 | 2.2 | 2.3 | 2.3 | 2.3 |
| Real GDP, percent change, Q4/Q4 | –2.3 | 5.1 | 3.8 | 2.5 | 2.1 | 2.0 | 2.0 | 2.0 | 2.1 | 2.2 | 2.3 | 2.3 | 2.3 |
| GDP chained price index, percent change, year/year | 1.3 | 3.9 | 3.3 | 2.1 | 2.0 | 2.0 | 2.0 | 2.0 | 2.0 | 2.0 | 2.0 | 2.0 | 2.0 |
| **Consumer Price Index,[2] percent change, year/year** | 1.2 | 4.6 | 4.7 | 2.3 | 2.3 | 2.3 | 2.3 | 2.3 | 2.3 | 2.3 | 2.3 | 2.3 | 2.3 |
| **Interest rates, percent:[3]** | | | | | | | | | | | | | |
| 91-day Treasury bills[4] | 0.4 | * | 0.2 | 0.9 | 1.6 | 1.9 | 2.1 | 2.2 | 2.3 | 2.3 | 2.3 | 2.3 | 2.3 |
| 10-year Treasury notes | 0.9 | 1.5 | 2.1 | 2.5 | 2.7 | 2.8 | 3.0 | 3.1 | 3.1 | 3.2 | 3.2 | 3.2 | 3.3 |
| **Unemployment rate, civilian, percent[3]** | 8.1 | 5.4 | 3.9 | 3.6 | 3.7 | 3.8 | 3.8 | 3.8 | 3.8 | 3.8 | 3.8 | 3.8 | 3.8 |

\* 0.05 percent or less

Note: A more detailed table of economic assumptions appears in Chapter 2, "Economic Assumptions and Overview," in the *Analytical Perspectives* volume of the Budget.

[1] The Administration's forecast was finalized on November 10, 2021.

[2] Seasonally adjusted CPI for all urban consumers.

[3] Annual average.

[4] Average rate, secondary market (bank discount basis).

## Table S–10. Federal Government Financing and Debt

(Dollar amounts in billions)

| | Actual 2021 | Estimate | | | | | | | | | | |
|---|---|---|---|---|---|---|---|---|---|---|---|---|
| | | 2022 | 2023 | 2024 | 2025 | 2026 | 2027 | 2028 | 2029 | 2030 | 2031 | 2032 |
| **Financing:** | | | | | | | | | | | | |
| Unified budget deficit: | | | | | | | | | | | | |
| Primary deficit | 2,423 | 1,058 | 758 | 724 | 766 | 680 | 622 | 725 | 565 | 667 | 663 | 692 |
| Net interest | 352 | 357 | 396 | 476 | 564 | 648 | 729 | 808 | 879 | 948 | 1,019 | 1,092 |
| Unified budget deficit | 2,775 | 1,415 | 1,154 | 1,201 | 1,330 | 1,328 | 1,352 | 1,533 | 1,443 | 1,614 | 1,682 | 1,784 |
| As a percent of GDP | 12.4% | 5.8% | 4.5% | 4.5% | 4.8% | 4.6% | 4.5% | 4.9% | 4.4% | 4.7% | 4.7% | 4.8% |
| Other transactions affecting borrowing from the public: | | | | | | | | | | | | |
| Changes in financial assets and liabilities:[1] | | | | | | | | | | | | |
| Change in Treasury operating cash balance | -1,567 | 535 | .......... | .......... | .......... | .......... | .......... | .......... | .......... | .......... | .......... | .......... |
| Net disbursements of credit financing accounts: | | | | | | | | | | | | |
| Direct loan and Troubled Asset Relief Program (TARP) equity purchase accounts | -18 | 147 | 42 | 32 | 38 | 11 | 24 | 19 | 17 | 17 | 20 | 27 |
| Guaranteed loan accounts | 310 | 219 | 3 | 7 | 8 | 7 | 6 | 6 | 5 | 5 | 5 | 5 |
| Net purchases of non-Federal securities by the National Railroad Retirement Investment Trust (NRRIT) | 4 | -1 | -2 | -2 | -2 | -2 | -1 | -1 | -2 | -2 | -1 | -1 |
| Net change in other financial assets and liabilities[2] | -237 | 238 | .......... | .......... | .......... | .......... | .......... | .......... | .......... | .......... | .......... | .......... |
| Subtotal, changes in financial assets and liabilities | -1,508 | 1,138 | 44 | 37 | 44 | 17 | 28 | 23 | 22 | 20 | 23 | 31 |
| Seigniorage on coins | -* | -* | -1 | -1 | -1 | -1 | -1 | -1 | -1 | -1 | -1 | -1 |
| Total, other transactions affecting borrowing from the public | -1,508 | 1,137 | 43 | 37 | 43 | 16 | 28 | 23 | 22 | 20 | 23 | 30 |
| Total, requirement to borrow from the public (equals change in debt held by the public) | 1,267 | 2,552 | 1,197 | 1,237 | 1,373 | 1,344 | 1,380 | 1,555 | 1,465 | 1,634 | 1,705 | 1,815 |
| **Changes in Debt Subject to Statutory Limitation:** | | | | | | | | | | | | |
| Change in debt held by the public | 1,267 | 2,552 | 1,197 | 1,237 | 1,373 | 1,344 | 1,380 | 1,555 | 1,465 | 1,634 | 1,705 | 1,815 |
| Change in debt held by Government accounts | 216 | 354 | 104 | 136 | 29 | 13 | -146 | -252 | -148 | -282 | -281 | -374 |
| Change in other factors | -2 | 1 | 1 | 1 | -* | * | 1 | * | * | -1 | -1 | -1 |
| Total, change in debt subject to statutory limitation | 1,481 | 2,907 | 1,302 | 1,374 | 1,402 | 1,358 | 1,235 | 1,304 | 1,317 | 1,352 | 1,423 | 1,440 |
| **Debt Subject to Statutory Limitation, End of Year:** | | | | | | | | | | | | |
| Debt issued by Treasury | 28,365 | 31,271 | 32,572 | 33,945 | 35,347 | 36,704 | 37,938 | 39,241 | 40,558 | 41,909 | 43,332 | 44,772 |
| Adjustment for discount, premium, and coverage[3] | 36 | 38 | 39 | 40 | 40 | 40 | 41 | 42 | 43 | 43 | 43 | 43 |
| Total, debt subject to statutory limitation[4] | 28,401 | 31,309 | 32,611 | 33,984 | 35,386 | 36,744 | 37,979 | 39,283 | 40,600 | 41,952 | 43,374 | 44,814 |
| **Debt Outstanding, End of Year:** | | | | | | | | | | | | |
| Gross Federal debt:[5] | | | | | | | | | | | | |
| Debt issued by Treasury | 28,365 | 31,271 | 32,572 | 33,945 | 35,347 | 36,704 | 37,938 | 39,241 | 40,558 | 41,909 | 43,332 | 44,772 |
| Debt issued by other agencies | 21 | 21 | 21 | 21 | 22 | 22 | 22 | 22 | 22 | 23 | 24 | 25 |
| Total, gross Federal debt | 28,386 | 31,292 | 32,593 | 33,966 | 35,368 | 36,726 | 37,960 | 39,263 | 40,580 | 41,933 | 43,356 | 44,797 |
| As a percent of GDP | 127.0% | 129.0% | 127.5% | 127.2% | 127.3% | 127.0% | 126.2% | 125.4% | 124.4% | 123.3% | 122.1% | 120.9% |

## Table S–10. Federal Government Financing and Debt—Continued

(Dollar amounts in billions)

| | Actual 2021 | Estimate 2022 | 2023 | 2024 | 2025 | 2026 | 2027 | 2028 | 2029 | 2030 | 2031 | 2032 |
|---|---|---|---|---|---|---|---|---|---|---|---|---|
| **Held by:** | | | | | | | | | | | | |
| Debt held by Government accounts ..... | 6,102 | 6,456 | 6,560 | 6,695 | 6,725 | 6,738 | 6,592 | 6,340 | 6,192 | 5,911 | 5,629 | 5,256 |
| Debt held by the public[6] ..... | 22,284 | 24,836 | 26,033 | 27,271 | 28,644 | 29,988 | 31,368 | 32,923 | 34,388 | 36,022 | 37,727 | 39,542 |
| As a percent of GDP ..... | 99.7% | 102.4% | 101.8% | 102.2% | 103.1% | 103.7% | 104.3% | 105.2% | 105.4% | 105.9% | 106.3% | 106.7% |
| **Debt Held by the Public Net of Financial Assets:** | | | | | | | | | | | | |
| Debt held by the public ..... | 22,284 | 24,836 | 26,033 | 27,271 | 28,644 | 29,988 | 31,368 | 32,923 | 34,388 | 36,022 | 37,727 | 39,542 |
| Less financial assets net of liabilities: | | | | | | | | | | | | |
| Treasury operating cash balance ..... | 215 | 750 | 750 | 750 | 750 | 750 | 750 | 750 | 750 | 750 | 750 | 750 |
| Credit financing account balances: | | | | | | | | | | | | |
| Direct loan and TARP equity purchase accounts ..... | 1,595 | 1,742 | 1,784 | 1,816 | 1,854 | 1,865 | 1,889 | 1,908 | 1,926 | 1,943 | 1,963 | 1,990 |
| Guaranteed loan accounts ..... | –156 | 63 | 66 | 72 | 80 | 87 | 93 | 99 | 105 | 110 | 115 | 120 |
| Government-sponsored enterprise stock[7] ..... | 221 | 221 | 221 | 221 | 221 | 221 | 221 | 221 | 221 | 221 | 221 | 221 |
| Air carrier worker support warrants and notes[8] ..... | 15 | 15 | 15 | 15 | 14 | 13 | 13 | 12 | 12 | 6 | ..... | ..... |
| Emergency capital investment fund securities ..... | ..... | 3 | 3 | 3 | 3 | 3 | 3 | 3 | 3 | 3 | 2 | 2 |
| Non-Federal securities held by NRRIT ..... | 28 | 26 | 25 | 23 | 22 | 20 | 19 | 17 | 16 | 14 | 13 | 11 |
| Other assets net of liabilities ..... | –307 | –69 | –69 | –69 | –69 | –69 | –69 | –69 | –69 | –69 | –69 | –69 |
| Total, financial assets net of liabilities ..... | 1,611 | 2,751 | 2,795 | 2,832 | 2,875 | 2,891 | 2,919 | 2,941 | 2,963 | 2,977 | 2,994 | 3,025 |
| Debt held by the public net of financial assets ..... | 20,673 | 22,085 | 23,238 | 24,439 | 25,769 | 27,097 | 28,449 | 29,982 | 31,425 | 33,045 | 34,732 | 36,516 |
| As a percent of GDP ..... | 92.5% | 91.0% | 90.9% | 91.6% | 92.7% | 93.7% | 94.6% | 95.8% | 96.4% | 97.1% | 97.8% | 98.6% |

\* $500 million or less.

[1] A decrease in the Treasury operating cash balance (which is an asset) is a means of financing a deficit and therefore has a negative sign. An increase in checks outstanding (which is a liability) is also a means of financing a deficit and therefore also has a negative sign. More information on the levels and changes to the operating cash balance is available in Chapter 4, "Federal Borrowing and Debt" in the *Analytical Perspectives* volume of the Budget.

[2] Includes checks outstanding, accrued interest payable on Treasury debt, uninvested deposit fund balances, allocations of special drawing rights, and other liability accounts; and, as an offset, cash and monetary assets (other than the Treasury operating cash balance), other asset accounts, and profit on sale of gold.

[3] Consists mainly of debt issued by the Federal Financing Bank (which is not subject to limit), the unamortized discount (less premium) on public issues of Treasury notes and bonds (other than zero-coupon bonds), and the unrealized discount on Government account series securities.

[4] The statutory debt limit is $31,381 billion, as enacted on December 16, 2021.

[5] Treasury securities held by the public and zero-coupon bonds held by Government accounts are almost all measured at sales price plus amortized discount or less amortized premium. Agency debt securities are almost all measured at face value. Treasury securities in the Government account series are otherwise measured at face value less unrealized discount (if any).

[6] At the end of 2021, the Federal Reserve Banks held $5,433.2 billion of Federal securities and the rest of the public held $16,850.9 billion. Debt held by the Federal Reserve Banks is not estimated for future years.

[7] Treasury's warrants to purchase 79.9 percent of the common stock of the enterprises expire after September 7, 2028. The warrants were valued at $5 billion at the end of 2021.

[8] Portions of the notes and warrants issued under the Air carrier worker support program (Payroll support program) are scheduled to expire in 2025, 2026, 2030, and 2031.

# OMB CONTRIBUTORS TO THE 2023 BUDGET

The following personnel contributed to the preparation of this publication. Hundreds, perhaps thousands, of others throughout the Government also deserve credit for their valuable contributions.

## A

Lindsay Abate
Bryan Abbe
Allison Abbott
Andrew Abrams
Amal Abukar
Chandana L. Achanta
Laurie Adams
Jeffrey Adarkwa
Nana Abena Serwah
 Addo
Drew Aherne
Saran Ahluwalia
Shagufta Ahmed
Benjamin Aidoo
Lina Al Sudani
Joseph Albanese
Isabel Aldunate
Erin Cheese Alejandre
Jason Alleman
Victoria Allred
Aaron Alton
Marc Alvidrez
Samantha Ammons
Michaela Amos
Starlisha Anderson
Kimberly Anoweck
Lisa Anuszewski
Kristine Arboleda
Nickole M. Arbuckle
Rachel Arguello
Alison Arnold
Aviva Aron-Dine
Anna R. Arroyo
Elham Ashoori
Emily Schultz Askew
Lisa L. August
Jeffrey Auser

## B

Eileen Baca
Samuel Bagenstos
Drew Bailey

Jessie W. Bailey
Ally P. Bain
Paul W. Baker
Carol A. Bales
Pratik S. Banjade
Avital Bar-Shalom
Zachary Barger
Carl Barrick
Jody Barringer
Amy Batchelor
Paula M. Becker
Alicia Beckett
Sarah Belford
Jennifer Wagner Bell
Sara Bencic
Joseph J. Berger
Danielle Berman
Elizabeth A. Bernhard
Katherine Berrey
Timothy Best
William Bestani
James Bickford
Samuel J. Black
Sharon Block
Kate Bloniarz
Mathew C. Blum
Tia Boatman
 Patterson
Brandon Bodnar
Amira C. Boland
Cassie L. Boles
Melissa B. Bomberger
Matthew Bowen
Derick A. Boyd Jr.
William J. Boyd
Michael D. Branson
Alex M. Brant
Victoria Bredow
Joseph F. Breighner
Nicholas Brethauer
Andrea M. Brian
Candice M. Bronack
Ashley A. Brooks
Katherine W. Broomell

Dustin S. Brown
Sheila Bruce
Michael T. Brunetto
Pearl Buenvenida
Tom D. Bullers
Coulton Bunney
Scott H. Burgess
Ben Burnett
Jordan C. Burris
Angela S. Burton
John C. Burton
Mark Bussow
Sean Butler
Dylan W. Byrd

## C

Steven Cahill
Greg Callanan
Lekesha Fay Campbell
Amy Canfield
Eric D. Cardoza
Laura Carollo
Kevin Carpenter
Christina S. Carrere
William S. S. Carroll
Scott D. Carson
Corryne C. Carter
Mary I. Cassell
David Cassidy
Terry J. T. Cathopoulis
David Cerrato
Christina Cervantes
Dan Chandler
David Chang
Suzanne Chapman
Anthony Chase
James Chase
Nida Chaudhary
Anita Chellaraj
Fonda Chen
Amy Chenault
Dana Chisnell
Sophia Choudhry

Alex Ciepley
Damon J. Clark
Michael Clark
Sean Coari
Porchetta Cody
Alyssa Cogen
Jordan Cohen
Pamela Coleman
Victoria W. Collin
Debra M. Collins
Kelly T. Colyar
Jose A. Conde
David C. Connolly
Kyle Connors
Mary Rose Conroy
Shila R. Cooch
LaTiesha B. Cooper
Nicole Cordan
Benjamin E. Coyle
Brian Coyle
Drew W. Cramer
Ayana Crawford
William Creedon
Jill L. Crissman
Rose Crow
Jefferson Crowder
Albert Crowley
Juliana Crump
Lily Cuk
Pennee Cumberlander
C. Tyler Curtis
William Curtis
Patricia Cusack

## D

Amanda Dahl
Nadir Dalal
Shaibya Love Dalal
J. Alex Dalessio
D. Michael Daly
Rody Damis
Neil B. Danberg
Elisabeth C. Daniel

Kristy L. Daphnis
Joanne C. Davenport
Kelly Jo Davis
Kenneth L. Davis
Margaret B. Davis-
  Christian
Karen De Los Santos
Kara DeFrias
Thomas Delrue
Tasha M. Demps
Paul J. Denaro
Catherine A. Derbes
Christopher DeRusha
Suzy Deuster
Kelly A. Deutermann
Joseph A. Di Rocco
Selene Diaz
John H. Dick
Jamie Dickinson
Amie M. Didlo
Rachel M. Diedrick
Cle Diggins
Jean Diomi Kazadi
Daniel Dister
Angela M. Donatelli
Paul S. Donohue
Cristin Dorgelo
Vladik Dorjets
Michelle Dorsey
Tobias A. Dorsey
Prashant A. Doshi
Celeste Drake
Megan Dreher
Carlton Drew
Lisa Cash Driskill
Mark A. Dronfield
Vanessa Duguay
Nathaniel Durden
Ryan Durga
Reena Duseja

### E

Matthew C. Eanes
Jeanette Edwards
Melissa Eggleston
Christopher Eldredge
Matthew Eliseo
Michelle Enger
Diana F. Epstein
Troy M. Epstein
Bianca Escalante
Jorge Escobar
Celeste Espinoza

Robert Etter
Beatrix Evans
Erica Evans
Gillian Evans
Patrick Evans

### F

Farnoosh Faezi-Marian
Edna Falk Curtin
Hunter Fang
Louis E. Feagans
Iris R. Feldman
Lesley A. Field
Sean C. Finnegan
Mary S. Fischietto
John J. Fitzpatrick
Cleones Fleurima
Daniel G. Fowlkes
Nicholas A. Fraser
Rob Friedlander
Christopher Froehlich
Laurel Fuller
Steven Furnagiev

### G

Ethan Joshua Gabbour
Scott Gaines
Christopher D.
  Gamache
Joseph R. Ganahl
Kyle Gardiner
Mathias A. Gardner
Arpit Garg
Marc Garufi
Anthony R. Garza
Alex Gaynor
Johannes J. Geist
Anna M. Gendron
Mariam Ghavalyan
Daniel Giamo
Carolyn Gibson
Brian Gillis
Jacob Glass
Porter O. Glock
Christopher Glodosky
Andrea L. Goel
Jeffrey D. Goldstein
Christopher Gomba
Anthony A. Gonzalez
Oscar Gonzalez
Alex Goodenough
Jonathan Sidney

Gould
Michael D. Graham
Anthony M. Grasso
David M. Gratz
Vivian Graubard
Colleen M. Gravens
Aron Greenberg
Brandon H. Greene
Robin J. Griffin
Justin Grimes
Hester C. Grippando
Stephanie F. Grosser
Benjamin Guhin
Kamari Guthrie

### H

Michael B. Hagan
Tia Hall
Victor Hall
Dean Halstead
William F. Hamele
Christine E. Hammer
Rachel Han
Anna Hansen
Brian J. Hanson
Jennifer L. Hanson
Dionne Hardy
Deidre A. Harrison
Christopher Hart
Edward Hartwig
Paul Harvey
Abdullah Hasan
Sara A. Hastings
Joseph
  Hatzipanagiotis
Laurel Havas
Nichole M. Hayden
Mark Hazelgren
Kelly A. Healton
Paul Heayn
Noreen Hecmanczuk
Andrew Heimowitz
Gary Hellman
Natalie D.
  Hengstebeck
John David Henson
Matthew A. Herb
Mitchel Herckis
Jacobo Hernandez
Rachel Hernández
Alex Hettinger
Michael J. Hickey
Michael Hildner

Amanda M. Hill
Jonathan Hill
W. Frankie Hill
Nathaniel Hillard
Michelle Hilton
Leni Hirsch
Elke Hodson-Marten
Jennifer E. Hoef
Stuart Hoffman
Troy Holland
Shane Holloway
Brian Holm-Hansen
Javay C. Holmes
Michele Holt
Nicholas Holtz
Jennifer Ann Hommel
Alexander Hoover
Jack Hoskins
Clinton T. Hourigan
Devany Howard
Andrew P. Howe
Peter Hoy
Mina Hsiang
Grace Hu
Christine Huanasca
Rhea A. Hubbard
Kathy M. Hudgins
Thomas Huelskoetter
Shristi Humagai
Ashley Hungerford
Sally J. Hunnicutt
Alexander T. Hunt
Ginny Hunt
Lorraine D. Hunt
Timothy H. Hunt
James C. Hurban
Veta Hurst

### I

Tae H. Im
Shelley Irving
Maya Israni

### J

Maia Ruth
  Jachimowicz
Charmaine Jackson
Scott W. Jackson
Aryeh Jacobsohn
Manish Jain
Harrison M. Jarrett
Ames R. Jenkins

Carol Jenkins
Connor Jennings
Julie D. Jent
Jeremy Etra Jick
Carol Johnson
Michael D. Johnson
Danielle Y. Jones
Denise Bray Jones
Lauren H. Jones
Lisa M. Jones
Devansh R.
 Jotsinghani
Shannon Maire Joyce
Hursandbek
 Jumanyazov
Hee Jun
Mark Junda

### K

Jason Kahn
Riyad Kalla
Kosta Kalpos
Daniel S. Kaneshiro
Jacob H. Kaplan
Jenifer Liechty
 Karwoski
Florence Kasule
Natalie Kates
Jason Kattman
Regina L. Kearney
Andrew Keeney
Christopher Keller
Mary W. Keller
Nancy B. Kenly
Moses I. Kennedy
Kameron Kerger
Blair W. Kessler
Jung H. Kim
Maria Kim
Michael B. Kim
Rachael Y. Kim
Kelly C. King
Kelly A. Kinneen
Marina Kirakosian
Jessica Elizabeth
 Kirby
Robert T. Klein
Hank Knaack
Carmen Knight
Ellen Knight
Bobby Kogan
Lara Kohl
Nick Koo

Andrea G. Korovesis
Katelyn V. Koschewa
Steven Kovacs
Anneli Faride Kraft
Charles Kraiger
Lori A. Krauss
Harold Krent
Alyssa Kropp
Megan K. Kruse
Steven B. Kuennen
Jennifer J. Kuk
Anshul Kumar
Tara Kumar
Christine J. Kymn

### L

Vincent La
Christopher D. LaBaw
Sherry E. Lachman
Leonard L. Lainhart
Chad A. Lallemand
Kristine Lam
Lawrence L. Lambert
Michael Landry
Daniel LaPlaca
Tracie B. Lattimore
Eric P. Lauer
Jessie L. LaVine
Daniel Lawver
Loc N. Le
Jessica K. Lee
Theodore Taewoo Lee
Susan E. Leetmaa
Carmine Leggett
Stephen Leibman
Bryan P. León
Daniel Leonardini
Kerrie Leslie
Ariel Leuthard
John C. Levock-
 Spindle
Sheila Lewis
Andrew Lewndowski
Thomas M. Libert
Andrew Lieberman
Jennifer Liebschutz
Jane C. Lien
Ming Ligh
Kristina E. Lilac
Erika Liliedahl
Michael Linden
John E. Lindner
Jennifer M. Lipiew

Adam Lipton
Kim Lopez
Sara R. Lopez
Zuzana Love
Adrienne Lucas
Alisa Luu
Kelvin Luu

### M

Steven Parsons
 Mackey
Ryan MacMaster
Christian MacMillan
Brett Maden
Claire A. Mahoney
Bianca Majumder
Dominic J. Mancini
Caroline Manela
Noah S. Mann
Iulia Z. Manolache
Roman Manziyenko
Italy Martin
Rochelle Martinez
Nicole Martinez Moore
Clare Martorana
Gina Mason
Stephen Massoni
Kimie Matsuo
Beth Mattern
Joshua May
Steven M. McAndrews
Jessica Rae McBean
Alexander J.
 McClelland
John L. McClung
Malcolm P. McConnell
Daniela McCool
Jeremy P. McCrary
Charquinta Regina
 McCray
Anthony W. McDonald
Christine A. McDonald
Katrina A. McDonald
Renford McDonald
Trevor R. McKie
Michael McManus
Frank McNally
William McNavage
Christopher McNeal
Maya Mechenbier
Andrea Medina-Smith
Edward Meier
Julie Meloni

Barbara A. Menard
Flavio Menasce
Ryan Mercer
Margaret Mergen
P. Thaddeus
 Messenger
Lauren Michaels
Daniel J. Michelson-
 Horowitz
Eric Mill
Jason Miller
Kimberly Miller
Scott William Miller
Sofie Miller
Susan M. Minson
Katherine Mlika
Abdullahi Mohamed
Emily A. Mok
Kirsten J. Moncada
Allyce Moncton
Claire E. Monteiro
Joseph Montoni
Andrea J. Montoya
Julia C. Moore
Natalie Moore
Betty T. Morrison
Savannah M. Moss
Austin B. Mudd
Robin McLaughry
 Mullins
Ian Munoz
Daenuka
 Muraleetharan
Jonathan J. Murphy
Molly Murray
Christian G. Music
Hayley W. Myers
Heather Myers
Kimberley L Myers
David D. Myklegard

### N

Andrew Nacin
Jeptha E. Nafziger
Larry J. Nagl
Katherine Nammacher
Barry Napear
Robert Nassif
Emma Nechamkin
Beverly Nelson
Kimberly P. Nelson
Michael D. Nelson
Anthony Nerino

Melissa K. Neuman
Travis Newby
Joanie F. Newhart
Kimberly Armstrong
  Newman
Annie Nguyen
Hieu Nguyen
Stephanie Nguyen
Thomas Nielsen
Greg Novick
Tim H. Nusraty
Joseph B. Nye

## O

Erin O'Brien
Kerry Clinton O'Dell
Melanie Ofiesh
Michael Ogren
Matthew J. O'Kane
Cassandra Olson
Kathryn Olson
Brendan J. O'Meara
Matthew Oreska
Timothy F. O'Shea
Jared Ostermiller

## P

Heather C. Pajak
Farrah N. Pappa
Jacob A. Parcell
Amy Paris
John C. Pasquantino
Michael Pauls
Brian Paxton
Casey Pearce
Michael D. Pearlstein
Liuyi Pei
Zachary T. Pendolino
Sean Pennino
Falisa L. Peoples-Tittle
Emma C. Perron
Michael A. Perz
Erik Brandon Peters
Whitney L. Peters
William C. Petersen
Andrea M. Petro
Laura M. Pettus
Amy E. Petz
Kathy Pham (Evans)
Stacey Que-Chi Pham

Carolyn R. Phelps
Karen A. Pica
Brian Pickeral
Alexandria Elise
  Pinckney
Brian Pipa
Joseph Pipan
Amy Pitelka
Megan Policicchio
Nicholas Polk
Mark J. Pomponio
Ruxandra Pond
Imani Pope-Johns
Meril A. Pothen
Larrimer S. Prestosa
Jamie M. Price
Alanna B. Pugliese
Robert B. Purdy
Hannah Pyper

## Q

Syeda Quadry

## R

Lucas R. Radzinschi
Kazi Sabeel Rahman
Zahid Rashid
Houman Rasouli
Johnnie Ray
Alex Reed
Maurice Reeves
Heather Regen
Thomas M. Reilly
Cody Reinold
Bryant D. Renaud
Keri A. Rice
Natalie Rico
Kyle S. Riggs
Glorimar Ripoll Balet
Jamal Rittenberry
Maria Roat
Becci Roberts
Beth Higa Roberts
Brian Roberts
Donovan Robinson
Marshall J. Rodgers
Drew J. Rodriguez
Jung Mary Roh
Samantha Romero
Meredith B. Romley

Andrea L. Ross
Jeffrey R. Ross
Alicia Rouault
Alexander Joseph
  Rougeau
David J. Rowe
Amanda Roy
Danielle Royal
Brian Rozental
Tamia Russell
Erika H. Ryan

## S

Julianna R. St. Onge
Adam N. Salazar
John Asa Saldivar
Sarah Saltiel
Zohaib Sameer
Mark S. Sandy
Nathan T. Sanfilippo
Ruth Saunders
Joel Savary
Jason K. Sawyer
Sarah Scheinman
Zachary Scherer
Kirsten Scheyer
Christina Schildroth
Tricia Schmitt
Andrea Schneider
Rio Schondelmeyer
Daniel K. Schory
Ian Schurr
Margo Schwab
Mariarosaria
  Sciannameo
Kristi Scott
Jasmeet K. Seehra
Owen Seely
Kimberly Segura
Robert B. Seidner
Andrew Self
Megan Shade
Vimal Shah
Shabnam
  Sharbatoghlie
Amy K. Sharp
Dianne Shaughnessy
Pooja Shaw
Paul Shawcross
Rachel Lee Shepherd
Gary F. Shortencarrier

Matthew Sidler
Becca Siegel
Jared Siegel
Leticia Sierra
Sara R. Sills
Celeste Simon
Daniel Liam Singer
Sarah Sisaye
Robert Sivinski
Benjamin J. Skidmore
Evan C. Skloot
Curtina O. Smith
Jennifer Smith
Matthew Smith
Sarah B. Smith
Stannis M. Smith
Silvana Solano
Roderic A. Solomon
Timothy Soltis
Suzanne Soroczak
Amanda R.K. Sousane
Megan Sowder-Staley
Candice G. Spalding
Rebecca L. Spavins
Valeria Spinner
Christopher Spiro
John H. Spittell
Sarah Whittle Spooner
Madhu Sreekumar
Langer Stacey
Travis C. Stalcup
Scott R. Stambaugh
Nora Stein
Christopher Paul
  Steiner
Erica Stephens
Meredith Stewart
Ryan Stoffers
Gary R. Stofko
Andrew Stoll
Kelly M. Strachan
Benjamin Strahs
Terry W. Stratton
Thomas J. Suarez
Kevin J. Sullivan
Patrick Sullivan
Abe Sussan
Ariana Sutton-Grier
Shelby Switzer
Katherine M. Sydor

## T

Jamie R. Taber
Naomi S. Taransky
Masrifa Tasnim
Andrea Taverna
Kelly Taylor
Myra Taylor
Whitney Teal
Jay F. Teitelbaum
Fatima Terry
Emma K. Tessier
Lan Thai
Amanda L. Thomas
Barbara E. Thomas
Jennifer Thomas
Judith F. Thomas
Payton A. Thomas
Will Thomas
Serita K. Thornton
Parth Tikiwala
Thomas Tobasko
Erika Tom
Gia Tonic
Gil M. Tran
Susanna Troxler
Patrick Trulock
Austin Turner

## U

Shraddha A.
  Upadhyaya
Darrell J. Upshaw

## V

Matthew J. Vaeth
Candace Vahlsing
Areletha L. Venson
Alexandra Ventura
Shaun Verch
Carl Vernetti
Jesus Vidaurri
Eileen Vidrine
Merici Vinton
Kalpana Vissa
Andrea Viza
Megha Vyas

## W

James A. Wade
Lucinda Wade
Brett Waite
Nicole Waldeck
Joseph Waldow
Rachel Wallace
Heather V. Walsh

Tim Wang
Ben A. Ward
Michelle Ward
Clarence Wardell
Benjamin Warfield
Peter H. Waterman
Gary Waxman
Bess M. Weaver
Jacqueline K. Webb
Daniel Week
William J. Weinig
David M. Weisshaar
Michael Weissman
Lillian Welch
Philip R. Wenger
Max West
Arnette C. White
Ashley M. White
Curtis C. White
Kim S. White
Sherron R. White
Alison Whitty
Amy Widman
Brian A. Widuch
Sabrina Williams
Alex O. Wilson
Kimberly Claire
  Wilson
Catherine Winters
Christopher Winters

Minzy Won
Alegra E. Woodard
Gwyneth Woolwine
Nicholas John
  Woroszylo
Christopher Wren
Sophia M. Wright
Bertram J. Wyman

## Y

Danny Yagan
Melany N. Yeung
David Y. Yi
Samantha Paige Yi
Christian T. Yonkeu
Xia You
Frank (Tom) Young
Rita Young
Shalanda D. Young
Susse Yuan
Janice Yun

## Z

Elizabeth Zahorian
Eliana M. Zavala
Erica H. Zielewski
Timothy Ziese
Jeremy Zitomer